The Grand Experiment

The Birth of the Railway Age: 1820-45

Stuart Hylton

Ian Allan
PUBLISHING

Contents

First published 2007

ISBN (10) 0 7110 3172 X
ISBN (13) 978 0 7110 3172 2

Published by Ian Allan Publishing

an imprint of Ian Allan Publishing Ltd, Hersham, Surrey KT12 4RG.
Printed in England by Ian Allan Printing Ltd, Hersham, Surrey KT12 4RG.

Code: 0704/A3

Front cover: Robert Stephenson's Primrose Hill Tunnel on the London & Birmingham Railway, opened in 1837/8. Lithograph by Edwin Thomas Dalby. *Ironbridge Museum Trust*

Visit the Ian Allan Publishing website at www.ianallanpublishing.com

ADVERTISEMENT

'By the establishment of a General Iron Rail-way in a direct line, the distance between the capital and the manufacturing districts and principal cities might be reduced one-quarter and in many cases one-third, instead of the ridiculously winding course the stage and mail-coaches now daily run.

'The permanent prosperity which would arise to commerce from this rapid communication would soon be felt in every corner of the United Kingdom. The mails from London to Manchester, Liverpool, and Leeds, might be conveyed within the space of twelve hours, and those to Glasgow and Edinburgh within twenty-four . . .

'. . . The farmer would likewise greatly participate in this national improvement. The land now required to produce food for his horses might be cultivated for other purposes far more profitable; the various products of the farm, as well as livestock of every description, might be conveyed to any market, and manures brought back, without employing a single horse, in one half the time and at one half the expense now incurred . . .

'As a permanently improving source of revenue to our capitalists, this plan would have no parallel; the diurnal returns, at the most moderate toll on each vehicle, would annually produce many millions; indeed no limits can be assigned to the increase of wealth which this change in our inland conveyance might produce; there is no branch of agriculture, no branch of commerce, or of arts, but would partake of its endless prosperity . . .

'One steam-engine, on an improved railway, would draw from London to Edinburgh three stage-coaches (each carrying twice the luggage and number of passengers of ordinary coaches) in thirty hours, which now require three hundred horses, and at least fifty hours' time for the performance of the journey.'

Part of an advertisement, placed by Thomas Grey in about 1820 to promote the case for a national network of railways in Britain.

The Grand Experiment: **Introduction**

'Even while it was being constructed, the Liverpool and Manchester line was viewed by many railway engineers and promoters as* The Grand British Experimental Railway, *the success or failure of which would have decisive influence in shaping plans for the lines of railways yet to be built.'

(Robert E. Carlson: *The Liverpool and Manchester Railway Project 1821–1831 — page 11)*

My love of railways began as a small child, when I used to watch, half-fascinated, half-terrified, as the Great Western steam expresses thundered through Slough station. Years later, my interest focused on the very earliest years of the railways, whilst I was writing a history of Manchester, in which the railways played a vital role. (*Stuart Hylton — A History of Manchester — Phillimore 2003*). But when I came to look among the wealth of excellent railway history for a book that gave an overview of those earliest pioneering railway days, I searched in vain. Hence my decision to write one.

For those first 25 years of railway history were unique. At the start of our story, the world had not seen a railway, as we would understand it. Some of the people who governed the nation literally did not understand the meaning of the word 'locomotive'. By the end of it, the broad outlines of a national railway network were in prospect and, in many cases, in place; railways were being constructed on every continent; the imagination of the world had been seized and people's lives had been changed in a thousand ways, many of which are set out in this book. It is hard to think of any development in transport — or indeed in anything else — that changed so much in so short a time. In that short period, the nation — and the world — learned what a railway was. More to the point, they had to work out from first principles how one operated. The process was one of trial and error — and the results were occasionally tragic, often comical and frequently unbelievable to modern eyes.

The period I have chosen to focus on is the quarter-century from 1820 to 1845. This choice of time period is not arbitrary, but neither is it hermetically sealed. At the start of it, the ideas for the Stockton & Darlington and the Liverpool & Manchester Railways — the latter, the first real modern railway — were just starting to take shape. By its end, we were well into the greatest period of railway mania known to history, and the idea of travelling on — and for many, investing in — the railways had taken root among a wide cross-section of the British public, and across the world. Nonetheless, I have not hesitated to trespass across my own time boundaries when the narrative seemed to require it.

My first thanks are due to the many fine historians who have recorded various aspects of this early history. They are listed in the bibliography and are directly credited as necessary. I hope my modest efforts will encourage the reader to delve further into their more detailed accounts. Second, thanks are due to the library staff up and down the country who have helped me to track down the wealth of material on which I have been able to draw.

I have tried to track down the copyright holders of the illustrations used in the book. If there are any omissions, I would be grateful if you would let me know via the publisher, and I will try to ensure that they are remedied in any future editions of the book.

I hope you will enjoy this journey through a unique period of history, and that you will share my wonder at the boldness, the shortsightedness, the vision, the duplicity and the ingenuity of a nation faced with the challenge of a life-changing possibility. If World War 2 is said to be Britain's finest hour, this period and its achievements — for all the shortcomings of governments and individuals — might rank as a worthy runner-up.

Stuart Hylton
October 2006

Chapter 1: Britain 1820 — another world

'A man born in 1800 would have grown up in a pre-railway world that was nearer to mediaeval England than it is to our own.'

(L. T. C. Rolt: *Victorian Engineering*)

'We who have lived before Railways were made belong to another world.'

(William Thackeray)

The Britain of 1820 seems a million miles removed from the railway age. As the year began, George III was still, in name at least, on the throne. Victoria, with whose reign the growth of the railways is most closely associated, was a babe in arms. It was the world of the genteel manners of Jane Austen, whose last novels, *Northanger Abbey* and *Persuasion*, were published after her death in 1817; and of the gentle landscapes of John Constable, whose *Haywain* was received with great acclaim at the Paris Salon of 1821. Napoleon Bonaparte was living out the last years of his exile on St Helena. Memories of his threatened invasion and subsequent defeat at Waterloo were still fresh in the minds of the nation, and the economic consequences of that prolonged war would continue to haunt Britain for years to come.

The nation's population was only around 14 million people, about a quarter of its current level. It was overwhelmingly a rural nation — over three-quarters of the people lived in the countryside. But theirs was a countryside that was changing. During the 18th century it had been tamed — ditched, drained, mediaeval strip farming phased out, and almost a million hectares of common land enclosed. New farming methods were being adopted, making the land more productive, but the loss of common grazing rights made it more difficult for the average agricultural labourer to eke out a living from the land.

A system of poor relief — known as the Speenhamland system —

provided publicly subsidised work for those in greatest need. Whilst it stopped them starving, it left those with regular jobs in agriculture pauperised and demoralised. It was also a significant drain on public funds, its cost increasing by around four-fold in the half-century to 1817. At the other end of the social scale, a new class of landed gentry was making its presence felt in the rural areas. These were people who had made their fortunes through trade and commerce, and who now sought the transition to a more traditional aristocracy. They often had no rural roots, no links with the communities in which they lived, and viewed their landholdings more in terms of a balance sheet, rather than of stewardship of the land and leadership of the rural communities in which they lived.

But agriculture was in an unstable state in 1820. The previous decade saw both the highest wheat prices of the 19th century and the widest fluctuations in price. During the French wars, landowners extended cereal production to moorlands and chalklands that would not normally be viable for this purpose. Their demands for protection after the war led to the passing of the 1815 Corn Laws, which prevented the import of foreign corn until domestic prices reached 80 shillings a quarter. The effect was to make bread a luxury food for many working people, and to goad into life what would become one of the century's great political pressure groups — the Anti-Corn Law League. This issue also highlighted a growing divide between rural and urban interests. Everyone wanted stable agricultural prices, but the manufacturers wanted them stabilised at a low level, to keep wages down and maintain international competitiveness, whilst farmers wanted them stabilised at a high level, to protect their incomes.

It may still have been a rural nation, but the balance between town and country was changing rapidly, as the great provincial manufacturing towns grew at breakneck speed. Manchester, Liverpool, Leeds, Birmingham and Sheffield all at least doubled their populations in the first 30 years of the century. The end of the Napoleonic Wars released about 400,000 people onto the labour market, just at a time when recession and technological advances were reducing the demand for their labour. Many of these, along with refugees from rural poverty, swelled the populations of the industrial towns and cities, searching for work and cramming themselves into slum housing with the horrifying consequences later described by James Kay, Friedrich Engels and others.

It was a narrow world for most people. The Napoleonic Wars may have broadened the horizons of those who took part in them, but most of the population would not have travelled much more than a day's walk from where they were born. There were no national newspapers, and those more local newspapers that were published were unaffordable to most people, even if they could read. Pamphlets, like William Cobbett's *Weekly Political Register*, had a larger readership, but even this numbered only in the tens of thousands. For most people, the only way that news and ideas could spread was by word of mouth.

Even then, the exchange of ideas could be a risky business. The examples of the French and American Revolutions weighed heavily on the minds of the governing classes. This was not without reason — in the years leading up to the 1832 Reform Act, according to Evans, 'Britain came closer to revolution… than at any time in the 18th, 19th or twentieth centuries'. George IV, while sane, did more than George III ever did during his period of insanity from 1811 to drag the reputation of the monarchy down to its lowest-ever level and sow the seeds of discontent. The repressive governments of the day were therefore likely to come down heavily on any expression of discontent, however peaceful and however justified it might be. The Home Secretary, Lord Sidmouth, sat at the centre of a substantial spy ring, gathering intelligence about civil unrest, particularly in the new — and, to him, uncharted — industrial areas of the north.

It was in part informants' scaremongering that led in August 1819 to a peaceful meeting at St Peter's Fields in Manchester taking its infamous place in history as the Peterloo Massacre. Those same spies also helped to uncover the Cato Street Conspiracy in 1820, a plot to kill the Prime Minister and his Cabinet. The Government's response was a variety of repressive laws, to stop what they regarded as seditious assemblies, to remove the right of habeas corpus and to prevent trade union activity. There were around 220 offences carrying the death penalty in the early 19th century, including (curiously) damaging Westminster Bridge or impersonating a Chelsea Pensioner. Under a new law of 1816, a hungry man poaching to feed his family could face transportation, or mutilation and death from the mantraps and spring guns that the gamekeepers were allowed to set for them.

Nor could it be described as a democratic country. The franchise of the day gave the vote to freeholders of land worth 40 shillings a year, but not to the great majority of working people, nor to any women. For many of those who could vote, it was seen as something to be sold to the highest bidder, or given to the local aristocracy as a form of traditional obligation. Whole areas of the country — notably booming industrial towns like Manchester — were entirely without representation in Parliament, whilst virtually unoccupied hamlets like Newton, between Manchester and Liverpool, elected two Members.

But the seeds of dramatic change were being sown, not least through science and technology. It was the age of *Frankenstein* (1818), as well as Jane Austen. Steam power was becoming widespread. It was first seen pumping out mines, then powering factories and mills. The first mill using steam power in Manchester had opened as long ago as 1780 and some 30,000 steam-powered looms were in use in the wider Manchester area alone by the 1820s. Steam power had also begun to be used on ships — the first commercial steamboat began trading on the Delaware River in the United States as early as 1790. By 1821, iron ships were starting to be made in the shipyards of the Clyde and a total of 188 steamboats were plying their trade around the coasts of Britain.

The age of the turnpikes...

Since 1660, the stagecoach had been the main means of public transport serving the nation. The first of these — between London and Oxford — initially covered the journey in about twelve hours on a good day, though accidents were not uncommon and the service was abandoned altogether when the weather got bad and the roads became impassable. Until 1835, the maintenance of most local roads depended upon a piece of legislation dating from 1555, using conscript labour from the parishes, supervised by unpaid — equally press-ganged — surveyors, with no sanctions over their unwilling workers. The result was a standard of maintenance that can most charitably be described as variable.

Turnpikes, on which maintenance was funded by tolls, became increasingly common after 1740, and John McAdam introduced an improved road surface that bore his name in 1815. By 1820 many major routes were turnpiked and had a macadamised surface. Fifteen years later, turnpike trusts managed about 22,000 miles of road — about a fifth of the national network. However, they were still relatively small-scale and localised, making a long journey a very hit-or-miss affair in terms of travelling conditions. One contemporary estimate classed the maintenance standards of 18% of the network as 'excellent' and a similar proportion as 'vile'. This 1825 letter to a newspaper suggests that the Liverpool to Manchester turnpike fell into the latter category:

> ***'It is circuitous, narrow and crooked, the soft part is uneven, the substance of it in many places quite worn through, and the pavement is infamous. It is constantly the subject of complaint with that great "tide of human existence", which is flowing in a ceaseless current between these two populous cities and it is observed with astonishment by all strangers***

who come from other parts of the kingdom...this road, connecting as it does two of the largest and most important towns of the kingdom, passing over a level country through populous districts remains almost in the same state it was in twenty years ago, as circuitous, crooked and probably as rough.'

(*Manchester Guardian — 13 August 1825*)

Even so, the turnpikes, and growing competition for customers among the stagecoach companies, produced their own modest revolution in journey times. Taking the example of the journey between Liverpool and Manchester, the first coach service between the two towns, started in the latter part of the 18th century, could take up to twelve hours. But, by 1825, twenty-two regular and seven occasional coaches were making the trip daily. They brought journey times down to three hours on a regular basis and, on occasions, two and a half. This was a breakneck speed for a horse-drawn coach, particularly on a road crowded with wagons, packhorses and private coaches. Accidents were commonplace, as they were in many parts of the road network. The same edition of the *Manchester Guardian* that carried the prospectus for the Manchester & Leeds Railway also gave details of 'a terrible accident' to the *Aurora* coach to Worcester. The coachman lost control of a heavily laden coach down a steep hill at Severn Stoke, leaving several people 'cut, bruised and dreadfully mangled' and two dead.

Similar improvements in speed, if not safety, were to be seen throughout the country. For example, in 1688 the London to Exeter coach took four days. A century later, this had been reduced to two days and by 1832 to $17^1/2$ hours (an average of around 10mph). The London to Shrewsbury coach of 1835, the *Wonder*, boasted an even more ambitious 12.1mph for its 153-mile journey. But, dramatic as these reductions were, they scarcely bettered the record for the distance travelled overland in a single day, which had rested with the Roman Emperor Tiberius since about A.D. 30. He had covered some 200 miles, using a relay of horses and chariots.

It was not only journey times that were transformed. The volume of traffic (in terms of the numbers of coaches) between ten of the nation's major towns and cities increased by eleven times between 1790 and 1835, giving some indication of the amount of pent-up demand for travel that the railways were about to unleash. Even this did not paint a full picture of the increase, for the stagecoaches individually also increased their carrying capacity significantly over this period. By 1835, some 700 mail-coaches and 3,300 stagecoaches were carrying an estimated ten million passengers a year around Britain. Some of the coach operators were substantial businesses. As late as 1838, W. J. Chaplin employed over 2,000 people and 1,800 horses and was operating 106 coaches daily out of London.

However, the stagecoach had just about reached the limit of its potential. The increasing volume of traffic on the turnpikes resulted in more rapid wear on the road surface, which in turn necessitated higher tolls (and hence increased coach fares). A sharp rise in the cost of horse feed after 1820 also added to travel costs. Speeds had reached the limit of the horse's capacity, and sometimes beyond — the horses were being over-driven to the point where their working lives were being shortened — and safety had become a real issue.

. . . and the canals

> ***'Canals superseded to a large extent the means of transport previously employed; if rail-roads are found better than canals, the latter must, in their turn, give way.'***
>
> (*The Times — 20 November 1824*)

The 18th and early 19th centuries had seen the construction of an extensive network of canals in Britain, which was virtually completed by 1815. As at 1820, the United Kingdom had 103 navigable canals with a total length of 2,690 miles, built in the face of determined opposition from the turnpike trusts and the coaching, wagon and other businesses that used the highways. Most parts of the country were within 10 miles of a navigable waterway.

Although their main purpose was the movement of goods, some canals also had significant passenger traffic. As late as the mid-1830s Scottish canals and rivers were carrying over 800,000 passengers a year. A number of these services were to survive for twenty-five years into the railway age. But transport by canal could be slow, inconvenient and subject to other problems, such as ice in winter and low water levels in summer, that could leave cargoes stranded for weeks. The problems were not limited to the elements. Francis Berry, a Bath linen draper, complained that the value of his cargo of clothing had depreciated by 20% in transit, since fashions had actually changed while they were being delivered (very slowly) by canal. There was also widespread pilfering — one example of which was known as 'sucking the monkey': the practice of siphoning off part of any cargo of alcohol and replacing

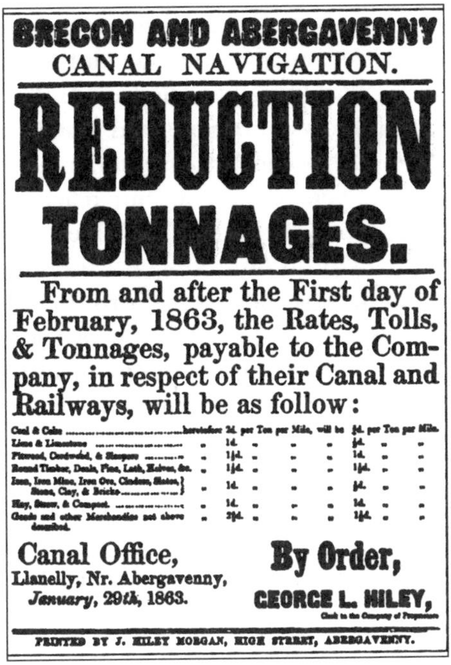

BRECON AND ABERGAVENNY
CANAL NAVIGATION.

REDUCTION
TONNAGES.

From and after the First day of February, 1863, the Rates, Tolls, & Tonnages, payable to the Company, in respect of their Canal and Railways, will be as follow:

Coal & Coke	heretofore	2d. per Ton per Mile,	will be	½d. per Ton per Mile.
Lime & Limestone	"	1d. " "	"	½d. " "
Pitwood, Cordwood, & Sleepers	"	1½d. " "	"	1d. " "
Round Timber, Deals, Fine, Lath, Halves, &c.	"	1½d. " "	"	1½d. " "
Iron, Iron Mine, Iron Ore, Cinders, Slates, Stone, Clay, & Bricks	"	1d. " "	"	½d. " "
Hay, Straw, & Compost.	"	1d. " "	"	1d. " "
Goods and other Merchandise not above described.	"	2½d. " "	"	1½d. " "

Canal Office,
Llanelly, Nr. Abergavenny,
January, 29*th*, 1863.

By Order,
GEORGE L. HILEY,
Clerk to the Company of Proprietors.

PRINTED BY J. HILEY MORGAN, HIGH STREET, ABERGAVENNY.

Competition with the railways forced the canal companies to cut their rates substantially.

it with water. One final problem for the sensitive traveller was the smell of some of the canals. Sir George Head describes sailing through the Runcorn area in 1835, where the canal was 'black as the Styx and absolutely pestiferous' and there was 'a compound of villainous smells past all endurance'.

The canals were built to address local needs, with little thought of forming a national network. The arrangements for the through movement of goods between canals were poorly developed and there were few timetabled services. Their different widths, depths and lock sizes meant that through traffic often had to be transhipped, and long-distance customers would end up paying tolls to a multitude of local companies. As late as 1913 there were three canal routes between London and Liverpool, two of which involved paying separate tolls to nine different companies and the third tolls to ten. (There were similar problems with the stagecoaches — for example, you could pre-book seats from the starting point of the journey, but not from intervening stops along the route. There was no standing room for unexpected extra stagecoach passengers.)

The canals lacked a George Hudson figure — whatever his other faults — to enforce amalgamation and standardise working practices. The law also worked against them operating efficiently. Until 1845, canal companies were forbidden to operate as carriers on their own waterways without special parliamentary permission, for fear of creating a monopoly. Only as the competition of a spreading rail network eased these fears were those restrictions removed. Much of the money that would be spent after 1820 on futile opposition to the railways might have been better used making the canals themselves more competitive.

So long as the horse remained the main source of traction, the canal had one considerable advantage over the railway. A packhorse on a road could carry just 2-3 hundredweight. Pulling a wagon on rails, its towing capacity was dramatically increased, to at least eight tons (or possibly even 38 — see the claims of the Surrey Iron Railway, later). But a horse harnessed to a barge could tow as much as fifty tons on the tranquil waters of a canal.

The British economy struggled to recover from the effects of the war after 1815. Hints of a recovery in 1817 were short-lived, but the economy began to pick up rapidly after 1820, heading towards a peak in 1825. This brought into relief the bottlenecks in the canal system. Nowhere was this clearer than the North West, where the cotton industry was booming, stimulating other industries in its wake, and where the canals between Manchester and Liverpool suffered from complacent and monopolistic management. In addition, two of the main routes were not entirely dead-water canals. This meant they suffered from the additional uncertainties, such as tides, affecting river navigation.

The Liverpool to Manchester route provides the clearest possible illustration of the fierce rivalry that would develop between the railways and canals. By 1820, the business communities of Liverpool and Manchester were heartily sick of their high-handed treatment by the canal interests. Trade between the two towns had grown enormously, but was being held back by slow and unreliable transport, despite the towns being linked by three waterways.

The first, the Mersey & Irwell Navigation, had received Royal Assent a century before, in 1720. The two rivers linking the towns were made navigable and the Act established them as a public highway, navigable by all for a payment of 3s 4d per ton of goods carried. Despite their having a monopoly until 1776, it was claimed that the cost of its construction, maintenance and improvement meant that the Navigation did not make a penny in profit before 1794. At this time the enterprise was financially restructured and the Navigation greatly improved, coinciding with the dramatic growth of the Lancashire cotton industry. The change in the Navigation's fortunes was equally dramatic. By 1825, shareholders of the Mersey & Irwell were receiving a dividend of 50% on their original investment each year.

This was despite the fact that, from 1776, the Mersey & Irwell had a rival in the Bridgewater Canal. The Mersey & Irwell interests originally opposed the newcomer with as much vehemence as the canal lobby later devoted to trying to stop the railways, but Parliament allowed the Duke of Bridgewater to construct a canal linking his coal mines at Worsley to Manchester. The Duke was able to construct the canal cheaply, since he owned most of the land through which it passed, thus avoiding the ruinous expense of the wayleaves that dogged so many transport projects at this time. Original plans to link it into the Mersey & Irwell Navigation were scrapped in favour of bringing it independently into Manchester via the Barton Aqueduct, at 600 feet long and up to 39 feet high one of the engineering wonders of the age. A further extension to the Mersey estuary at Runcorn Gap was approved in 1762, making it into a self-contained rival route between Liverpool and Manchester.

As a condition of the enabling Act for the new canal, the Duke was required to supply coal to Manchester at a cost of no more than 4d a hundredweight, compared with the then going rate of 7d. In fact, he was able to supply it profitably for just 3½d. Like the Mersey & Irwell, the canal was to be a public highway, open to all for a payment of 2s 6d a ton. Initially, the Bridgewater could massively undercut the Mersey & Irwell, charging just half the Mersey & Irwell's rate. But despite their initial opposition, the two companies soon became conspirators in price-fixing. The cost of transporting grain between the two towns rose to up to 13s per ton, sugar to 16s 8d and cotton up to 20s a ton. Even at these prices, they could still undercut packhorses and wagons, which charged 40s a ton.

These prices encouraged private shipping operators to set up in competition, but the Duke's ownership of the land along the canal enabled him to prevent rivals building the warehouses they needed to operate efficiently. (Having said this, it was claimed at the parliamentary inquiry into the Liverpool & Manchester Railway that the Duke's boats carried less than a third of the total tonnage using the Canal in 1824.) The Duke himself had died in 1803 and ownership of the Canal passed to his nephew, the Marquis of Stafford. But the Duke's will provided that, on the death of the Marquis, the interest would pass not to his eldest, but to his second, son. Perhaps even more importantly, the running of the Canal was taken away from the Marquis. It became the responsibility of three trustees, including the man who had managed it for the Duke for 33 years: Robert Bradshaw.

Bradshaw was a bully and a profiteer. Secure in his near-monopoly, he was happy to ignore the needs of his customers. Shortage of barges and other operational difficulties could lead to goods taking anything up to six weeks to move between the two towns. Bradshaw's philosophy was described as 'profit extraction to the utmost limit, regardless of the feelings and interests of the users of the Canal' *(Young — page 87)*. As one contemporary concluded, the public highway envisaged by the Bridgewater Act was, in fact, an effective private monopoly:

> ***'When we consider that one of the practical results of this system has been, to place one of the most important avenues of commerce in Great Britain, the Bridgewater Canal... at the disposal of one individual, as his private property, and that this individual is precluded from any interference or management of the property in which he alone possesses a beneficial interest, — we may form some notion of the absurdities and evils to which the system leads.'***
>
> (Thomas Grahame: *A Treatise on Internal Intercourse and Communication in Civilised States, and Particularly in Great Britain — 1834*)

The third, and quite possibly least, of the waterways linking Liverpool and Manchester, the Leeds & Liverpool Canal, was primarily designed for trans-Pennine traffic. It was linked to the Bridgewater only from 1821, and provided a circuitous and expensive route that had relatively little impact on trade between the two towns. In fact, none of these canals was very direct: the Mersey & Irwell was the shortest, at 43 miles, compared with the Bridgewater's 46 and the Leeds & Liverpool's 58 miles. But none of them would be able to compete for directness with the 31-mile route of the proposed new railway.

'Mischief in those tram-roads . . .'

Up to 1820 (and for some time afterwards, in many people's eyes), there was no automatic presumption that a railway was superior to a canal. In many cases both were investigated as alternatives and, in some of these, a canal was preferred. In one extreme example, the respective cases for a ship canal and a railway linking Newcastle and Carlisle were compared. It will come as no surprise that the railway, at £252,500, came in at less than a third of the estimated cost of a large-scale ship canal across the Pennines (£888,000). Sometimes railways were built as feeders to the canal, where it would be impractical or uneconomic to build a branch of the canal itself. These could be quite substantial pieces of engineering in their own right. The Lancaster Canal Company, for example, built a railway of five miles in length between Walton and Preston in 1799, linking its canal with the Ashby Canal across the Ribble Valley. Most parliamentary Acts authorising canals contained a parallel authority for the canal company to set up and run ancillary railways.

By the end of the 18th century, some major railway schemes were already taking shape — at least as ideas. A scheme was even proposed in 1799 (driven partly by military needs) to build a horse-drawn railway from London to Portsmouth, as a supplement to the recently opened Basingstoke Canal. In its revised 1803 version, the capital cost of the scheme was estimated at as much as £430,000. There were even suggestions (for example, from correspondents to the *Liverpool Mercury*) that the canals should be filled in, wheels fitted to the canal barges and sails or horses used to propel them along a railway made in the canal bed. This almost came about in one case, through an 1831 Act that permitted the Bolton & Bury Canal Navigation Company to convert its canal into a railway. The Act authorised it to fill, stop up or drain as much of the canal as was required, except for the Bolton to Bury section, which they were required to maintain. In the event, the route was changed, and the company built its railway alongside, rather than in or on, the canal.

However, like the stagecoaches, the canals were approaching the limits of their potential. The more locks there were, and the more traffic trying to get through them, the slower the journeys became. Even the potential for steamboats to increase speed between the locks was limited by the damage their wash caused to the canal banks. The king of the canals, the Duke of Bridgewater, shrewdly saw the competition the railways represented long before it materialised. In his later years, some three decades before the opening of the Liverpool & Manchester Railway, he said of the canals: 'They will last my time, but I see mischief in those damned tram-roads'.

This was the world into which the railways were about to make their dramatic entrance.

Chapter 2:
The first railways

The wooden railways

Although the impact of the railways on the nation was to be revolutionary, the main elements of them had been in place for a long time. The first record of something resembling a railway is to be found in a stained-glass window in the Minster of Freiburg im Breisgau, Germany, and dates from about 1350. Other references are to be found, in books and illustrations, from the 16th century onwards.

The first British reference dates almost from the time of the first Queen Elizabeth. Documents from 1597 and 1598 describe exports of coal from the mines of Sir Francis Willoughby at Wollaton and Strelley to the River Trent in Nottinghamshire. There, between 1603 and 1604, a mining engineer named Huntingdon Beaumont built a two-mile line from the pit to the river, at a cost of £166. An agreement of 1609 refers to 'Wollerton Lane at the new rayles end'. Within a decade, the idea had been exported to the mining areas of the North East, and there was one operating between pits at Cowpen and Bewley and the River Blyth near Bedlington. A mine at Whickham, County Durham, reported what were possibly the world's first recorded railway fatalities in 1650, when two boys were 'slain with a wagon' on a wooden railway. These early railways could be relatively costly for their time — records from 1726 show one coming out at £785 a mile. They suffered from heavy wear, but they were found to improve the productivity of the wagon drivers by a factor of five and to make them less dependent upon the weather.

Iron gradually came to be used, first as a wearing surface on top of the wooden rails and eventually instead of wood, for the rails. By 1758, the Whitehaven Colliery used iron to line their wooden rails, and wheels with flanges were introduced by William Jessop in 1789. When the Coalbrookdale Ironworks found themselves with a surplus of iron in 1767, they used the excess to make cast-iron rails for their works railway. The original idea had been to take them up and re-cast them, as and when demand for iron picked up. Another iron railway, installed in the

Duke of Norfolk's colliery near Sheffield in 1776, provoked a riot among the colliery workers, who tore it up. Wrought iron, a more durable product for rail making, was introduced in the Bedlington Ironworks, Northumberland, in 1805. Meanwhile, early references to points — originally known as 'pointers' — were seen on a tramway from Denby Colliery to Little Eaton in 1799.

By the dawn of the 19th century, an extensive network of tramways already covered the country's growing industrial and mining areas. Conservative estimates put the national mileage at 133 miles by 1750 and 292 miles by 1800. By 1820, Tyneside alone had some 225 miles. Most of these were lightly constructed, suitable only for horse-drawn traffic, and single-tracked. The parallel development of the idea of plateways, using L-section rails with the flange facing in, meant that ordinary road-going carts of the right gauge could become railway wagons without adaptation.

The first public railway, in the sense of being approved by Act of Parliament, was the Leeds & Middleton wagonway, which dated from 1758. The Act was granted to assist the owner, Charles Brandling, in obtaining wayleaves. This was the iniquitous practice of landowners charging huge sums for allowing wagonways or canals to cross their land. In some cases, the landowner could earn more from the passage of coal than did the mine-owner who had extracted it. The six-mile Surrey Iron Railway opened for horse-drawn traffic in July 1803, serving an early industrial area along the River Wandle between Croydon and Wandsworth. This was as an alternative to canalising the river, which was not practicable since it was used as a source of waterpower to the many industries bordering it, and contained many millponds and weirs. Tests on this railway suggested that a horse could draw 38 tons over a six-mile track in two hours, and could actually move up to 58 tons.

Passenger transport by rail — again horse-drawn — began in March 1807, when the Oystermouth Railway began operations between Mumbles and Swansea. The Act authorising this,

One of the first images of a steam locomotive — Richard Trevithick's *Catch Me Who Can* of c1808 (from Dendy-Marshall).

passed in 1804, (the year of Trevithick's nearby experiment in steam locomotion, covered later), refers intriguingly to the traction being by 'men, horses *or otherwise'*. This railway was to be rail's earliest victim to competition from the roads. When, in about 1826, horse buses started operating along a nearby turnpike, they put the railway's passenger services out of business, though it continued its function of delivering stone from the quarries. Passenger travel was later revived as a tourist attraction and survived until 1960.

Steam propulsion was an idea almost as old as the railways. The first steam-propelled vehicle — it involved a jet of steam being blown onto a vaned wheel — was built around 1665 by a Jesuit missionary in Peking called Father Verbiest. The first full-sized model using more conventional steam technology was the work of Frenchman Nicholas Cugnot. He built a steam tractor in 1769, designed to pull gun carriages, but it proved to be unsteerable and required stops for water too frequently to be a practicable proposition on a battlefield. James Watt started work on one in 1786, based upon his steam engine patent of two years before, but never finished it. At the same time, his patent stifled other initiatives in this field. William Murdoch developed a model steam carriage in the 1790s, but his position as Watt's agent in Cornwall prevented him from developing it further.

It was Cornishman Richard Trevithick who pioneered the working steam railway, shortly after James Watt's patent ran out. He had previously developed road-going steam carriages, but they were both unsteerable (nobody had had to think about steering before — you just pulled the reins and the horse turned) and unstoppable (like the early locomotives, they had no brakes). After testing a first prototype at Coalbrookdale, he took his idea to the Penydarren Iron Works, initially to settle a bet about the practicability of steam locomotion between the proprietor, Samuel Homfray, and another ironmaster, William Crawshay.

This local newspaper report is thought to be the first-ever published description of a steam railway at work:

> ***'Yesterday the long-expected trial of Mr Trevithick's new-invented steam engine, for which he has obtained His Majesty's letters patent, to draw and work carriages of all descriptions on various kinds of roads, as well as for a number of other purposes, to which its power may be usefully applied, took place near this town (Merthyr Tydfil) and was found to perform, to admiration, all that was***

expected from it by its warmest advocates. In the present instance, the novel application of steam, by means of this truly valuable machine, was made use of to convey along the Tram-road ten tons long weight of bar iron, from Penydarren Iron Works to the place where it joins the Glamorganshire Canal, upwards of nine miles distance... It is not doubted but that the number of horses in the kingdom will be very considerably reduced, and the machine, in the hands of the present proprietors, will be made use of in a thousand instances never yet thought of for an engine.'

(The Cambrian — 24 February 1804)

One feature of this early prototype was that it had no footplate. It is thought the driver would have walked alongside it, much as a carter leading a carthorse might have done. Four years later and Trevithick's invention reached London, albeit in the form of a novelty fairground ride. His new locomotive, *Catch Me Who Can*, gave pleasure rides on a circular track near the Euston Road. By now, walking alongside it was no longer an option for the driver and Trevithick had an interesting new angle for publicity:

'We are credibly informed that there is a Steam Engine now preparing to run against any mare, horse or gelding that may be produced at the next October meeting at Newmarket; the wagers at present are stated to be 10,000:l; the engine is the favourite. The extraordinary effect of mechanical powers is already known to the world; but the novelty, singularity and powerful application against time and speed has created admiration in the minds of every scientific man. TREVITHICK, the proprietor and patentee of this engine, has been applied to by several distinguished personages to exhibit this engine to the public, previous to its being sent to Newmarket; we have not heard this gentleman's determination yet; its greatest speed will be 20 miles in one hour, and its slowest rate will never be less than 15 miles.'

(The Times — 8 July 1808)

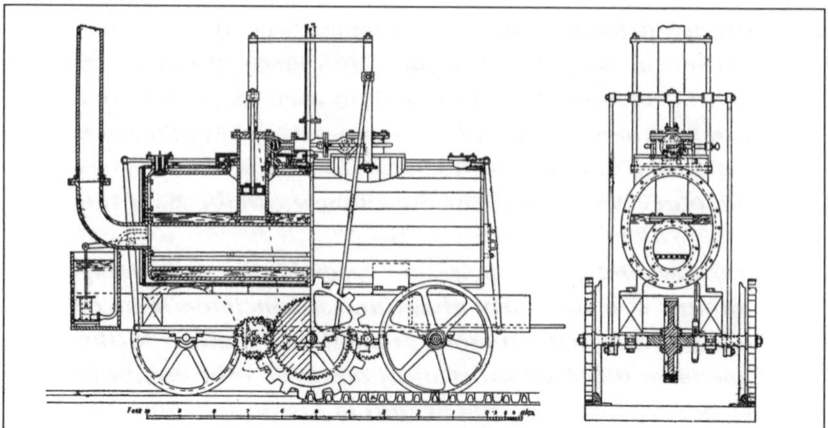

Drawings of a Blenkinsop Engine (1815).

Technical drawings of a Blenkinsop locomotive from 1815, using the rack system.

A few working locomotives began to appear in collieries around the country over the next few years, but Trevithick would not be the man to make the breakthrough for steam. Although he was in some ways even more important than George Stephenson as an innovator in steam locomotion, he was a poor businessman, and his Penydarren locomotive proved to be so prone to breaking the cast-iron rails of the day that its owner took its wheels off and used it as a stationary engine. Nonetheless, Christopher Blackett, the owner of Wylam Colliery on Tyneside, made enquiries about purchasing a locomotive, but Trevithick had by now moved on to other projects.

The first recorded commercial use of steam locomotion, albeit using the rack system, was on the Leeds & Middleton Colliery line in 1812. A 21-year-old colliery worker went to see it in action the following year, and young George Stephenson was greatly impressed by the principle, if not the detail, of the rack system. His own first locomotive, *Blucher*, appeared the following year. However, the wider initial enthusiasm for steam locomotives rather petered out, probably not helped by things like the lethal explosion of William Brunton's curious 'walking' locomotive in 1815.

One man who did not abandon the idea was Christopher Blackett and, in the absence of Richard Trevithick, he had his colliery overseer William Hedley and his blacksmith Timothy Hackworth develop locomotives. Hackworth was later to be an important figure in the development of locomotives, being responsible for many of the improvements to them in the years before the opening of the Liverpool & Manchester Railway. Two of Hedley's engines, *Puffing Billy* and

Wylam Dilly, dating from 1813/14, continued in use until the 1860s. The former can now be seen in the Science Museum. (One of Stephenson's colliery locomotives had an even longer life, not being withdrawn from service until 1912.) There was, however, relatively little evolution in their design up to 1820.

Thomas Grey describes seeing one of these early 'walking horses':

> ***'. . . certainly . . . it bears no resemblance to a living animal . . . the superabundant steam is emitted at each stroke with a noise something similar to the hard breathing or snorting of a horse — the escaping steam representing the breath of his nostrils and the deception altogether aided by the regular motion of the beam.'***
>
> (From *Observations on a General Iron Rail-way* — 1820, possibly reproduced from a report in the *Leeds Mercury* in 1812)

George Stephenson was one of the few unswerving champions of steam locomotion during this period. This newspaper report suggests that he at least was starting to make some progress with their design by the 1820s:

> ***'On Monday last a number of scientific gentlemen attended at Killingworth Colliery, to witness the first experiment of the improvements made by the ingenious Mr George Stephenson upon the locomotive steam engine invented by him when, notwithstanding the unfavourable state of the weather, the engine conveyed with the utmost facility (upon a railway having an elevation of one-eighth of an inch to a yard) twenty laden coal wagons, the aggregate weight of which, with the engine itself, may be estimated at nearly 100 tons, with an amazing degree of rapidity, and with an effect, upon the whole, which beggars all description. Too much credit cannot be given to Mr Stephenson for having brought this engine to such a state of perfection, and we heartily hope that he may ultimately reap the full benefit to which his extraordinary talents entitle him — The party afterwards dined with Mr Stephenson and found that his ingenuity was only exceeded by his hospitality.'***
>
> (*Newcastle Chronicle — 2 June 1821*)

If railways, passenger carrying and steam traction all pre-dated the Stockton & Darlington Railway, then so too did the large-scale thinking and major engineering works that were later to become associated with the railway age. The Standedge canal tunnel through the Pennines, dating from 1811, was over three miles long, a feat not equalled by the railway builders until 1886. As a measure of the ambition of these early engineers, it is worth noting that the idea of a Channel Tunnel was first conceived as early as 1802, and that it was politics that killed the idea, rather than concerns over the engineering difficulties. (The fact that Britain was in the middle of a period of war with France cannot have helped.)

The Tanfield Wagonway, opened in 1726 to serve a series of Durham mines, involved the diversion of a river — the Beckley Burn — and the construction of an embankment over its former bed that, at its fullest extent, stood some 100 feet high and 300 feet wide. Another of its notable features was the Causey Arch, a stone bridge with a span of some 105 feet. This wagonway carried substantial amounts of traffic — by 1732 it was conveying 1,000 tons of coal daily from pithead to wharf. Even more grandiose was the horse-drawn Central Junction Railway, promoted in 1819 or 1820 to link the Coventry coalfields with Stratford, Oxford, London and other locations. It was approved just six weeks after the Stockton & Darlington and opened in September 1826.

The Stockton & Darlington Railway

Periculum privatam utilitas publica

(*'Private risk for public service'* — the motto of the Stockton & Darlington Railway)

'The proprietors of the above concern, hereby give notice, that the main line of the Railway commencing at Wilton Park Colliery, in the west of this county, and terminating in Stockton–on-Tees, with several branches to Darlington, Yarm, &c, being in extent nearly 27 miles, will be formally opened for the general purposes of trade, on Tuesday 27th instant . . .'

'. . . An elegant dinner will be provided for the company who may attend, by Mr Foxton, in the Town's Hall, Stockton at three o' clock, to which the Proprietors have resolved to invite the neighbouring

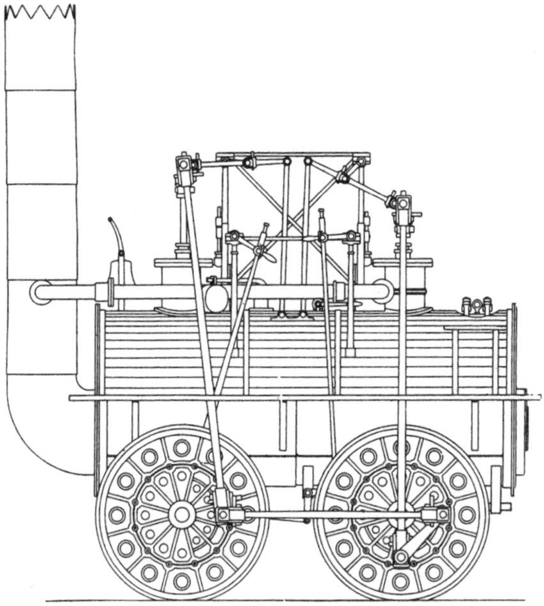

"THE ENGINEER" SWAIN SC.
"LOCOMOTION NO. 1"—STOCKTON AND DARLINGTON RAILWAY, 1825.

Locomotion No 1. It was not known as No 1 until 1833 as, at the time of the railway's opening, the company possessed only one locomotive. Its original title was therefore 'the Company's locomotive engine'. It operated on the Stockton & Darlington until 1841 and last moved under its own steam in 1846.

Nobility and Gentry who have taken an interest in this very important undertaking.

'. . . A superior locomotive engine, of the most improved construction, will be employed, with a train of convenient carriages, for the conveyance of Proprietors and strangers.'

(From the opening announcement of the Stockton & Darlington Railway, published in the *Manchester Guardian* — 24 September 1825)

In 1725, coal from the Etherley Colliery, near Bishop Auckland, cost 2½d a bushel (80 pounds) at the pithead and 8d on the streets of Darlington, 12 miles away. This difference in cost resulted from the mode of delivery, by packhorses. Wayleaves also hugely inflated the cost of delivery.

The Stockton & Darlington Railway first saw life in opposition to a proposed canal that would have by-passed Darlington. A link of some kind was first mooted in 1810 and John Rennie was bought in to survey the route and consider the respective merits of a canal and a tramway. His recommendation (which was not delivered until 1815) was the construction of a canal, but the cost and the effects of the Napoleonic Wars on the economy prevented the idea from being taken up. The people of Darlington were naturally never as keen as their Stockton neighbours on the canal idea, and when a public meeting was called in September 1818 to advocate the railway option, it was decided to apply for the necessary Act of Parliament. At this stage, the intention was to use horsepower, and the corporate seal of the railway in fact shows a horse-drawn railway.

The route was initially surveyed by George Overton, the man who had built the Penydarren tramway along which Trevithick's locomotive made its historic journey in 1804. The railway's leading promoter, Edward Pease, was a wool merchant from Darlington. As a Quaker, he was debarred from swearing oaths and therefore could not hold public office. His contribution to civic life was therefore to pursue his two great passions — the abolition of slavery and the promotion of a public railway. He took no payment for his work on the railway and at one stage even paid the wages of the construction workers from his own pocket when the company ran out of money.

The scheme faced some substantial opposition. Lord Eldon was the Lord Chancellor, and was one of the landed interests that benefited greatly from existing wayleaves along the route of the railway. The railway also had to be diverted to avoid trespassing on the land over which the Earl of Darlington fox-hunted with such great enthusiasm. The latter described the first scheme in 1819 as 'harsh and oppressive and injurious to the interests of the country through which it is intended that the railway should pass'.

The first Bill was vague as to the means of power. It offered the options of wagons being drawn by 'men or horses'. Steam power was also raised as a possibility, but many of the legislators in London, including the secretary to Lord Shaftesbury, had no conception of what a *loco-motive* was, and struck the offending word from the Bill. Even without it, the first Bill was narrowly lost in Parliament, in 1819.

The prospectus for the second Bill made clear the public benefits that the scheme would bring:

> ***'The cost of carriage of coal will be halved for a district of 40,000 people. A great nuisance will be removed from the roads by removing the numerous one-horse carts and carrying horses and asses which now infest them, for about 1/10th of this number on rail.'***

The death of George III in 1820 delayed the passage of the second Bill until April 1821, when it became the 21st railway Act to be passed since the turn of the century. With so many precedents, why has the Stockton & Darlington been singled out as historic? Its main purpose, like so many of the tramways of the day, was to open up the potential of a mining area — in this case, around Bishop Auckland. The means of traction was still far from clear. George Stephenson, who had re-surveyed the route, still referred to motive power by 'men, horses or otherwise', although elsewhere it did allow for the possible use of 'loco-motive or moveable steam engines'. For some, like George Overton, whom Stephenson had displaced as engineer of the railway, steam was an abomination. In his view: 'an engine on the public (rail) road would be a perpetual nuisance'. To the extent that steam locomotive and horse-drawn traffic proved to be fundamentally incompatible, he had a point. It was only when revisions to the route were made, requiring a second parliamentary approval, that consent was obtained at the same time for the radical possibility of passengers being conveyed by steam.

The parliamentary draftsmen did not exactly record the historic decision to allow steam-drawn passenger trains in a suitably memorable manner:

> ***'It shall and may be lawful for any person or persons permitted by them, from and after the passing of this Act, to make and erect such and so many loco-motive or moveable engines as the said company of proprietors shall from time to time think proper and expedient, and to use and employ the same in and upon the said railways or tramroads or any of them, by the said recited Act, and by the Act directed and authorised to be made, for the purpose of facilitating the transport, conveyance and carriage of goods, merchandise and other articles and things upon and along the said roads, and for the conveyance of passengers upon and along the same roads.'***

But, as we shall see, this was no guarantee for the railways that followed that steam locomotion would be either the preferred or even the permitted form of motive power.

The engineering of the railway was no small feat. There were embankments up to 48 feet high; a swamp — Myers Flat — which could almost rival Chat Moss on the Liverpool & Manchester, and which swallowed hundreds of tons of stone until a firm track-bed was found; and collieries like Brusselton and Etherley, which had to be linked to the railway by stationary engines, hauling goods wagons up steep inclines. But its most striking feature was the bridge over the River Skerne at Darlington; designed by a local architect, Ignatius Bonomi, it was a stone structure with a span of 39 feet 6 inches and a 30-foot clearance over the river.

In the end, the railway had a combination of locomotive, stationary engine and horse power, and a horse preceded Stephenson's engine, *Locomotion*, for the inaugural trip. Passengers had not yet mastered the discipline of rail travel. On the opening day, an estimated 450 people boarded a train with a capacity of 300 (for which 300 tickets had been issued) for the outward journey. The return journey was even more crowded, with 550 on board. One of the brakemen fell off his wagon and got his foot crushed. On the day of Darlington Races, would-be passengers clung to the side of any coach they could find.

Possibly the main contribution the Stockton & Darlington Railway made to the cause of steam locomotion in its early years was to suggest (the word *demonstrate* would perhaps overstate the case) that they could haul coal 30% more cheaply than horses. These early locomotives certainly did not prove themselves to be dramatically quicker than the competition. In fact, they were still so slow that children were in the habit of chasing after them and hitching a free ride on the wagons. The company had to issue a reward for the arrest of the guilty parties. On a number of the railways opened between 1825 and 1830, the locomotive lost out to horses, or to a combination of horses and stationary engines. In the case of the Canterbury & Whitstable Railway, as we shall see, Stephenson's locomotive *Invicta* hardly provided a ringing endorsement for the technology. The case for the locomotive was far from being won. The promoters of the Newcastle & Carlisle Railway were still struggling to make up their minds about steam locomotion as late as 1834.

Even after the Act was passed, the railway still faced the opposition from the Establishment, in all its forms. Two owners of the Stockton to Darlington road took exception to the way in which the railway crossed their property and a number of the workers found themselves being taken to court for trespass, where the Magistrates turned out to be precisely the same people who had made the original objection. The words 'natural justice' appeared not to be understood by these gentlemen, and the result of the court case was never in doubt.

Working on the railway

The first locomotive-men on the Stockton & Darlington were tough; they had to be. There was no weather protection of any kind on the early locomotives and, until 1840, when the first forlorn signal was introduced on the Railway (a second did not follow for many years) no real warning of danger ahead. There were not even any timetables that could be relied upon. The first George Stephenson locomotives had no brakes — in an emergency, the engineers had to try and reverse the direction of the locomotive, and the firemen to engage the primitive brakes on the wagons, to slow the juggernaut. Only when Timothy Hackforth's improved design of locomotives was introduced did stopping the locomotive itself become a possibility. Even changing the points was a health hazard; before 1839, the points were just a movable piece of rail that had to be held in place with a stick or rod as the train went over them. There was a real risk of derailment to the train and of injury to the railwayman operating them.

The dangers of operating the railway were not helped by the management regime. The mainly Quaker proprietors of the railway operated a harsh version of the Protestant work ethic. The long hours the railwaymen worked in bad conditions, and the experimental nature of the railway, made it all too easy for staff to break the company's many rules — and any worker found so doing was instantly fined. These fines were used to pay any compensation due to other workers injured in the course of their work, or to provide amenities like Sunday Schools for their families. In this way, the 'charity' of the Directors did not become a burden on the company balance sheet.

The line proved to be very popular with local business, despite all the early operational problems described in various parts of this book. In its first three months the Stockton & Darlington managed to deliver 10,000 tons of coal to Stockton, which could be sold — profitably — at 8s 6d per ton, compared with the pre-railway price of 18s. But the chaotic overcrowding that was the result of its heavy use led to accusations of favouritism. It was claimed that this colliery or that was being allowed to jump the queues that built up. Before long, the average time taken for a wagon to cover the $26^3/4$ miles between Bishop Auckland and Stockton had risen to $4^1/2$ days. There were even cases where the lack of siding space resulted in trucks being stored on the main line, blocking it completely.

Neither did all this activity make it an immediate commercial success. Despite the level of use, nobody was making much money out of the railway. Between 1825 and 1832, the maintenance of the track was costing them slightly more than they were earning in passenger contracts. As for the independent operators themselves, competition between them cut profit margins wafer-thin. All in all, investment in both track and rolling stock was being stifled.

In November 1830, Thomas Hall of the Black Boy Colliery wrote to the company with ideas for improving its operation. He wanted a Chief Manager appointed, who would resolve the competing demands of the users in a disinterested manner; substantial sidings at Stockton and Shildon, with separate provision for each colliery; places between Stockton & Darlington where wagons could be left overnight without blocking the line; and a complete ban on horse-drawn traffic to allow locomotives freer passage.

This latter proposal was the most radical, because it would effectively bar most independent users from the railway. It ran counter to the public access principle that was central to the Act setting up the railway, but that same public access was the prime cause of the chaos. Central control was essential. In 1833, a General Manager was appointed — the former blacksmith Timothy Hackworth, who had originally been appointed to look after their locomotives. He was also identified as the sole contractor to operate on the line.

He quickly set about removing the independents, by making steam locomotives the sole means of haulage and thus pricing them out. Most went without too much of a fight, given the lack of profit in the business and aided by payments from the company totalling £316 7s 8d. They were 'persuaded' to sign a document saying that they would not 're-establish any service without the consent of this company'. The legality of this document was open to question, since it deprived them of rights granted under the original parliamentary Act. Some of the colliery owners complained about restrictions on their freedom of operation. One colliery owner, denied access to the railway after dark, cited the turnpike analogy, claiming that 'on the same principle, Trustees of turnpike roads might close the gates at night except for their own carriages'.

Initially at least, the line was used overwhelmingly to serve the local collieries. Only 3% of its revenue in the period 1826 to 1828 came from passenger traffic. By contrast, 65% of the gross revenue of the Liverpool & Manchester in its first full year was passenger traffic. Despite everything, the line gradually became a commercial success.

The Canterbury & Whitstable Railway

The Stockton & Darlington and the Liverpool & Manchester are the most famous of the early railways, but there is another that can claim to be a pioneer. It was the first to take fare-paying passengers in steam-hauled trains and the first passenger railway of any kind in the south of England. It was built by George Stephenson, or at least by his apprentice, and also played a role in Brunel's construction of the Great Western Railway.

As long ago as 1783 plans were drawn up for a waterway linking Canterbury with the coast at Whitstable, and extending down through Kent as far as Ashford. The proposal failed, in part due to its high capital cost (£61,872), but the seeds of an idea had been sown. It was revived in 1825, in the form of a plan to make the River Stour navigable from Canterbury to Sandwich. This got as far as receiving Royal Assent on 22 June 1825, though there was much scepticism about its viability. Detractors said it involved a 70-mile navigation to reach a coast that was only six miles from Canterbury as the crow flies. Again, there was a high capital cost involved — over £80,000. But this time, the scheme had a rival — a railway, that its proponents claimed could be built for less than a third of the cost — £25,000. It received Royal Assent just twelve days before the navigation.

The scheme was the brainchild of William James, the pioneer of early railways who was to play such an important part in the Liverpool & Manchester Railway and was also an early advocate for a national network of routes. He was not only an advocate of railways, but also of steam locomotion. After a visit to George Stephenson at Killingworth Colliery in the late summer of 1821, he declared: 'here is an engine that will, before long, effect a complete revolution in society'. By 1823, among his many other activities, James had drawn up a report advocating direct inland communication between Kent, Surrey, Sussex and Hampshire.

On 5 November 1824, The Canterbury Rail Road Company was launched. It was floated on a share capital of £25,000 (in the form of 500 £50 shares) and a positive tidal wave of optimism, as Article 11 of its prospectus shows:

> ***'There cannot exist a doubt that not only the great landed interest, but even the Government itself will give their fostering support and powerful patronage to a measure teeming with national good.'***

More worryingly for the shareholders, they also assumed that the market would give them its universal backing. Their calculation was that 20,000 tons of goods moved annually between Whitstable and Canterbury, and they happily assumed that every last ounce of this traffic would transfer to rail, producing (at 5s a ton) an annual revenue stream of £5,000. This, and their estimate of the construction costs, was to prove seriously at odds with reality.

It is thought that three routes were originally considered. The most direct involved a tunnel of some half a mile through Tyler Hill. However, it was decided that the cost of this could be offset by fewer earthworks elsewhere along the line, and the direct route was chosen. This relative lack of engineering was achieved by the use of stationary steam engines to haul the trains up some of the steepest inclines, which were as much as 1:49. Elsewhere haulage would be by a combination of horses, steam locomotives and gravity.

Compared to the Liverpool & Manchester, the Canterbury & Whitstable seems to have had a relatively easy passage through Parliament. Certainly, the *Kentish Gazette* gave it a warm welcome, at a time when the Liverpool & Manchester had just lost its first, bitterly contested parliamentary Bill:

> ***'It is not so long since we gave an extract of a well-written article in the Quarterly Review, proving the great superiority of Railways over Canals with reference to the rapidity and regularity of the conveyance of goods, and it is now generally admitted that Railways are preferable to Canals for even where canal navigation is and has been for many years carried on with the greatest advantages, namely, in the neighbourhood of Manchester and Liverpool, a railway it is well known, is anxiously desired . . .'***
>
> (*Kentish Gazette — 14 June 1825*)

It was given parliamentary approval. One odd provision of the enabling Act was that no shareholders' meeting would be valid if held more than ten miles from Canterbury. George Stephenson was appointed to oversee the project but, so long as his attentions were fully occupied by work on the Stockton & Darlington, he was little more than a figurehead. He appointed as his on-site supervisor one John Dixon, a young man in his twenties, scarcely out of his apprenticeship. But even he was considerably delayed in leaving his responsibilities on other railway projects up north, and irate correspondence passed between the parties before he took up his post. In late October 1825, the first shipment of rails arrived from Northumberland and construction finally began.

The works — in particular, the tunnel through Tyler Hill — soon became a local tourist attraction, but equally quickly it became clear that they had seriously under-estimated the cost. Before long, work was being undertaken on a haphazard basis, as and when some money could be raised to pay the workers. During the winter of 1827/28, no work whatsoever was undertaken. Stephenson made it his priority to get the railway into some sort of state where it could start to generate revenue — using purely horsepower if necessary.

At one stage, there were thoughts of the entire railway being worked by stationary engines, but the success of locomotives at the Rainhill Trials led to them purchasing a locomotive — named the *Invicta* (or 'Undefeated', the motto of Kent). Built by Stephenson, it was a close relative of *Rocket*. It was trialled on 2 May 1830, and was initially an outstanding success, according to the *Kentish Chronicle,* achieving speeds of up to 17mph:

> ***'. . . On Sunday, the vehicle made several trips between Clowes Wood and Church Street, performing the distance with astonishing rapidity... Frequently a distance of two miles was made in the space of seven minutes and the speed might have accelerated very considerably, but as the trial was only intended to ascertain the disposition of the machinery that no failure might take place, the engine was not put to the full test of its power, which is that of ten horses . . .'***

The railway opened on 3 May 1830, months before the Liverpool & Manchester. A train, consisting of one closed carriage (for the Aldermen and Council officials) and several open ones, containing the directors of the railway, plus 'ladies, a band, proprietors of the railway and other invited guests' was hauled 'as it were by magic' up the slope by the first stationary engine. Passengers cheered (possibly nervously) as they were plunged into the darkness of the Tyler Hill Tunnel. Later in the trip, they were hauled behind *Invicta,* history's first steam-hauled passengers on a public railway.

Once the railway was opened for normal business, provision for passengers was much more prosaic — open wagons until 1832, when they tried to provide weather protection on the cheap. This consisted of four poles holding up a canvas roof. The effect of these was to create violent air currents around the wagons, which all too often blew the roof off! The company was eventually forced to incur the expense of properly built closed carriages (for which, naturally, an extra charge was made). Other facilities for passengers were equally rudimentary at first. Whitstable initially had no proper station — just a basic platform and a hut — and there were no timetables.

The railway was single track with just one passing place, at Clowes Wood. There, the trains would be divided in two. The passenger coaches descended under the control of gravity, achieving speeds of up to 30mph. Their only form of control was by the brakemen who rode on them. The goods wagons followed, at least having the restraint of the rope used by the stationary engine.

Or, at least, they were supposed to — operating practices were often lax, and the goods wagons would sometimes descend without the rope, relying purely on the brakemen. Normally this would be sufficient but, on 16 October 1840, a train of six fully loaded wagons on a wet and greasy track found themselves out of control as they approached North Lane station at a horrifying speed. The terrified brakemen leapt clear of the wagons — all except for one Charlie Curd, who clung on for dear life as the train hurtled through the station, shot off the end of the track and plunged into a yard, twelve feet below. They found the wagons, horribly mangled, and Charlie Curd equally so. Brian Hart, the railway's historian, records that he 'expired the following day in what must have been terrible agony'.

Safety had already proved a problem for a public unaccustomed to railways. They would attempt to board the trains while moving, or would walk in front of them. This had resulted in the railway's first fatal accident, in 1833, when a young girl called Jane Hazell came off second best in a collision with a train of descending wagons.

At first, in common with many early railways, they offered no service on a Sunday, but there was found to be a demand for leisure travel. The introduction of Sunday services led to an outcry from the local clergy about breaching the Sabbath, though this did not stop one of them — the Revd Spencer Braham — from asking to be given a free season ticket. He did not get one, but the idea caught on. From 1834, customers could buy a seven-month season ticket for £2 2s (or £5 5s for a family ticket).

Financial problems dogged the railway from the start. It had been under-capitalised and suffered from being a pioneer. The build costs, at £14,350 a mile, had been almost three times the £5,000 a mile estimate. Their hopes of monopolising road traffic proved ill founded. The road hauliers could offer the great benefit of door-to-door shipment, which offset much of the advantage of a relatively short rail journey. Then, after barely a year of operation, a bridge at Church Road in Whitstable was found to be in imminent danger of collapse. In lieu of the expensive repairs it needed, the bridge was shored up with timbers, a temporary solution which remained in place for the rest of the life of the railway, and beyond.

Problems also emerged with *Invicta*, which, contrary to its name, was defeated by the task of hauling loads up the hill out of Whitstable Harbour. Despite being nominally rated at 10 horsepower, it was found that four strong horses could do the job better than the locomotive. This they did until a new stationary steam engine was installed, while *Invicta* was retired to lighter duties elsewhere on the line. By 1836, it was found to be in need of expensive repairs, but an ill-advised attempt to do the work on the cheap turned out to be a total failure. The locomotive — the only one on the railway — was mothballed and, in 1839, unsuccessful attempts were made to sell it.

The other great problem with the railway was the lack of proper harbour facilities at Whitstable. A new harbour was duly opened on 19 March 1832. In an early example of integrated transport, it offered lower tolls for ships offloading goods for onward transmission by railway.

Isambard Kingdom Brunel visited the line in 1835. He had become engaged in a heated debate over the safety of the Box Tunnel, which he was building on the Great Western line. An opponent of the Great Western Railway, Dr Dionysius Lardner, claimed that a train suffering brake failure in the tunnel would emerge from it at 120mph, at which speed the passengers would be unable to breathe. Brunel tested this hypothesis by a group of people in a wagon freewheeling down the 1:49 incline that led to the Tyler Hill Tunnel and going through it at maximum speed. Naturally, no such fate befell them, and the brakesman was able to stop the wagon within sixty yards of leaving the tunnel.

Not all reviewers were complimentary about the service. *The Steam Packet and Coast Companion* talks of passengers as travelling in 'a kind of omnibus with coal carts behind' and describes the section where the passengers freewheel downhill in the following terms:

> ***'They are detached from the machine and set down an inclined plane, until they arrive at the ascent of the second hill, going with the most frightful velocity, to those unaccustomed thereto, being nearly a mile in a minute . . .***

'. . . This is a journey very expeditious, but requires strong nerves, particularly for ladies.'

The railway's financial problems continued into the 1840s, by which time its technology of stationary engines was outmoded. The railway was now facing competition from other lines with more efficient locomotive-hauled services. It was eventually leased to the South Eastern Railway in 1844. This was the start of it being converted into a conventional locomotive-hauled line that survived until 1952. The railway's claim to fame survived beyond its closure, until 1969, when the world's oldest surviving railway bridge — the one over Church Road, temporarily propped-up in 1831 — was finally demolished.

The Liverpool & Manchester Railway

Iron railway between Manchester and Liverpool

'For many years past, an undertaking of this sort has, at different times, been a subject of consideration; but there has not hitherto been a sufficient combination of interest or property engaged in favour of the plan, to admit of its being commenced. We understand, however, that the attention of a great number of the leading merchants, both in Manchester and Liverpool, has recently turned to the subject, and that a variety of calculations have been made to show the great public advantage which may be expected to accrue from the undertaking being carried into effect. The result, it is probable, will be, that public meetings of the inhabitants of this town and Liverpool will speedily be called to consider the scheme. And that early application will be made to Parliament for the powers requisite to carry it into effect. It is, perhaps, scarcely necessary to add, that the use of steam carriages is contemplated.'

(*The Times — 29 July 1822,* reprinting an item from the *Manchester Guardian*)

'The great work of the Liverpool & Manchester Railway, advancing towards completion, seemed, by a common unanimity of opinion, to be deemed as the

experiment which was to decide the fate of rail-ways. The eyes of the whole scientific world were upon that great undertaking.'

(Nicholas Wood, Manager of Killingworth Colliery, 1832)

The Liverpool & Manchester was not the first public railway, nor even the first public railway in Lancashire (the Bolton & Leigh opened in August 1828). But it can lay claim to being the world's first real railway, as we would understand it. It was fully operated by steam locomotives, double tracked and worked to a timetable (even though the timetable told you the time of your departure, but not that of your arrival). The idea of a railway between the two towns (as they then were) had been put forward in the late 18th century, when William Jessop, who built the Surrey Iron Railway, surveyed the route (no trace of his survey remains). But when Thomas Grey published his *Observations on a General Iron Rail-way* in 1820, he saw this route as a prototype for a national (and, indeed, Europe-wide) network of railway lines.

It was a wealthy corn merchant, Joseph Sandars, and a lawyer and land agent, William James — the man behind the Canterbury & Whitstable Railway — that took the first serious steps towards its construction. As we saw earlier, the case for the railway company rested very heavily upon the poor service provided by the existing carriers. As the evidence put before Parliament said:

'It will be shown that it has taken longer to pass goods from Liverpool to Manchester, than to bring them over from America to Liverpool. It will be shown, that what is stated, takes place not once occasionally, but often; that goods have taken twenty-one days in coming from America to Liverpool. And that they have staid (sic) on the wharfs before they could get the means of conveyance to Manchester for more than six weeks...

'...It is not that the water companies have not been able to carry goods on more reasonable terms, but that, strong in the enjoyment of their monopoly, they have not thought proper to do so. Against the most arbitrary exactions the public have hitherto had no protection, and against the indefinite continuance or recurrence of the evil, they have but one security — IT IS COMPETITION THAT IS WANTED.'

As evidence that this was the case, the Bridgewater reduced its rates by 1s 6d a ton, immediately before the first Liverpool & Manchester Railway

Bill went before Parliament. As soon as it was thrown out, they were raised back to their old level.

James originally surveyed the route in 1822. He had previously visited George Stephenson and was later to describe him as 'the greatest genius of the age'. It was therefore no surprise that Stephenson was brought in to work up the detailed scheme, experiencing considerable difficulty with sometimes violent opposition from the landowners in doing so, as this letter from October 1824 shows:

> ***'We have sad work with Lord Derby, Lord Sefton and Bradshaw the great Canal Promoter whose ground we go through with the projected railway. Their Ground is blockaded on every side to prevent us getting on with the Survey — Bradshaw fires guns through his ground in the course of the night to prevent the surveyors coming on in the dark... we are going to have a grand field day next week, when the Liverpool Railway Company are determined to force a survey through if possible — Lord Sefton says he will have a hundred men against us — the Company thinks these great men have no right to stop a survey.'***

Stephenson had to conduct parts of his survey by stealth — sometimes by night — and with the use of violence to counter violence — one of his surveyors hired a prizefighter to accompany him. He ended up in a fist-fight with a miner from St Helens, which the pugilist won, but the rest of his team were driven off by a volley of stones from the miner's supporters, and the surveyor's theodolite was smashed.

The detailed story of the battle to secure the consent of Parliament, and then to build it, has been well documented elsewhere (See, for example, *The Liverpool and Manchester Railway Project 1821-1831* by Robert E. Carlson). The problems with conducting the survey, along with his lack of education and his heavy commitments elsewhere, may help to explain Stephenson's lack of mastery of his brief when the first Liverpool & Manchester Railway Bill came before Parliament. The eminent engineer William Cubitt was produced to testify that none of Stephenson's levels were correct, and that the track level on a bridge across the River Irwell was actually below the maximum flood level of the river. Counsel for the objectors, Edward Alderson, exposed a catalogue of errors in his survey and Stephenson's ignorance of its contents, in what must be one of the most spectacular and humiliating cross-examinations in legal history.

> ***'Did any ignorance ever arrive at such a pitch as this? Was there ever any ignorance exhibited like it? Is Mr Stephenson to be the person upon whose faith this Committee is to pass this Bill, involving property to the extent of 400,000£ or 500,000£, when he is so ignorant of his profession, as to propose to build a bridge not sufficient to carry off the flood water of the river, or to permit any of the vessels to pass which must of necessity pass under it, and to leave his own railroad liable to be several feet under water?'***

Stephenson said of the experience afterwards:

> ***'I began to wish for a hole to creep into. Some members of the Committee asked me if I were a foreigner, and another hinted that I was mad.'***

Alderson won fame and fortune on the back of his cross-examination. He ended his days as a judge and a Baron. Stephenson claimed that the errors in his initial survey of the route were the result of skulduggery. He thought that the Bridgewater Canal interests had planted two of the surveyors involved on him as an act of sabotage. Sadly, another of those responsible for the errors took the humiliation to heart even more than Stephenson himself: a young engineer named Hugh Steele in Stephenson's Newcastle office committed suicide.

Not surprisingly, the first Bill was thrown out. Equally unsurprisingly, Stephenson was relieved of his duties as chief engineer for the submission of the second Bill. The prestigious engineers George and John Rennie were bought in to re-survey the route, after having snootily refused the Stockton & Darlington contract, on the grounds that they were far too busy dealing with public works 'of infinitely greater magnitude and importance than the Darlington Railway'. Their assistant, who did the work, Charles Vignoles, proved to be not only a competent and politically aware surveyor, but also a rather smoother operator in the face of cross-examination in Parliament. He re-routed the line around some of its major opponents, and others were bought off. In particular, the possible use of steam locomotives was played down. But the greatest coup was in getting the Marquis of Stafford, the heir to the Duke of Bridgewater and thus an important figurehead in the canal interest, to invest no less than £100,000 in the railway. The second Bill received parliamentary approval on 5 May 1826. It cost the promoters over £70,000 to secure parliamentary approval, and led for calls for a review of the system:

> ***'The moment a scheme that is likely to be beneficial to the country is proposed, it is treated as a public nuisance by the parliament... as a general offence against the nation, which is only to be expiated by a huge tax.'***
>
> (*Monthly Review*, quoted in Garfield, page 99)

The Rennies set unacceptable conditions for their appointment as engineers to the new line (such as wanting to employ the doyen of their profession, Thomas Telford, as their 'assistant'). After shopping around for an alternative, the company eventually went back to George Stephenson and re-appointed him. By this time, the Stockton & Darlington Railway was open and his reputation was somewhat restored. They appointed Charles Vignoles as his assistant. Neither of them was pleased with this arrangement. George Stephenson eventually eased Vignoles out, and Vignoles in turn said of his former superior:

> ***'He did not look on the concern with a liberal and expanded view but with a microscopic eye; magnifying details and pursuing a petty system of parsimony very proper in a private colliery line or in a small undertaking but wholly inapplicable to this national work.'***

The crossing of Chat Moss, a silted-up lake west of Manchester that had become a watery swamp in which the unwary could easily perish, has become part of railway legend. Opponents of the railway saw it as one of their trump cards and Stephenson's talk of 'floating' the railway over the Moss had done much to undermine his credibility at the first parliamentary inquiry. During the construction, opponents spread alarming stories of hundreds of construction workers, horses and wagons being swallowed up by the Moss, and of work being abandoned. Even the railway's backers looked on in alarm as Stephenson poured what seemed to be endless quantities of foundation materials into an alleged bottomless pit. In total, 670,000 cubic yards of material was tipped onto Chat Moss, most of which was never seen again.

In fact, the method used to cross Chat Moss was a well-established engineering technique. Whole areas of housing along the Thames, not far from the Houses of Parliament, were built on land reclaimed on similar principles. In simple terms, it involved laying two drains along the line of the route, putting woven hazelwood hurdles along it and covering them with brushwood and gravel. As they sank, they squeezed some of the water from the moss into the drains, and so the process went on until the structure came to rest on the firm clay bottom (in this case, up to thirty-four feet down). Although it took a long time — work started in July 1826 and was not completed until December 1829 — it was in fact the cheapest part of the railway to construct. The four-mile section cost just £28,000 — below even Stephenson's estimate of £40,000 — and some said the ride over that section was smoother than on 'firm ground'.

The first Act had imposed a range of operating restrictions on the Railway. No steam locomotives were to be used in Liverpool and the Manchester end of the line was originally required to terminate in Salford, across the River Irwell from Manchester itself. Elsewhere, any locomotives must 'consume their own smoke'; gated level crossings had to be provided at all road crossings, and had to be set in favour of road traffic and against trains. The Act laid down maximum charges for the use of the railway and, in an echo of the turnpike roads with which they were compared in many contemporary minds, the Railway was expected to install tollgates across the line.

If dividends from the railway exceeded 10%, charges had to be reduced accordingly (by contrast, the Bridgewater Canal for many years paid an annual dividend of close to 100%). In addition, 10% of all profits from the railway had to go into a fund, to be used to top up dividends in the event that they fell below 10%. The company had to raise all of the £510,000 estimated cost of building the railway before construction could start, and limits were placed (£127,000) on the additional amount they could borrow in the event of a cost overrun.

Further parliamentary approvals were obtained in March 1828 and May 1829. Among other things, these made minor alterations to the route, established the gauge of the railway and allowed an extension of the line into Manchester. (The choice of Liverpool Road for the station site was determined by what they saw as the vital need for them to be located close to the warehousing area of the canal companies.) Importantly, the 1829 Act also allowed the company to act as a common carrier on the Railway, while still requiring them to maintain it as a public highway, should others wish to operate it independently.

'All persons shall have free liberty to use with carriages all Roads, Ways and Passages for the purposes of carrying goods, wares, merchandise and other things, passengers or cattle... and to pass along the said railway with carts or wagons properly constructed.'

As with the Stockton & Darlington, a majority of the Directors had initially wanted the company to limit itself to being the track authority, rather than being the sole carrier. They were understandably nervous about the additional investment required in locomotives, rolling stock, lifting gear, warehousing and staff, especially since they had already had to borrow an additional £100,000 in April 1827 from the Exchequer Loan Commissioners, just to finance the construction of the railway.

Against this, they were keenly aware of the chaos being experienced on the Stockton & Darlington as a result of multiple carriers; they knew they would have to make some investment in rolling stock and warehousing in any event; and they could see the cost savings and increased profits that could be realised as sole carrier. More generally, having a variety of operators operating the same track, with different allegiances, equipment of different standards and equally diverse operating practices, was a recipe for danger. A railway was not like a canal or a turnpike; it needed a single set of rules and a single authority to apply them.

Early in 1831, the company therefore nominally fulfilled its legal obligation under their Act to provide for the possibility of independent operators running their own trains along the line. They learned from the early mistakes of the Stockton & Darlington, and closely specified the design of the locomotives and rolling stock to be used. The independent operator would have been at a disadvantage in a number of ways: the cost of providing this rolling stock would have been high, possibly prohibitively so if it could not be intensively used; the standard of maintenance was set equally high and the independent operator would have been constrained in his operation by the Railway's timetable and by competition from the Railway's own rolling stock. The Railway was opened to independents, on these restrictive terms, from the beginning of May 1831.

Before long, a number of branch lines had been connected to the Liverpool & Manchester, each of them operated by a separate carrier who would want to extend his routes along the main line. The company made punitive charges for the use of the track and generally made life as difficult as possible for rival operators. It will come as little surprise that very few independent operators survived long, and that the railway was left, in effect, as sole carrier.

Steam locomotion and the Rainhill Trials

The choice of motive power on the Liverpool & Manchester was far from clear-cut. The possibility of using steam locomotives had been played down during the passage of the successful Bill through Parliament, in order to remove one possible source of opposition. In any event, the few steam locomotives in use on other public railways had not shown themselves to be decisively better than the alternatives.

Benjamin Thompson's patent 'reciprocating' rope haulage system was favoured by some interests. It had worked reliably on mining railways in County Durham (something steam locomotives could not always claim at this time). It could pull wagons at 7mph over undulating tracks. But George Stephenson could see its limitations. Stationary engines could not cope with substantial increases in the volume and weight of traffic, whereas locomotives could be developed (and purchased) incrementally, in line with need. They presented particular complications when constructing branch lines or sidings, and a problem with one of them brought the whole railway line to a standstill. Others considered them to be unsuitable for passenger use.

The Directors of the Liverpool & Manchester Railway commissioned trials of the steam locomotives at Killingworth Colliery early in 1825, while the final form of motive power for the railway was still under consideration. There was clearly a good deal of black propaganda being circulated about the outcome of these trials, prompting a report in *The Times* on 8 February. This talked of 'tests made with an old and imperfect engine, the results of which gave a speed of not more than 4 miles an hour with a moderate load. Later tests with a superior engine gave an average velocity of nearly 7 miles an hour and the greatest speed 9½ miles an hour'. James Walker, the leader of the engineers supervising the tests, complained about the misrepresentation surrounding them, and was at pains to point out that 'had the railway been good and well fixed, the result would have been higher'. At around the same time as these trials were taking place, the proprietors of the Mersey & Irwell Navigation were conducting their own demonstrations, showing how horse-drawn barges could make a return trip between Liverpool and Manchester in twenty-four hours.

The delegation reported in favour of stationary engines, and Stephenson produced a detailed counter-argument. A second and more expert delegation, sent in March 1829 and including the engineer John Rastrick, again found marginally in favour of stationary engines, despite seeing an improved Stephenson locomotive, the *Lancashire Witch*, in action. Again Stephenson sought to rebut their arguments.

The following month, the company announced that a trial would be held that October. The section of the railway around Rainhill included a level stretch and an incline. A stationary engine would be built at the incline and the competing locomotives could run on the flat section. They advertised for competitors:

> ***'To engineers and iron founders.***
>
> ***The Directors of the Liverpool and Manchester Railway hereby offer a premium of £500 (over and above the cost price) for a LOCOMOTIVE ENGINE, which shall be a decided improvement on any hitherto constructed, subject to certain stipulations and conditions, a copy of which may be had at the Railway Office, or will be forwarded, as may be directed, on application for the same, if by letter, post paid.'***
>
> (*Advertisement from the Liverpool Mercury — 1 May 1829*)

The competition brought a bewildering variety of eccentrics out of the woodwork. According to Henry Booth, the treasurer of the railway company:

'Communications were received from all classes of persons, each recommending an improved power or an improved carriage... every element and almost every substance were brought into requisition, and made subservient to the great work. The friction of the carriages was to be reduced so low that a silk thread would draw them, and the power to be applied was so vast as to rend a cable asunder.

'Hydrogen gas and high-pressure steam — columns of water and columns of mercury — a hundred atmospheres and a perfect vacuum — machines working in a circle without fire or steam... to the **ne plus ultra** ***of perpetual motion. Every scheme which the restless ingenuity or prolific imagination of man could devise was liberally offered to the Company.'***

The competition was eventually whittled down to five finalists, two of which soon proved not to be serious contenders. The Stephensons' entry was, of course, the famous *Rocket.* It incorporated at least two important improvements. The first, claimed as the brainchild of Henry Booth (though many others had experimented with the idea) was the multi-tube boiler. One of the main shortcomings of earlier locomotives was their inability to raise enough steam, and the multi-tube boiler provided a larger surface area for heating the water. The other major improvement was the blastpipe exhaust, something Stephenson had patented in February 1815. This injected the waste steam from the cylinders up the chimney, helping the fire to burn more efficiently, so that full benefit could be extracted from the multi-tube boiler. These improvements are discussed in more detail later.

The other entries were:

> The *Sans Pareil*, developed by Timothy Hackworth, then in charge of the locomotives on the Stockton & Darlington Railway. He had a considerable reputation — his *Royal George* was the most powerful and advanced locomotive built up to that time and *Sans Pareil* was a scaled-down version of it, built to try and comply with the competition weight rules. However, it failed on the grounds of being too heavy, though it was still allowed to compete. It was also untried — Hackworth had built it at the last minute and on a shoestring budget, as a spare-time activity over and above his day job. More importantly, it was perhaps a final development of the old design of locomotives, whereas *Rocket* pointed the way to the future.
>
> *Novelty* was entered by John Braithwaite and John Ericsson of London, whose main business was pumps and other high-pressure steam engines. One of their fire engines put out a blaze at the House of Commons, and Ericsson would go on to design the *Monitor*, the revolutionary iron-clad battleship used in the American Civil War. They built the *Novelty*, their first locomotive, in just seven weeks, and it was partly based on their fire engines. There was no track in London on which they could test *Novelty* beforehand and it turned out to have a basic design fault, in that it tended to fill up rapidly with clinker. Contemporary detractors also said it looked more like a tea urn than a serious locomotive.

> *Perseverance*, entered by Timothy Burstall of Edinburgh, was damaged *en route* to the trials and played little part in them. Even had it been in pristine condition, it was a blind alley in design terms.
>
> The *Cyclopede* was the most bizarre entry — a light cart, driven by a treadmill powered by two horses, and entered by T. S. Brandreth, a director of the Liverpool & Manchester Railway.

At the pre-trial displays, the lightweight *Novelty* showed an unexpected turn of speed and soon became the favourite of the huge crowd. Stephenson, however, dismissed it as having 'no guts', and on the first day of the trials proper it broke down; *Sans Pareil* also had minor problems; and *Perseverance* did not run. When *Sans Pareil* did run, its fuel consumption was found to be far in excess of that of *Rocket*. Only *Rocket* was able to meet the conditions of the trial — even exceeding them by achieving a maximum speed of 29mph, compared with the 10mph required as the average for the trial. More importantly, *Rocket* pointed the way to the development of the locomotive over the next century in a way that none of the others did — as *Planet* and the other locomotives that were derived from it were to show. In addition to the £500 prize, the Stephensons won orders for four more *Rocket*-class locomotives. Under the influence of James Cropper, a member of the Liverpool & Manchester board who opposed the Stephensons, two replicas of *Novelty* were also ordered, but they failed in their trials. The *Sans Pareil* had a working life on other railways until 1863.

Running the railway

'Never was there such an assemblage of wealth, rank, beauty and fashion in this neighbourhood.'

(*From a contemporary account of the opening of the Liverpool & Manchester Railway*)

The railway was opened on 15 September 1830, amid much ceremony and in the presence of many dignitaries, including the Prime Minister, the Duke of Wellington. One of the eminent guests, the local Member of Parliament and former President of the Board of Trade, William Huskisson, slipped and fell beneath the wheels of one of the trains. He was rushed by train to the nearest medical help, but died the following day. This cast a major shadow on the proceedings, which were also used by radical elements in the crowd to protest against the Government's policies (to many in Manchester, the Duke of Wellington was seen more as the villain of Peterloo, rather than the hero of Waterloo). It was said that the crowds at the Liverpool end of the opening ceremony watched it with patriotic fervour, while those in Manchester displayed 'looks of sullen or insolent indifference' (*Blackwood's Edinburgh Magazine*).

The railway was built primarily to carry goods in competition with the canals, so it is perhaps surprising that its first impact on its rivals was to destroy the passenger business of the turnpikes. Within two years of it opening, all but one of the stagecoaches operating between Liverpool and Manchester had gone out of business, and that survivor was carrying only parcels. The tollgates on the turnpike, hitherto leased for up to £1,500 each, became unlettable. The railway was overwhelmed by the unexpected public demand for passenger travel. In the first full calendar year of operation (1831) it carried 445,057 passengers. From December 1830, the price of a first-class trip was reduced from 7s to 5s and second-class from 4s to 3s 6d, though an 'extra-first-class' option, travelling in luxury by express train for 7s, was also introduced. It also started carrying animals in 1831. For the purpose of comparison with a second-class human passenger, a pig made the trip for 1s 6d and a sheep for 9d.

The canals, meanwhile, had been forced to drop their goods rates by 30% to compete, but they at least still had plenty of business. Goods traffic, the railway's original purpose, did not even start as a separate enterprise until 4 December 1830, when the first 30-ton load of cotton, oatmeal and malt made its way by rail to Manchester. By the end of the month, 1,432 tons of goods had been carried and, by the following March, the figure was up to 5,500 tons a month. Before long, individual trains 120 yards long carrying 151 tons were being hauled (quadruple-headed up the Rainhill incline) and income from freight began to cross-subsidise passenger fares. Freight trains had to leave between 15 and 30 minutes before any following passenger service, and had to be shunted off into a siding if the passenger train caught up.

The Liverpool & Manchester would eventually merge in 1845 with the Grand Junction Railway. Given the national and international interest that surrounded its opening, it is perhaps surprising that it did not immediately start a flood of similar schemes. Some twenty-five new railways had been approved between 1826 and 1830, but only ten new lines received parliamentary approval in 1831 and 1832, three of which were never built, and another being a branch line to the Liverpool & Manchester. Five of the remainder had a combined length of less than sixty miles, and included the first line in Ireland. This reticence was partly due to people waiting to see whether the Liverpool & Manchester was a success before embarking on such a costly undertaking. But it was also a reflection of the unsettled politics of the day, with large-scale public unrest in the run-up to the Reform Act of 1832.

The Grand Junction and London & Birmingham Railways

Two schemes that were also unsuccessful in their first attempt at securing parliamentary approval — the Grand Junction and the London & Birmingham Railways — brought Stephenson's grand vision of a national network an important step closer.

A line south from the Liverpool & Manchester, linking it to Birmingham and thence to London, was first proposed by William James in 1808. An attempt was made in 1824 to secure parliamentary approval for the northern half of the route, but it was seen off by the canal lobby, which had just started constructing the Birmingham & Liverpool Junction Canal. However, once the Liverpool & Manchester Railway was trading successfully, it was an idea whose time had come. In similar vein, the London to Birmingham Railway had an unsuccessful trial run through Parliament in 1830, before the two separate Acts for the building of the Grand Junction and London & Birmingham Railways were passed in May 1833. This is not to say that the opposition was not fierce, because the canal owners as well as the turnpike, coach and wagon interests now knew from the experience of the Liverpool & Manchester what the likely commercial consequences of its construction would be for them.

As with a number of the early railways, the Grand Junction concentrated solely on making the most direct possible link between the major centres at either end of the line. The potential custom from the large towns along the route was ignored, and places like Walsall, Wolverhampton and Nantwich found themselves stranded, some miles off the route. George Stephenson was once again engaged as the Chief Engineer of the Grand Junction, and appointed as a relatively junior assistant the 28-year-old Joseph Locke. Stephenson was by now in great demand, and increasingly distanced himself from the project, much to the annoyance of the Directors. As relations between the two steadily worsened, Locke by contrast greatly impressed the company, and was appointed as the line's engineer under Stephenson, and then in November 1834 as Chief Engineer of equal status to Stephenson, who promptly refused to have anything further to do with the Railway and subsequently resigned.

Despite all these complications, Locke brought the 78-mile Grand Junction in on time. It opened in July 1837, and (most unusually for any major civil engineering project of that or any other era) was within budget. Locke's own estimate of the cost was just £25,000 a mile — others put the cost even lower — and this despite having to pay out £211,862 in land costs and compensation. He even arrived in Birmingham before the terminus at Curzon Street was finished, and the service had to begin operations from a temporary station in the Vauxhall Pleasure Gardens.

Locke was fortunate to have Thomas Brassey (1805–70) as one of his major contractors for the Grand Junction. Brassey was 'discovered' by George Stephenson running a stone quarry, was lured into the railway industry, and went on to become one of the greatest railway contractors, a byword in the industry for both his skill and his integrity. He also went on to become hugely rich. When he died in 1870, he left a fortune of £3.2 million, the second largest personal estate ever recorded up to that time.

The 112-mile London & Birmingham took almost a year longer to complete, opening in June 1838. Its cost, at £5½ million, or £53,000 per mile, was more than double that of the Grand Junction and twice the original estimate. Their bill for land purchase and compensation was correspondingly higher, at over £500,000 (for land valued at less than half that sum) and the costs involved simply in obtaining parliamentary approval came to £73,000. There was the usual opposition to the railway from landed interests — the surveyors avoided the wrath of one clerical landowner by surveying his property only when they knew he would be conducting church services. Unexpected problems with the geology along the route added to the cost, as did Robert Stephenson's conservatism as the railway's engineer. Stephenson was also the country's leading manufacturer of steam locomotives at this time. Mindful of the limitations of his early locomotives, he set himself the design criterion of having no gradient on the railway of more than 1:330 (with one exception, mentioned below). This necessitated some major engineering works along the route, which Nock suggests might have been avoided or at least greatly reduced with a relaxation to 1:200.

The London & Birmingham had as its London terminus the

architectural spectacle of Euston station, though it was not the best advertisement for the early locomotives. The slope of 1 in 70 on the approach to the station proved too much for them and, up to 1844, they had to use a stationary engine to get the trains out of the station. In Birmingham, the two railways met up at Curzon Street, some distance from the heart of the town centre.

In July 1846, the Grand Junction, London & Birmingham and Manchester & Birmingham Railways would amalgamate to form the nucleus of one of the giants of British railways — the London & North Western Railway. The new company's locomotive superintendent bore a famous name — Francis Trevithick, the son of the locomotive pioneer.

The Great Western Railway

The first proposal to link London and what was then the second city in England — Bristol — emerged in 1824. A company was formed and an initial survey carried out by a man better known as a road-builder, John McAdam. It should perhaps not be a surprise that what emerged were parallel proposals for a railway, carrying goods only, that skirted around the principal towns along the route, and a turnpike road for passengers, which took them through the towns.

The scheme never got as far as a parliamentary Bill, but it was revived in 1832. This time, an inexperienced 27-year-old was appointed Engineer, on the strength of a local track record in Bristol that included the, as yet unbuilt, Clifton Suspension Bridge and improvements to the Floating Harbour. His name was Isambard Kingdom Brunel. The initial Bill was opposed by a wide range of interests — they included the usual local landowners and canal and coaching interests; the promoters of the rival London & Southampton Railway; the residents of Brompton, who would have the terminus located among them; farmers, who feared the competition of the cheap imports the railway would bring; the Corporation of Maidenhead, who would lose tolls on their bridge; and the Provost of Eton College, who thought the railway would cause London to pour forth:

> ***'...the most abandoned of its inhabitants to come down by the railway and pollute the minds of the scholars, whilst the boys themselves would take advantage of the short interval of their play hours to run up to town, mix in all the dissipation of London life, and return before their absence could be discovered.'***

The initial Bill, for only part of the route, was lost in July 1834. A second Bill, this time for the entire route, was quickly drawn up. The new prospectus spoke of negotiations with the London & Birmingham Railway for a junction near Wormwood Scrubs, enabling the GWR to share their new terminus at Euston. When negotiations for this later fell through, the unplanned need to provide a separate London terminus was one of the main factors that pushed the railway's cost through the roof. By August 1838, the original £2.5 million estimate had grown to £4.28 million, even before any locomotives and rolling stock had been purchased. Paddington was chosen as the location for the terminus, being at that time both semi-rural and one of the less exclusive parts of the London hinterland.

The second Bill got Royal Assent in August 1835. Notable among its provisions were the concessions needed to buy off Eton College, whose alumni no doubt featured prominently among the parliamentarians considering the Bill. They included 'a good and sufficient fence on each side' of the four-mile stretch of the line nearest to the College and 'a sufficient additional number of persons for the purpose of preventing or restricting all access to the said Railway by the Scholars of Eton College'.

The company was also refused the right to construct a station at nearby Slough, to discourage the scholars from rail travel. They easily got round the problem of having no station, at first by using some rooms in

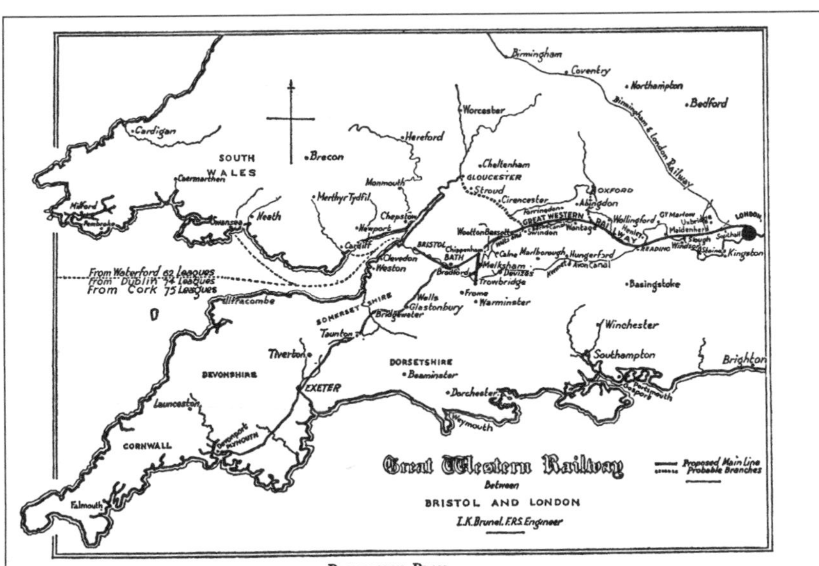

PROSPECTUS PLAN

The original plan for the Great Western Railway, as set out in their prospectus (from MacDermot).

the nearby Crown inn as an office and waiting room, and simply stopping the trains on the adjacent piece of track for people to board. Later, they bought their own pub, the New Inn, part of which they leased back to the licensee, the remainder being given over to station activities. A furious Provost of the College took the matter to court, but was told by the Lord Chancellor that the Company could do anything not expressly forbidden in the Act (which this was not). Within a month of this court defeat, the College had overcome its principled opposition to the railway to such an extent that it chartered a special train to take its pupils to see Queen Victoria's Coronation. The railway would later (1848) secure permission for a branch line to Windsor, running dangerously close to the College. This was subject to even more stringent access controls, again designed to save the souls of Eton pupils.

The railway also faced similar opposition from another educational establishment — this time the University of Oxford and its Chancellor, the Duke of Wellington. Their influence was able to ensure that the nearest station to the dreaming spires was initially at Steventon, some ten miles away, adding an hour and a half to the journey time to London. By 1842, some 77,567 passengers a year were being forced to endure the three-shilling coach ride between city and distant station.

By July 1842, the Great Western Railway was open as far as Taunton, 163 miles from Paddington. *En route* it had sown the seeds of one of the great railway towns, Swindon; had met one of the great engineering challenges of the age in the Box Tunnel; and had laid the ground for the gauge wars of the 1840s — all of which are described elsewhere in this book.

Chapter 3:
The railway pioneers

George Stephenson (1781–1848) and Robert Stephenson (1803–59)

'I will do something in coming time which will astonish all England!'

(George Stephenson, c1814)

If George Stephenson was not born with railways in his blood, he was certainly born with them in his front garden. He was the son of a fireman at Wylam Colliery, just to the west of Newcastle, and the mine's wooden tramway ran directly in front of his house. His first job, aged eight, was to stop the cows from straying onto the line. Two years later, he was put in charge of a horse on the tramway and by the age of fourteen he had become assistant to his father. He soon displayed an aptitude for fixing machinery and progressed within three years to become the plugman (in charge of one of the mine's stationary steam engines, and senior to his father).

Illiterate until the age of 18, Stephenson took evening classes in English and mathematics, but never became proficient. However, his biographer Hunter Davies suggests that self-doubt was never a major feature of Stephenson's make-up. The words 'dogmatic', 'opinionated' and 'vengeful' describe some of the less attractive aspects of his character. In 1804, by this time a widower in his twenties with a son, Robert, he moved the few miles to Killingworth Colliery. By 1812, at the age of 31, he had become the enginewright to the colliery, with a salary of £100 a year and — that most coveted of fringe benefits — a company horse. More importantly, his employers allowed him free rein to develop his ideas. Within two years, he had introduced steam locomotives to the pit, just at a time when many colliery engineers were losing faith with this newfangled mode of traction. As he gradually improved the steam locomotives his fame spread, and many came to inspect his work.

When the original parliamentary consent was obtained for the Stockton & Darlington Railway, Stephenson was engaged to re-survey the route. In the course of so doing, he was also instrumental in winning the proprietors over to the idea of locomotive power. This was somewhat at odds with the terms of his appointment, in which Edward Pease said:

> ***'In making this survey, it must be borne in mind that this is for a great public way, and to remain as long as any coal in the district remains. Its construction must be solid, and as little machinery introduced as possible.'***
>
> (*George Stephenson's letter of appointment to the Stockton & Darlington Railway — 28 July 1821 — author's emphasis*)

Notwithstanding this, in 1823 Stephenson was able to open a locomotive manufacturing works in Newcastle, with Edward Pease providing a large part of the £4,000 initial capital. Stephenson's son Robert, still only aged twenty but with a good training in engineering (from his father and Edinburgh University), took on an important role as the director of the business. One of the reasons for setting it up was the lack of interest shown by other manufacturers in producing locomotives for them. As the leading figure in early railway construction (indeed, one of the very few people with any real experience in building and running them), Stephenson soon found himself being stretched in all directions, with railway schemes in Kent, Bolton, Wales and, most important, the Liverpool & Manchester, where he worked a 14-hour day trying to complete the survey in the face of fierce local opposition. This was in addition to part-ownership of a coal mine and his locomotive manufacturing interests. The demands of the latter were compounded when his son and business partner decided in 1824 to go off mining in South America.

His over-commitment was one of the factors behind his humiliation at the first attempt to secure parliamentary approval for the Liverpool & Manchester. Throughout his working life, he found it difficult to say no to any project that was put before him. The Liverpool & Manchester Company in 1827 increased his salary to £1,000 per annum, on condition that he took on no new projects, but this does not appear to have had much effect on him. Stephenson's reputation went into something of a decline with the failure of the first Liverpool & Manchester Bill, but was restored by the successful opening of the Stockton & Darlington.

Robert returned home from South America in 1827, drawn back partly by the news that the locomotive manufacturing business was in serious trouble, due to lack of proper management. On the way home, he chanced to meet a near-destitute Richard Trevithick in Colombia, and gave him £50 for his passage back to England. From January 1828, and for the next five years, Robert was back in charge of the locomotive manufacturing company. They were to be some of the most important years for the development of steam locomotion.

The Liverpool & Manchester was probably George Stephenson's greatest achievement, though he built many railways subsequently. The next was the Leicester & Swannington, opened in 1833. His association with the Grand Junction Railway was a less happy one, with Stephenson's perennial over-commitment leading to the delays that resulted in him resigning and his protégé Joseph Locke taking over the project. Locke would go on to become in turn one of the great railway builders, but there was a long period of enmity between the Stephensons and Locke. This had its origins in Locke finding errors in parts of Stephenson's survey for the construction of the tunnel into Liverpool Lime Street, and was not resolved until after George's death.

Stephenson's business methods were not beyond reproach. He had difficulty delegating, and would negotiate one-off deals with individual contractors, so that everyone was working on different rates. When the Liverpool & Manchester was forced to make use of an additional Exchequer loan of £100,000, the eminent engineer Thomas Telford was brought in to investigate the justification for it. He did not like much of what he saw, and forced a reluctant Stephenson to accept many changes to his working practices as a condition of the loan. At the same time as he was trying to build the railway, Stephenson was fighting the cause of using locomotive power for it, described elsewhere in the book.

George Stephenson also had his flaws as a builder of railways. One consequence of his over-commitment was that his surveys tended to be somewhat superficial. He surveyed the London-Brighton line from a post-chaise, but lost that contract to another of his perpetual rivals, Sir John Rennie. He also got rather out of touch with improvements in locomotive technology, which meant that railways could follow the most direct route, rather than the flattest. In his report for the proposed railway from Liverpool to Carlisle (1839) Stephenson proposed a very indirect route via Morecambe Bay and west Cumberland, to avoid the mountainous parts of the Lake District. 'This is the only practicable line from Liverpool to Carlisle. The making of a railway across Shap Fell is out of the question', he insisted. The project was awarded to Joseph Locke, who successfully routed it over Shap with a gradient of 1:75 over one four-mile stretch.

Another person whom Stephenson at first befriended, and was then alienated from, was George Hudson. The two of them co-operated on a number of schemes, and the combination of Stephenson's engineering skills and prestige, and Hudson's entrepreneurial and (up to a point) financial genius was a potent one. By 1845 the two were estranged, with Stephenson claiming that Hudson had grown 'much too grand' for him. Stephenson also managed in his later years to fall out with Brunel, first over the battle of the gauges and then over Brunel's plans to introduce an atmospheric railway. The rivalry between the two engineers got as far as them putting competing schemes for a railway between Newcastle and Berwick before Parliament in 1845. Stephenson's more conventional proposal defeated Brunel's atmospheric scheme.

Stephenson nonetheless completed many successful railway projects in the following years, including those between Derby and Leeds, Normanton and York, Manchester and Leeds, Birmingham and Derby, and Sheffield and Rotherham. During his survey of the Leicester & Swannington, he discovered rich coal seams on some of the land the railway crossed. In partnership with others, (including Joseph Sandars of Liverpool & Manchester fame) Stephenson bought the land and mined it successfully. He bought himself a country estate, Alton Grange near Ashby de la Zouch, and opened offices in London. As an employer, Stephenson was always mindful of his own modest beginnings. He took a personal interest in his workers' wellbeing, paying them fair wages and providing them with such amenities as cottages, schools and places of worship.

Stephenson spent most of his last ten years at another country seat, Tapton House near Chesterfield. He carried out his last railway survey in Spain in 1845. Despite being aged 64, he spent 33 days on horseback, crossing and re-crossing the Pyrenees. He was widely respected among the ordinary people of Britain, who dubbed him 'the Father of the Railways', or even (wrongly) their inventor. He also won much popular acclaim abroad, including a Belgian title, but never received quite the same respect from the British Establishment, who thought him 'something less than a gentleman'. He was not eligible to become even a Member of the Institution of Civil Engineers, due to his lack of formal qualifications, though his son Robert would in time become their President. George was, however, made the first President of the Institution of Mechanical Engineers.

George Stephenson died on 12 August 1848 at the age of 67, and is buried at Holy Trinity church, Chesterfield.

Robert Stephenson had assisted his father in surveying the Stockton & Darlington and Liverpool & Manchester Railways, but had always been somewhat in his father's shadow as a railway (as distinct from locomotive) engineer, until he secured the job of building the London & Birmingham Railway. This, with its level running and wide curves, has proved eminently suitable for modern railway operation. Thereafter he won great acclaim for his railway building and other engineering exploits (his successes included the Britannia Bridge across the Menai Strait, the Royal Border Bridge across the Tweed at Berwick, the railway bridge at Conway and the Newcastle High Level Bridge). In later life he was to gain the recognition of the Establishment that had eluded his father, becoming the President of both the Civil and Mechanical Engineers and the Member of Parliament for Whitby from 1847 to 1859. He is buried in Westminster Abbey.

George Hudson (1800–71)

> ***'There are some dogs who can't endure one particular note on the piano. In like manner I feel disposed to throw up my head and howl whenever I hear Mr Hudson mentioned... If you can let me know anything bad of him, pray do. It would be a great comfort. Something intensely mean and odious would be preferred, but anything bad, will be thankfully received.'***
>
> (Charles Dickens: *Letters, Volume IV*)

> ***'His conceptions as regards the future development of the English railway system were as grandiose and far-reaching as were those of Brunel in the field of engineering, and there is no doubt that the rapid progress in railway construction made in some districts was due to his foresight and energy.'***
>
> (*Lewin, page 46*)

> ***'The Railway King'***
>
> (*Hudson's nickname — before his fall*)

George Hudson was possibly the most important figure from the early years of the railways and certainly quite the most extraordinary. As one of his biographers, Robert Beaumont, puts it, he 'could have walked straight out of the pages of a Charles Dickens novel'. As we have just seen, Dickens himself was one of the many who came to hate him with a vengeance.

Hudson was born near York in 1800, the fifth son of a farmer. His father died when George was nine, leaving the family penniless and, at

15, he was apprenticed to a draper in York (partly, it seems, to flee the opprobrium of having fathered an illegitimate child in his home village). He did well in the business in every respect, working his way up to become a partner in it and marrying one of the other partners' daughters. But the turning point in his life came when, at the age of 27, he inherited a fortune of some £30,000 from a great uncle (by nefarious means, some said later, at a time when the world was prepared to believe almost anything bad about him). With this windfall, he instantly changed religion, politics and his station in life, becoming Church of England (though his alleged earlier non-conformism was never conclusively proven), high Tory and a pillar of the local establishment.

It was in 1833 that he was appointed treasurer of a company formed to promote a railway between York and Leeds. On a visit to Whitby the following year, he chanced to meet George Stephenson, who enthused Hudson with his idea of a national network of railways. Within two years, Hudson had changed the route of their railway to tie in with one Stephenson was planning to build, and had harnessed the great man's prestige to his scheme. Hudson's own prestige grew as the scheme passed its parliamentary scrutiny. He became Chairman of the company and Mayor of York, making much of his association with Stephenson.

Hudson then set out on a campaign of building or taking over control of any number of railway companies. He was helped in so doing by the fact that, until 1849, no independent audit of railway companies was required by law. He was therefore able (highly illegally) to use each influx of new investment to pay his existing shareholders, doctoring the accounts and packing the shareholder meetings with his supporters. He was notorious for the vagueness of his accounting but his shareholders were at this stage happy to accept his unrealistically high dividends and not ask too many questions (he even paid a dividend on one line, the Yorkshire & North Midland, that was not yet even fully operational). 'I will have no statistics on my railway!' he is said to have shouted at one shareholder who attempted to confuse a meeting with facts. Such was his personal prestige that, in October 1844, he was able to raise £2.5 million to fund proposed railways without even publishing such minor details as where they went. His first major, and possibly greatest, amalgamation was the Midland Railway, formed in 1844. The idea for it came from Robert Stephenson, but it was Hudson's energy and forcefulness that drove it through.

He was equally ruthless in his management of railway projects, driving down costs to the absolute minimum and sometimes beyond, often at the expense of the safety of his employees and passengers. Under his control, the North Midland Railway earned the unenviable reputation as the nation's most dangerous line, attracting a detailed investigation by the Board of Trade. They reported that:

> ***'...A reduction of wages had been enforced, which had led to the whole of the engine drivers and firemen employed on the line resigning in a body, whose places had been filled, at a few days' notice, by other men, who were represented in various quarters as incompetent...'***

The Superintendent of the Board of Trade Locomotive Department went to investigate, but was assured by the Chairman and several of the Directors of the company that the rumours were baseless and 'the new enginemen and firemen had all produced good characters, and were perfectly competent for their situations'.

Within days of this, 'information was received of a fatal accident which occurred at the Barnsley station of the North Midland Railway, by a luggage train running with great violence against a passenger train which was standing in the station'.

From the investigation which followed

> ***'...abundant evidence was obtained, of the extreme danger and inexpediency of such measures as those which had been resorted to... Twenty-eight new enginemen were engaged by the North Midland Railway Company in the space of three weeks, of whom 18 were engaged ...to supply the places of the former enginemen, who resigned in a body. Of these 18 men, the Company were obliged to discharge no fewer than ten, after a few days' trial, on account of incompetence or misconduct, after having in several cases occasioned accidents.'***
>
> (Quotes from the reports of the Railway Department to the President of the Board of Trade)

Six of them had been discharged from other companies for similar reasons. In one instance, not only had Hudson appointed a fireman who had been sacked in short order from other railways, he had promoted the man to driver, and within three weeks he was involved in a fatal accident.

This led to the Board of Trade issuing a general warning to railway companies, about not letting pecuniary interests override their duty of care to their customers. After repeated crashes on Hudson railways, rival coach operators took to putting up spoof posters by stations, advertising the establishment of a cemetery at the station and inviting passengers to book their plot at the same time as their ticket.

Even so, by 1843 Hudson was the most important man in the railway world. He controlled a network of lines from York down to Rugby and Birmingham, and it was in this year that his nickname — *The Railway King* — was first coined. He was called as a witness to Gladstone's 1844 parliamentary committee into the railways, which sought to impose greater Government control on them, and was instrumental in getting the Bill which followed (the so-called 'Railway Plunder Bill') emasculated, before it came into law.

There seemed to be no end to his meteoric rise, nor to his ambition. In 1845, Hudson was elected Member of Parliament for Sunderland and Deputy Lord Lieutenant of Durham. He bought the Duke of Devonshire's 12,000-acre estate at Londesborough for £500,000 and had his own private branch line installed, bringing the railway to his back door. As his London residence, he acquired the largest private house in the city — Albert House in Knightsbridge, near Hyde Park (today occupied by the French Embassy) — from which he conducted a social life that was glittering and vulgar in equal proportions. For, while the Establishment laughed behind his back at his and his wife's provincial vulgarity and ignorance, referring to him as the *Yorkshire Balloon*, most of them wanted to benefit from his enormous influence. Prince Albert asked to be introduced to him and the Archbishop of Canterbury invited him to dine. Even the Duke of Wellington was not above coming to him for help for a member of his family who had unwisely purchased some dubious railway shares. (Hudson spread the word that he was investing in them, until their price had risen sufficiently for the Wellington relative to sell them at a profit.)

Hudson was by now possibly the second most famous man in the kingdom, after the Duke of Wellington himself. W. M. Thackeray, writing in *Punch*, created a comic character named James Plush, a domestic servant who made a fortune from speculating in railway shares, whose adventures were a thinly disguised and quite vicious satire of the life of Hudson. The story was even turned into a West End play. Hudson himself was more concerned about the growing attacks on rail speculation in *The Times,* and even went so far in 1846 as to throw his weight behind its rival, the *Daily News,* in a bid to promote his interests. In retrospect, this was to prove a bad move, one which only reinforced *The Times'* opposition to him.

Hudson's power had created a large number of other influential enemies. The whiff of corruption had hung over him since his early days.

In 1835 he had been summoned before a parliamentary Select Committee to answer charges of corruption over his part in getting Sir John Lowther elected MP for York (charges only dropped when they became politically embarrassing). He had alienated George Stephenson and the powerful Liverpool railway lobby, as well as those elsewhere who still held out against the spread of his empire. Others, such as the eminent Quaker Joseph Rowntree, had challenged the vagueness (to put it no stronger) of his accounts. Hudson responded to his call for independent auditors in typically bombastic style:

> ***'The accounts are always audited by the directors themselves. Does anyone doubt these worthy gentlemen? Are not the books always open for every shareholder to inspect for himself?'***
>
> *(Beaumont — page 47)*

As the heat of railway mania cooled in 1847, Hudson began to realise that his railway empire was built upon unstable foundations. He tried — and failed — to get the Government to bail him out by giving him £16 million for the construction of railways in Ireland, which he presented as part of the solution to the potato famine. Shortly after this, he was forced to admit liabilities of £14 million for his Midland Railway (the true figure was later thought to be nearer £30 million). He also faced liabilities of £13.5 million on the financial bottomless pit that was the Eastern Counties Railway (not helped by the fact that he had used some £294,000 of that company's share capital to fund dividend payments due elsewhere).

The major recession of 1848 was to prove the final nail in his financial coffin, added to which Hudson himself fell seriously ill at this time. His empire was then paradoxically at its height: of the nation's 5,007 miles of railway, Hudson directly controlled 1,450, stretching from Berwick to London, and from Yarmouth to Bristol. At a cost of some £30 million, he had created several of the nation's largest railway companies. As he struggled to balance the books, attacks on him and his family began to multiply at every level. The shareholders, who had been happy enough to take his generous dividends and ask few questions, began to disown him as their holdings began to lose value. His wife was even vilified in the press for delaying the Darlington-York express for 27 minutes one night, in order to have a pineapple delivered to their country estate. Then, in what seemed like a small matter at first, he was accused of corruption in York.

Two stockbrokers called Robert Prance and Horatio Love, who had lost money on a Hudson scheme, went through the accounts of the York

& North Midland Railway in some detail. They found that the company had bought shares in another railway at a higher price than they had ever reached on the Stock Exchange. The total sum involved was only £9,000 but Hudson was forced at a shareholder meeting to admit guilt, to offer to repay the sum and to have a committee of investigation. This started a bandwagon. At subsequent shareholder meetings for his other companies, further investigations of his dealings were set in motion, which began to reveal many more serious abuses.

In the summer of 1848, one Arthur Smith produced a pamphlet *The Bubble of the Age or The Fallacies of Railway Investment, Railway Accounts and Railway Dividends.* This put Hudson's practice of paying dividends out of capital into the public domain for the first time. His conflicts of interest, as Chairman of many railway companies with diverging or even competing interests began to be exposed; when the Midland had acquired the Leeds & Bradford in 1846, Hudson had been the Chairman of both companies. In whose interest had the merger been — one company, the other, or simply Hudson's own?

Hudson's position was not helped by his brother-in-law (and accomplice in many of these scandals) committing suicide. He was eventually found guilty of embezzlement and of bribing MPs. Embezzlement totalling £598,785 was proven, but it was thought there might have been much more. The whole of Victorian society now turned on Hudson and he was stripped of all the honours and prestige that had previously been bestowed upon him. Lord Macaulay may have summed up society's view in 1849 when he called Hudson 'a bloated, vulgar, insolent, purse-proud, greedy, drunken blackguard'.

Hudson, to his credit, did not try to deny his wrongdoings and sold up all his possessions to pay off such creditors as he could, before fleeing to France. Only after twenty years' poverty overseas did he return in 1868 to his home village of Scrayingham, where he died three years later.

Hudson was undoubtedly deeply corrupt and deserved some form of retribution. He was also personally obnoxious and charmless, which did not win him public sympathy when adversity came. But Britain's railways owe him a considerable debt. He had the vision to realise the need for the amalgamation of the small early railways, and the initiative (and several other less charming qualities) to make it happen. His drive towards amalgamation rescued them from the kind of fragmented and disorganised state in which the canals found themselves at the start of the railway age, and gave the nation a railway system which was much more convenient and cost-effective than it threatened to be, under the Government policy of laissez-faire.

As one contemporary said of him:

> ***'Mr Hudson is neither better nor worse than the morality of 1845. He rose to wealth and importance at an immoral period; he was the creature of an immoral system; he was wafted into fortune upon the wave of a popular mania; he was elevated into the dictatorship of railway speculation in an unwholesome ferment of popular cupidity, pervading all ranks and conditions of men.'***
>
> (Frederick S. Williams: *Our Iron Roads — 1852*)

Isambard Kingdom Brunel (1806–59)

'The Little Giant'

(*Brunel's nickname*)

Marc Isambard Brunel was a French engineer and inventor, who fled post-revolutionary France in the late 18th century. He eventually ended up in England, where he married an English woman, Sophia Kingdom. Their third child, Isambard Kingdom Brunel, was born in Portsmouth in 1806. Isambard was something of a child prodigy, learning technical drawing at the age of four. He completed his education in France and, after some work experience with the great French engineer Breguet, returned home to work with his father.

In 1822/23 Marc Brunel won a commission to construct a tunnel under the Thames, using his patented tunnelling shield. The project ran into serious problems, due to ground conditions and, when the Thames burst in, Isambard narrowly escaped drowning. The tunnel itself was not completed until 1843 and, whilst recuperating in Bristol from his injuries, Brunel entered a competition to design a bridge across the Avon Gorge. His proposal was for a suspension bridge, half as long again as the recently completed Menai Bridge, at that time the world's longest. One small problem was that Thomas Telford, the designer of the Menai Bridge, was on the judging panel for the competition. He was so rude about Brunel's design (and, indeed, those of all the other contestants) that the committee ended up offering Telford the job. It took a second competition before Brunel was awarded the contract, though it later ran into money problems and was not completed until after his death. A commission for improvements to Bristol docks further reinforced Brunel's reputation locally.

This helped persuade the promoters of the proposed new railway between Bristol and London to award the job of Chief Engineer to this young and (in railway terms) untried man. Brunel even threatened to withdraw his candidacy when it was rumoured that the committee were going to award it to the candidate offering the lowest price for the project. The 27-year-old told the distinguished appointment board:

> ***'You are holding out a premium to the man who will make you the most flattering promises. It is quite obvious that the man who has either least reputation at stake, or who has the most to gain by temporary success, and least to lose by the consequences of disappointment, must be the winner in such a race.'***

He took up the post in August 1833, having completed the preliminary survey for the line in record time by dint of working 20-hour days. The same intense and largely self-imposed pressure continued, as the main survey was carried out and preparation made for the submission to Parliament. The first Bill, for just part of the railway, was lost, but Brunel demonstrated his encyclopaedic grasp of his subject at the inquiry.

At the hearing for the second Bill, this time for the entire railway, the London & Southampton Railway put up Dionysius Lardner to present their opposition. Professor of Natural Philosophy and Astronomy at London University, Lardner was famously 'clever', and willing to pontificate on almost any subject with complicated pseudo-mathematical underpinnings for his case. It was here that Lardner produced his pompous and overblown case for the deadly effects of the Box Tunnel, discussed earlier. Brunel dismissed it contemptuously as 'the most absolute drivel'. As one engineer who witnessed Brunel's performance during 11 days of cross-examination put it:

> ***'His knowledge of the country surveyed by him was marvellously great, and the explanation he gave of his plans, and the answers he returned to questions suggested by Dr Lardner showed a profound acquaintance with the principles of mechanics. He was rapid in thought, clear in his language, and never said too much, or lost his presence of mind. I do not remember ever having enjoyed so great an intellectual treat as that of listening to Brunel's explanation...'***

The first ever view of a British railway? Prior Park, near Bath, the seat of Ralph Allen Esq in 1752. He used the railway to move stone from his quarries to the River Avon. (AE185.792)

An illustration of an early wooden
railway dating from between 1532 and
1562, by Heinrich Gross. (642/217/92)

Above: A fully laden colliery wagon descending under gravity — drawn by William Beilby in about 1773. (Elton Collection) (page 52)

Below: The Denby Canal Tramroad. (642/504/7/56)

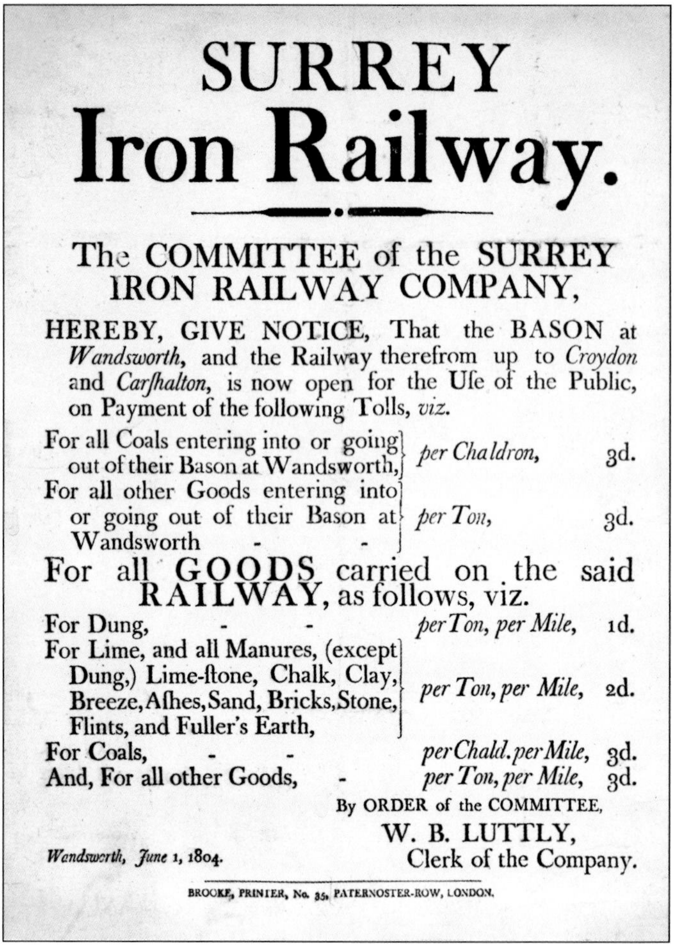

SURREY Iron Railway.

The COMMITTEE of the SURREY IRON RAILWAY COMPANY,

HEREBY, GIVE NOTICE, That the BASON at *Wandsworth*, and the Railway therefrom up to *Croydon* and *Carfhalton*, is now open for the Ufe of the Public, on Payment of the following Tolls, *viz.*

For all Coals entering into or going out of their Bason at Wandsworth,	*per Chaldron,*	3d.
For all other Goods entering into or going out of their Bason at Wandsworth - -	*per Ton,*	3d.

For all GOODS carried on the said RAILWAY, as follows, viz.

For Dung, - -	*per Ton, per Mile,*	1d.
For Lime, and all Manures, (except Dung,) Lime-ftone, Chalk, Clay, Breeze, Afhes, Sand, Bricks, Stone, Flints, and Fuller's Earth,	*per Ton, per Mile,*	2d.
For Coals, - -	*per Chald. per Mile,*	3d.
And, For all other Goods, -	*per Ton, per Mile,*	3d.

By ORDER of the COMMITTEE,

W. B. LUTTLY,
Clerk of the Company.

Wandsworth, June 1, 1804.

BROOKE, PRINTER, No. 35, PATERNOSTER-ROW, LONDON.

Right: The 1804 schedule of rates for the Surrey Iron Railway. Dung travelled at half the price of other types of manure, and a third of the price of coal.

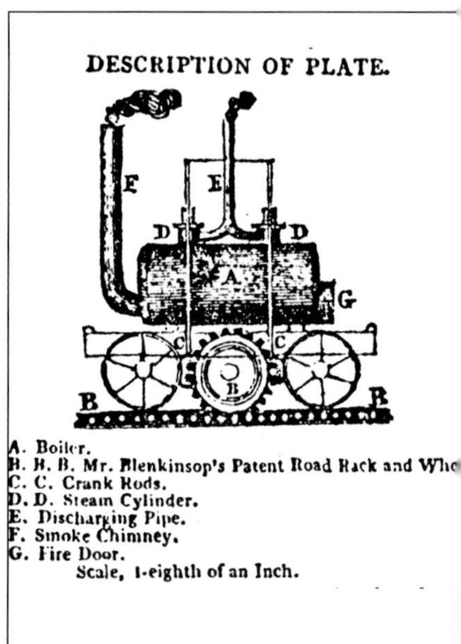

DESCRIPTION OF PLATE.

A. Boiler.
B. B. B. Mr. Blenkinsop's Patent Road Rack and Whe
C. C. Crank Rods.
D. D. Steam Cylinder.
E. Discharging Pipe.
F. Smoke Chimney.
G. Fire Door.
Scale, 1-eighth of an Inch.

Left: One of the earliest published accounts of the working of a steam locomotive, from the *Leeds Mercury* of 18 July 1812 (from Dendy-Marshall).

Top: A model of Nicholas Cugnot's prototype steam road carriage of 1769.

Above: The prototype steam vehicle started but never completed by William Murdoch, who worked for James Watt.

Richard Trevithick, (1771–1833) whose contribution to the early development of railways is not always fully recognised. (699/2646/52)

Above: A replica of Richard Trevithick's Penydarren locomotive of 1804, at the ceremony in 1981 to name a British Rail locomotive after Trevithick.

Below: A model of the Blenkinsop locomotive of 1812, using the rack system on the Leeds Wagonway.

Left: A not particularly flattering sculpture of the locomotive engineer Timothy Hackworth, who took part in the Rainhill Trials and had previously built one of the most advanced locomotives of its day.

Below: Timothy Hackworth's *Royal George*, built for the Stockton & Darlington in 1827, and regarded as the finest locomotive of its day.

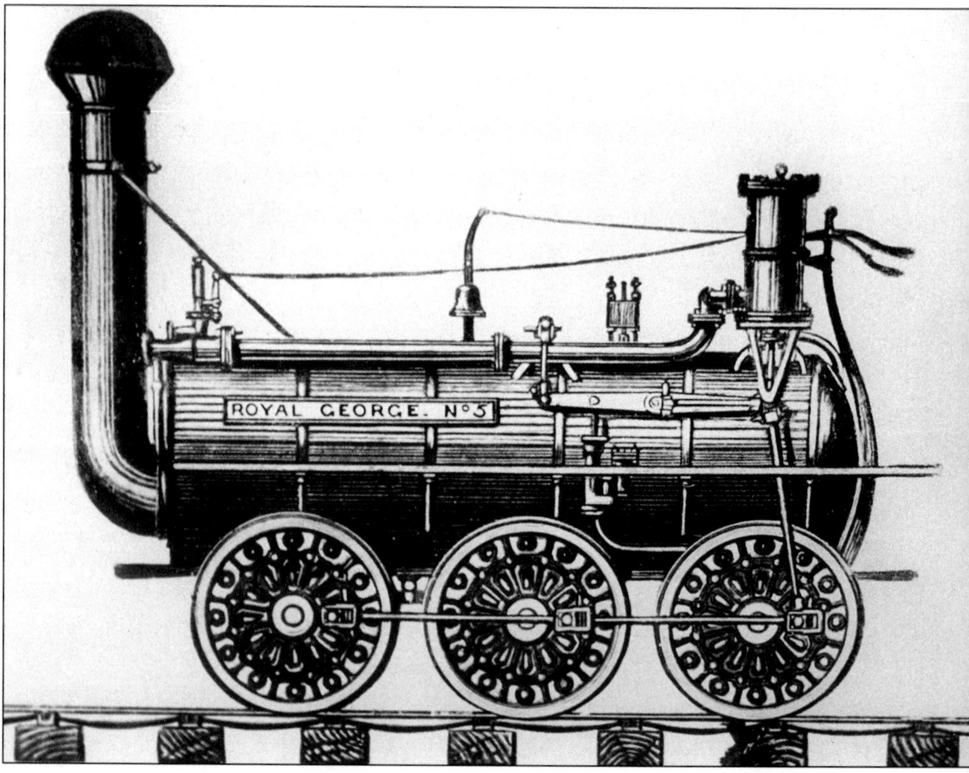

William Hedley's *Puffing Billy* at work. Built for the Wylam Colliery in 1813, it continued in use until the 1860s.

Above: Puffing Billy and its sister *Wylam Dilly*, are the oldest surviving locomotives in the world. *Puffing Billy* now resides in the Science Museum. The complicated and inefficient valve gear on these early locomotives has echoes of the stationary beam engines of Boulton and Watt. *NRM*

Below: The Wylam Colliery locomotive *Wylam Dilly,* pictured in its final working days in the 1860s. The top-hatted gentlemen are the sons of the man who built it, William Hedley.

Even the most utilitarian structures, like this railway bridge at Rugby, could be turned into imposing pieces of architecture.

MEETING

OF

GENTLEMEN, MERCHANTS, AND OTHERS, FOR THE PURPOSE OF PROMOTING A

Canal or Railway

FROM STOCKTON, BY DARLINGTON,

Westwards,

HELD AT THE

HOUSE OF MR. SCOTT, THE KING's HEAD, IN DARLINGTON, IN THE COUNTY OF DURHAM,

On Friday, the 17th day of January, 1812,

Pursuant to advertisement,—

(The Resolutions of the general Meeting, held on the 18th day of September, 1810, having been read, and the Report of the Committee then appointed having been received and taken into Consideration)—

RESOLVED,

THAT a Survey of the Country or District, through which the proposed Canal or Railway is intended to pass, be forthwith made by Mr. RENNIE. That he be instructed to make a Report as to the practicability of those several measures, their comparative advantages, and the best line or course and extent for each; with an estimate of the expence which will attend the carrying it into effect.

That a Subscription be entered into, in order to defray the expence of such survey, and any other reasonable charges which have already been, or shall hereafter be, incurred relative to the projected undertakings; and that the Committee shall have power to call for such proportion thereof as they shall find necessary, and to direct to whom the same shall be paid.

Left: The minutes of the meeting in January 1812, at which it was decided to appoint Mr Rennie to evaluate the respective merits of a railway or a canal to link Stockton & Darlington. Rennie preferred a canal (from Emett).

Right: Edward Pease (1767–1858), one of the founding fathers of the Stockton & Darlington Railway. From the *Illustrated London News*.

Below: A contemporary sketch, showing the opening of the Stockton & Darlington Railway in 1825.

thereof and Persons interested therein respectively (other than and except those specified in the Schedule annexed to this Act).

Power for the Company to erect Steam Engines, and to purchase Land, not exceeding Two Acres in the whole, for that Purpose.

VII. And whereas it will be expedient and necessary for the said Company of Proprietors to erect Steam Engines or other proper Machines in certain Places upon or near to the said Railways or Tramroads by the said recited Act and this Act directed or authorized to be made, for the Purpose of facilitating the Transport, Conveyance, and Carriage of Goods, Merchandize, and other Articles and Things upon and along the same; be it therefore further enacted, That it shall and may be lawful for the said Company of Proprietors, and they are hereby authorized and empowered, from and after the passing of this Act, by themselves or by their Deputies, Agents, Officers, Workmen, or Servants, to make, erect, and set up one permanent or fixed Steam Engine or other proper Machine, in such convenient Situation at or near each of the inclined Planes, which shall be made by virtue or in pursuance of the said recited Act or of this Act, as the said Company of Proprietors shall think proper, and to take and purchase from any Person or Persons, Bodies Politic, Corporate, or Collegiate, or Corporation Aggregate or Sole, who shall be willing to sell the same, any Lands, Tenements, or Hereditaments which may be necessary or convenient for that Purpose, so as the entire Quantity of the Lands, Tenements, or Hereditaments to be taken and appropriated for the Purpose aforesaid do not exceed in the whole Two Acres for any one Engine; and also, with the Consent of the Owner or Owners of the Lands in or through which the same shall be made, to make such and so many Wells, Watercourses, Drains, and other Works for supplying the said Steam Engines and other Machines with Water, as shall be deemed requisite or convenient, and for the Purposes aforesaid, or any of them, to purchase, take, and use the Lands and Grounds of any Person or Persons, Bodies Politic or Collegiate, who shall be willing to sell the same.

Power to make and use loco-motive or moveable Engines on the Railway.

VIII. And be it further enacted, That it shall and may be lawful to and for the said Company of Proprietors, or any Person or Persons authorized or permitted by them, from and after the passing of this Act, to make and erect such and so many loco-motive or moveable Engines as the said Company of Proprietors shall from Time to Time think proper and expedient, and to use and employ the same in or upon the said Railways or Tramroads, or any of them, by the said recited Act and this Act directed or authorized to be made, for the Purpose of facilitating the Transport, Conveyance, and Carriage of Goods, Merchandize, and other Articles and Things upon and along the same Roads, and for the Conveyance of Passengers upon and along the same Roads.

Repealing the Part of the recited Act which relates to the Quantity of Land to be purchased for Wharfs.

IX. And whereas it is in and by the said recited Act enacted, that the said Company of Proprietors shall have full Liberty and Power to purchase any Parcel of Land, not exceeding Five Acres in the whole, for the Purpose of making a Wharf or Wharfs: And whereas it may tend to the public Advantage and Accommodation if the said Company of Proprietors be empowered to purchase a greater Quantity of Land than Five Acres, and also to purchase any Messuages or other Buildings for the Purpose of making and erecting a Wharf or Wharfs; and also for the

Left: The historic extract from the Act, permitting the use of steam locomotives on the Stockton & Darlington Railway (from Emett).

Above: The daddy of them all, *Locomotion* on display at the museum in Darlington.

Below: *Locomotion* and its train, seen at the 1925 centenary celebrations of the opening of the Stockton & Darlington Railway. (812/CCE (YORK) 18343)

RAPID, SAFE, AND CHEAP TRAVELLING

By the Elegant NEW RAILWAY COACH,

THE UNION,

Which will COMMENCE RUNNING on the STOCKTON and DARLINGTON RAILWAY, on MONDAY the 16th day of October, 1826,

And will call at Yarm, and pass within a mile of Middleton Spa, on its way from Stockton to Darlington, and *vice versa.*

FARES. Inside 1½d.—Outside, 1d. per Mile. Parcels in proportion.

No gratuities expected by the Guard or Coachman.

N. B. The Proprietors will not be accountable for any Parcel of more than £5. value, unless entered and paid for accordingly.

The UNION will run from the Black Lion Hotel and New Inn, Stockton, to the New Inn, Yarm, and to the Black Swan Inn, near the Croft Branch, Darlington; at each of which Inns passengers and parcels are booked, and the times of starting may be ascertained, as also at the Union Inn, Yarm, and Talbot Inn, Darlington.

On the 19th and 20th of October, the Fair Days at Yarm, the Union will leave Darlington at six in the morning for Yarm, and will leave Yarm for Darlington again at six in the evening; in the intermediate time, each day, it will ply constantly between Stockton and Yarm, leaving each place every half hour.

Above: Although the Stockton & Darlington Railway was built primarily for freight traffic, private operators were quick to cater for the demand from passengers (from Emett).

Right: The opening day on the Canterbury & Whitstable line, 3 May 1830, and *Invicta* hauls the inaugural train back from Whitstable.

Left: Invicta, the Canterbury & Whitstable's only (and not conspicuously successful) steam locomotive, built by Robert Stephenson. (941/4388/577)

Above: Another view of *Invicta*, built by Stephenson, the one locomotive bought by the Canterbury & Whitstable Railway in 1830. Although related to *Rocket*, it was not a great success.

Below: The featureless bog that was Chat Moss, which many thought would defeat George Stephenson. (Shaw 1831)

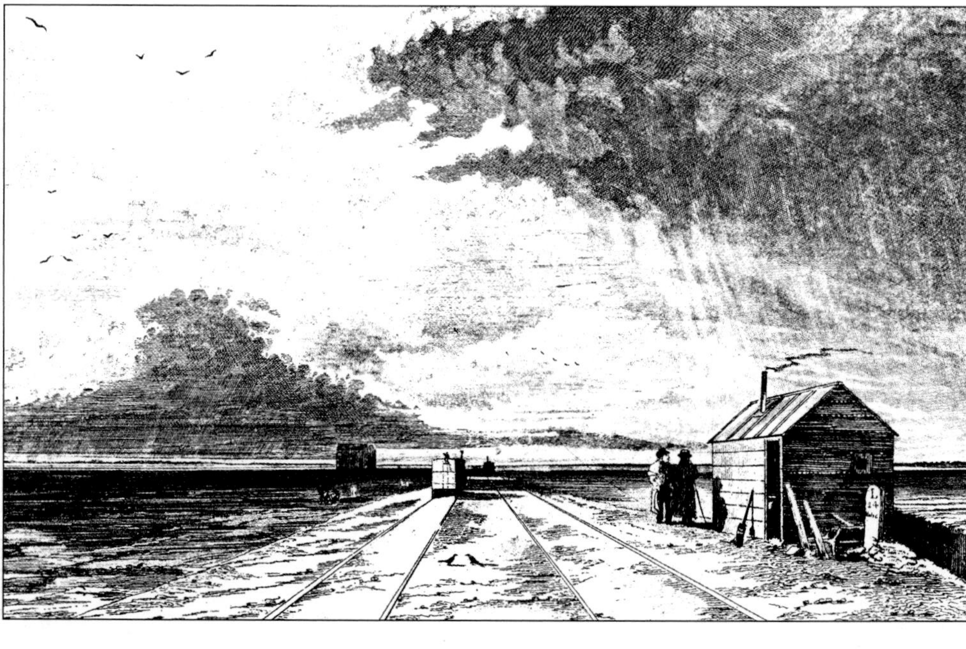

The entrance to the Box Tunnel on the Great Western line.

Above: The viaduct that carried the Liverpool & Manchester Railway over the Sankey Canal. (Shaw 1831)

Below: The opening day of the Liverpool & Manchester Railway. The Moorish Arch at Edge Hill dominates the scene and the Duke of Wellington's ornate coach can be seen on the left of the picture. (Shaw 1831).

Right: A contemporary print of *Rocket.*

The **ROCKET** *of M^r. Robt. Stephenson of Newcastle.*

Above: An early (1831) engraving of Rainhill Bridge on the Liverpool & Manchester Railway (from Shaw).

Below: Olive Mount on the Liverpool & Manchester Railway — another Shaw engraving.

The trackless wastes of Chat Moss now have tracks. This part of the route represented a major challenge to the engineering skills of George Stephenson on the Liverpool & Manchester Railway.

1829.

GRAND COMPETITION

OF

LOCOMOTIVES

ON THE

LIVERPOOL & MANCHESTER RAILWAY.

STIPULATIONS & CONDITIONS

ON WHICH THE DIRECTORS OF THE LIVERPOOL AND MANCHESTER RAILWAY OFFER A PREMIUM OF £500 FOR THE MOST IMPROVED LOCOMOTIVE ENGINE.

I.

The said Engine must "effectually consume its own smoke," according to the provisions of the Railway Act, 7th Geo. IV.

II.

The Engine, if it weighs Six Tons, must be capable of drawing after it, day by day, on a well-constructed Railway, on a level plane, a Train of Carriages of the gross weight of Twenty Tons, including the Tender and Water Tank, at the rate of Ten Miles per Hour, with a pressure of steam in the boiler not exceeding Fifty Pounds on the square inch.

III.

There must be Two Safety Valves, one of which must be completely out of the reach or control of the Engine-man, and neither of which must be fastened down while the Engine is working.

IV.

The Engine and Boiler must be supported on Springs, and rest on Six Wheels; and the height from the ground to the top of the Chimney must not exceed Fifteen Feet.

V.

The weight of the Machine, WITH ITS COMPLEMENT OF WATER in the Boiler, must, at most, not exceed Six Tons, and a Machine of less weight will be preferred if it draw AFTER it a PROPORTIONATE weight; and if the weight of the Engine, &c., do not exceed FIVE TONS, then the gross weight to be drawn need not exceed Fifteen Tons, and in that proportion for Machines of still smaller weight—provided that the Engine, &c., shall still be on six wheels, unless the weight (as above) be reduced to Four Tons and a Half, or under, in which case the Boiler, &c., may be placed on four wheels. And the Company shall be at liberty to put the Boiler, Fire Tube, Cylinders, &c., to the test of a pressure of water not exceeding 150 Pounds per square inch, without being answerable for any damage the Machine may receive in consequence.

VI.

There must be a Mercurial Gauge affixed to the Machine, with Index Rod, showing the Steam Pressure above 45 Pounds per square inch; and constructed to blow out a Pressure of 60 Pounds per inch.

VII.

The Engine to be delivered complete for trial, at the Liverpool end of the Railway, not later than the 1st of October next.

VIII.

The price of the Engine which may be accepted, not to exceed £550, delivered on the Railway; and any Engine not approved to be taken back by the Owner.

N.B.—The Railway Company will provide the ENGINE TENDER with a supply of Water and Fuel, for the experiment. The distance within the Rails is four feet eight inches and a half.

The rules issued to entrants in the Rainhill Trials.

Left: Sans Pareil by Timothy Hackworth, one of the entrants in the Rainhill Trials.

Below: A replica of Timothy Hackforth's *Sans Pareil* in steam at the 150th anniversary of the opening of the Liverpool & Manchester Railway, in 1980.

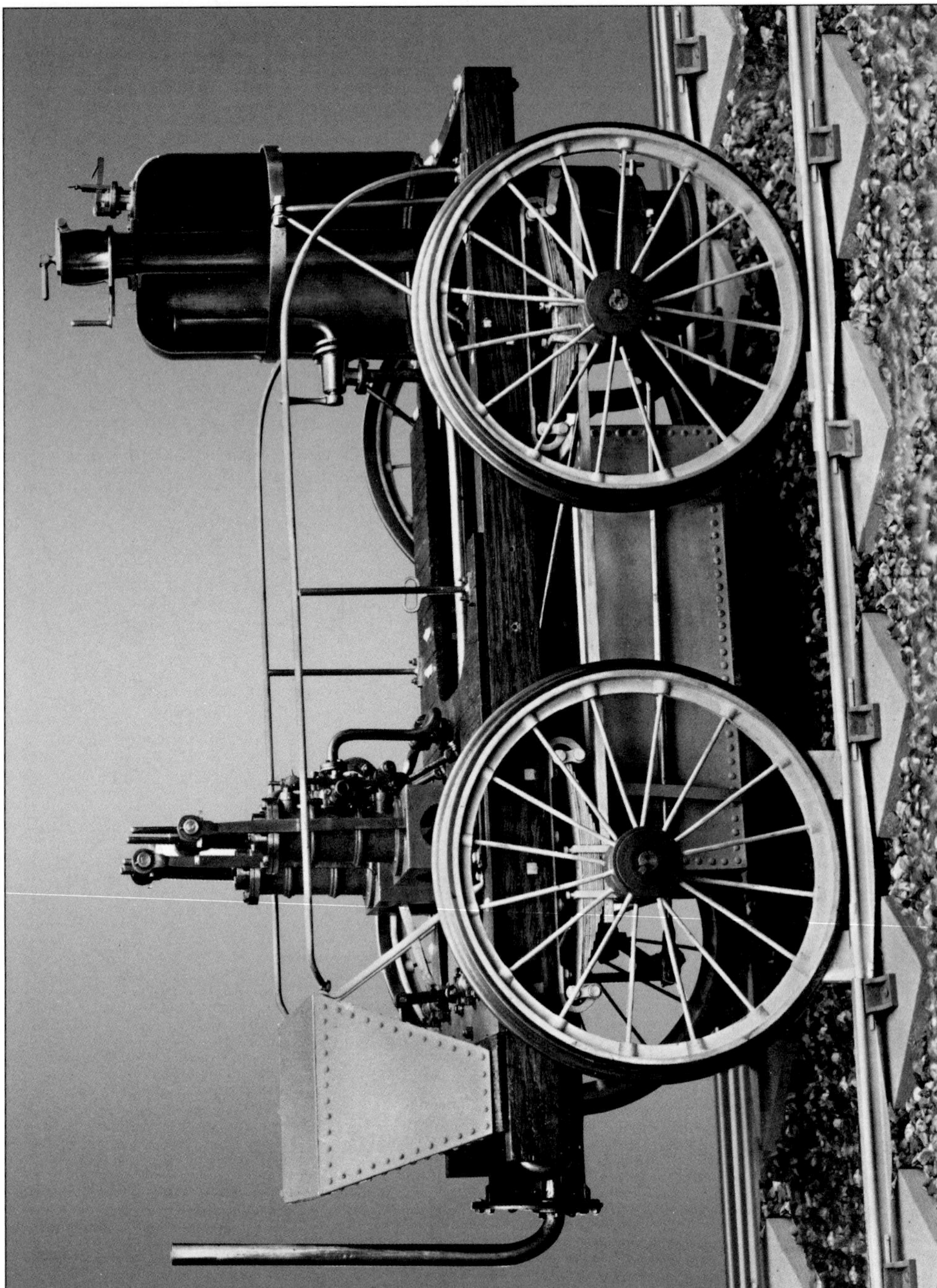

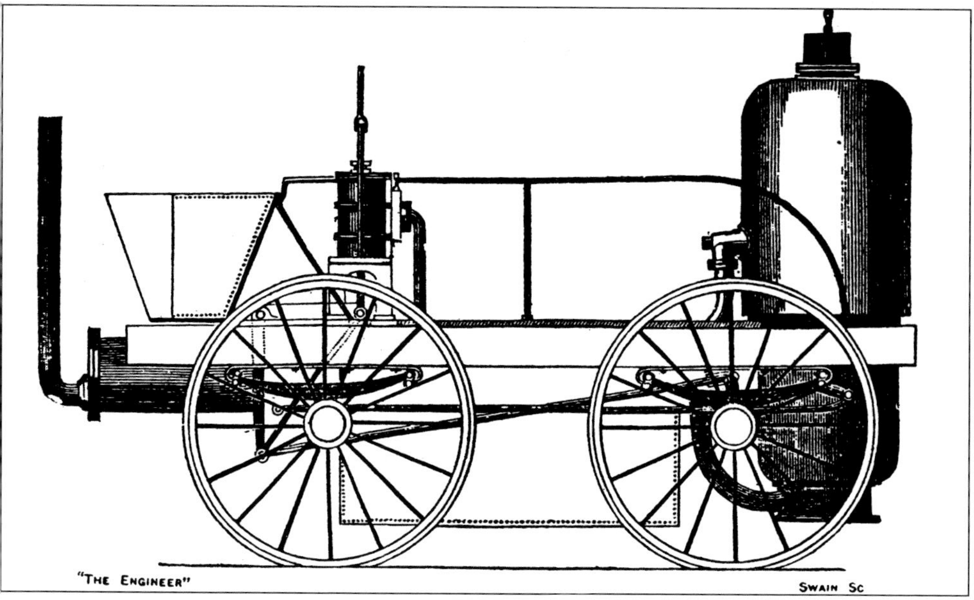

Above: The *Novelty*, built by Braithwaite and Ericsson for the Rainhill Trials and an early favourite with the crowds.

Left: A model of *Novelty*.

Below: *Planet*, the next stage in locomotive design after *Rocket* (from Shaw).

The 1930 centenary celebrations of the opening of the Liverpool & Manchester Railway. The locomotive *Northumbrian* is pulling a replica of the Duke of Wellington's state coach.

Above: The famous 1831 print of passenger trains on the Liverpool & Manchester Railway.

Right: William Huskisson, (1770–1830) whose death cast a shadow over the opening of the Liverpool & Manchester Railway. (697/2657/52).

Below: The Roundhouse at Chalk Farm, built in 1847 by Robert Stephenson. *BR*

The eastern end of the tunnel from Primrose Hill on the London & Birmingham Railway, drawn in October 1837.

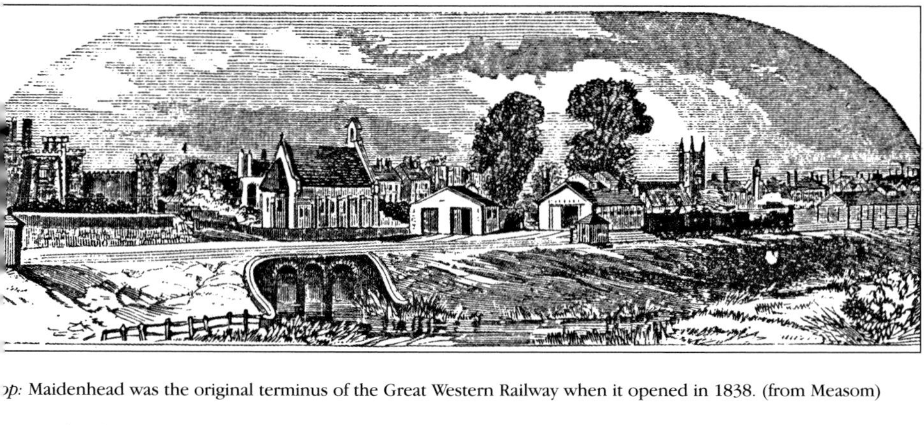

›p: Maidenhead was the original terminus of the Great Western Railway when it opened in 1838. (from Measom)

entre: Slough was not originally permitted to have a station, for fear of the potential moral pollution to the
ıupils of nearby Eton. However, traffic into Windsor became an important part of the railway's income; a station
ʼas eventually provided and, by 1849, the Great Western had a branch line whose terminus lay within the
ıadow of the castle walls. (from Measom)

bove: In order to maintain the levels on his line, Brunel built the section that passes the centre of Reading on an
ɪnbankment, as is shown by Measom's illustration.

A 1960s re-enactment of the opening of the Great Western line to Maidenhead. The locomotive is a replica of *North Star*.

George Stephenson was among those who went along to hear the evidence, and was one of the first to congratulate him on his performance. Brunel won — the Great Western got Royal Assent on 31 August 1835 — but he and Lardner were to cross swords several times more in his lifetime.

Brunel married Mary Horsley in 1836, but she was to see little of him. In addition to his railway duties, he was taken up by a project to extend the Great Western from Bristol much further to the west — in fact to New York, by means of the first purpose-built transatlantic steamship, also called the *Great Western*. Lardner had, of course, demonstrated that it was mathematically impossible for a ship to carry enough coal to make the journey, but Brunel proved him wrong again in 1838.

The first phase of the Great Western Railway — from Paddington to Maidenhead — opened in May 1838. In another piece of daring engineering dictated by the constraints of the site, the brick arches of the Thames bridge at Maidenhead were the flattest ever built. The entire engineering world waited expectantly for the bridge to collapse. They are still waiting, with locomotives eight times the size of Brunel's passing over it daily.

Despite the successful progress of the railway, a strong Liverpool faction on the board was out to get Brunel (and the broad gauge), and they forced through an 'independent' evaluation of the scheme so far by John Hawkshaw (a strong supporter of the Stephenson camp). In addition, they required an evaluation of the Great Western's locomotives (by Dionysius Lardner again). This concluded that, because of their larger frontal area (and hence wind resistance), broad gauge locomotives were incapable of economic operation at much more than 35mph. Lardner was wrong again — Gooch discovered that the problem was a combination of inept driving of the locomotive and an easily rectified design fault on the particular example they had driven — but Brunel barely survived this twin onslaught on his reputation.

Brunel and Atmospheric Railways

'I think they're a 'umbug, Your Royal 'Ighnes.'

George Hudson's considered opinion on atmospheric railways, as given to Prince Albert.

The Great Western was undoubtedly Brunel's railway masterpiece. His great failure was his espousal of the idea of an atmospheric railway. This was a system whereby a large-bore pipe was laid between the rails. There was a slit running along the top of the pipe, sealed by a leather flap. Through this slit the locomotive connected with a piston inside the pipe. Pumping stations

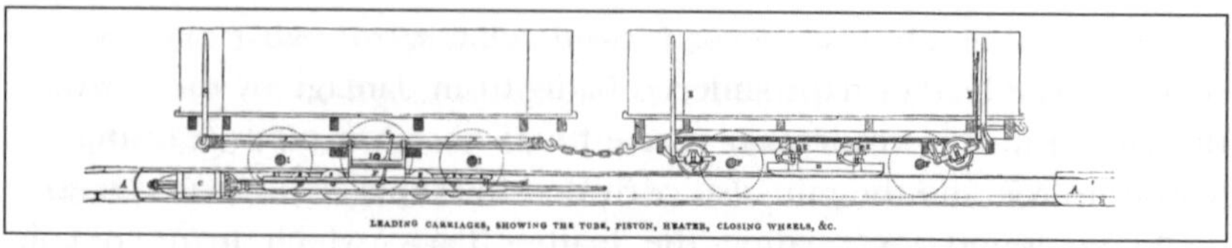

A contemporary illustration explaining the working principles of an atmospheric railway. *Illustrated London News*

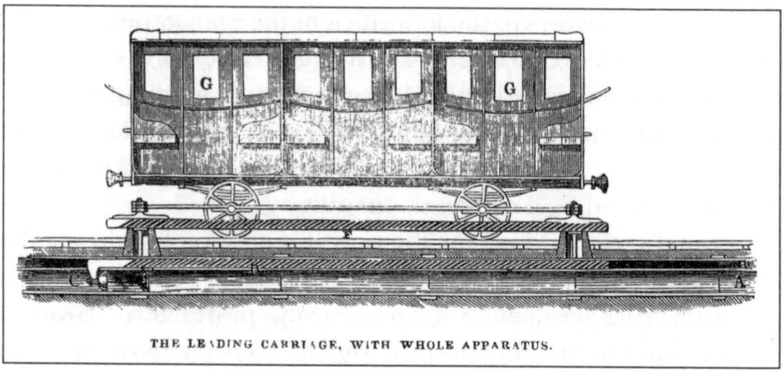

An 1845 illustration of one of several methods for the operation of an atmospheric railway. *Illustrated London News*

were located at around three-mile intervals along the track. They would suck all the air out of the pipe and the vacuum would draw the train along. The idea had been shown to work on an experimental basis on a short stretch of line in Dun Laoghaire in Ireland, and was patented in 1839. Despite it achieving over 60mph in early trials (84mph in one trial that went wrong!), the Board of Trade later concluded that, whilst the system might be a mechanical possibility, it was somewhat premature to regard it as a commercial success. Stephenson dismissed the idea more robustly — and correctly — as just another stationary engine, but drawn by a rope of air.

The idea undoubtedly had strengths — it could provide rapid, quiet and (unless you were living next to the pumping station) non-polluting transport. It was particularly good on gradients, and Brunel was able to plan some as steep as 1 in 36 on the South Devon Railway, where the scheme was first tried in earnest. The idea had many supporters at the time, including the Prime Minister, Sir Robert Peel. But on the debit side, the system was very inflexible — no crossings or points were possible, and an alternative form of traction was needed for the lengthy process of assembling a train at the start of the journey, or for moving it from one section of the railway to the next; there was also no reverse gear. It needed to run frequent services (for example, on a heavily used commuter line) to make it economic, yet Brunel installed it on a sparsely populated rural route.

Most serious of all, it never proved reliable enough to be used in practice. The leather flaps suffered badly from damage by the weather: the tannin in the wet leather reacted with the iron pipes, causing the leather to rot, and the rain also corroded the pipes. No suitable sealant could be found for treating the leather flaps, which froze in cold weather, making the railway unusable. (However, stories about the leather being eaten by rats were apparently not true.) The more the sealing system broke down, the less efficient the railway became, forcing the pumps to work ever harder and driving up operating costs to twice that of a locomotive-hauled line. The system had a working life that was measured in just months and a breakdown in one section tended to close the whole line down for the day. It had to be removed within about a year, and replaced by a conventional railway.

But Brunel was by no means the only one to look for alternatives to steam railways. The newspapers of the day carried reports of a 'patent aerial steam carriage which is to convey passengers, goods and dispatches through the air, performing the journey between London and India in four days, and travelling at the rate of 75 to 100 miles per hour'. Others offered 'an entirely new system of railway carriage' combining low costs, speeds of more than 60mph and an (unspecified) propulsion system involving no moving parts. The Edinburgh & Glasgow announced plans for an electro-magnetic carriage, whose practicality was 'placed beyond doubt', water power was proposed for

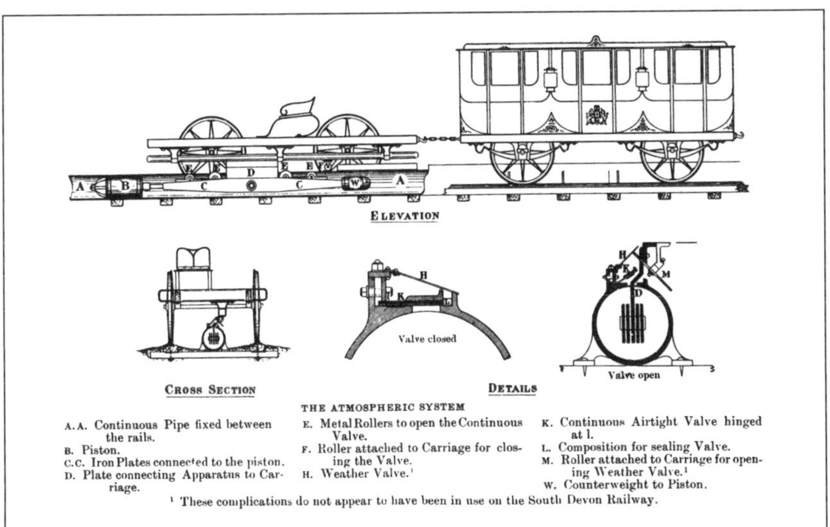

A contemporary illustration of the principles of the atmospheric system.

the line between Exeter and Plymouth, whilst another system was worked by two men inside the carriage pulling on a continuous rope. One inventor, convinced that conventional locomotives had insufficient grip to climb slopes, proposed that the driving wheels of the locomotive should be rough rollers running along a gravel bed laid between the tracks. Another overcame this same problem with switchable magnets, which gave the locomotive additional adhesion when required. Where ice was the cause of loss of traction, one solution proposed was hollow rails filled with water, which could be heated in freezing conditions. Others took the view that advances in ship and marine engine design would soon give the world ships as fast as trains, rendering many rail services unviable.

In later years Brunel himself turned increasingly to the construction of ocean-going ships. These culminated in the *Great Eastern*, the forerunner of the modern passenger liner, which was undergoing trials as he died. His last great railway work was the Royal Albert Bridge at Saltash. It was opened in 1859 and Brunel was later wheeled over it in a truck, a dying man, worn out by years of prodigious industry.

He was a complex man, charming, humorous and boundlessly energetic, but also ruthlessly ambitious, conceited and not above using dubious business practices to achieve his ends. He was obsessive in his quest for total control of the railway, refusing to accept that anyone but he was capable of doing anything properly. As he once admitted:

> ***'Robert Stephenson is* decidedly *the* only *man in the profession whom I feel disposed to meet as my equal or superior.'***

This led him to over-commit himself wildly, causing delay and confusion. Recognising this, the Directors of the Great Western made the locomotive depot at Swindon a separate entity under Daniel Gooch from 1840, reporting direct to the Board. This did not stop Brunel trying to interfere with the detailed running of the works, sending Gooch patronising and arrogant letters. Despite his small stature, Brunel was also not above using physical violence to achieve his ends. In a dispute with a contractor at Mickleton Tunnel, he incited some three thousand navvies to a riotous assembly, an offence that could in theory have cost him transportation to Australia.

In terms of his approach to railways, he shared George Stephenson's overweening belief in his own genius and his inability to delegate. In every other respect, there could hardly have been a greater contrast between them. As O. S. Nock put it, Stephenson advanced cautiously, gradually improving upon the practices he had grown up with from childhood. Brunel, a trained engineer, thought out every aspect of his railway from first principles. His sketchbooks teemed with ideas — detailed designs for stations, down to the elaborate lamp posts that would illuminate them; even a new profile for the cross-section of the rails and new ways of laying the permanent way. His attention to detail and design skills produced some of the finest examples of railway architecture — on his atmospheric railway, even the chimneys of the pumping stations were based on Italianate campaniles, in an attempt to overcome environmental objections. On one of the rare occasions the Great Western board got him to cut back on the architectural detail to save money (at Reading station) Brunel's revenge was to ensure that the buildings looked as nasty as they were cheap. The tragedy was perhaps that Brunel was not the absolute pioneer of British railways in the way Stephenson was. Under his influence, a very different, and better, national network might have emerged.

Chapter 4:
No way to run a railway

The first operators struggled to work out how to run a railway. These pioneers had no real precedents on which to base their operations. Neither the colliery tramways, the canals, nor the turnpikes and stagecoaches offered an appropriate model, and the operators had to make up the rules as they went along, with sometimes comical and sometimes disastrous results.

Some small oversights

The problems of working in uncharted territory sometimes showed even before the railway was operating. The promoters of the Leicester & Swannington Railway found themselves going back to the shareholders for more money on the grounds that, not only had they forgotten to budget for the cost of getting their railway Bill through Parliament, they had also overlooked the need to purchase small matters like locomotives and rolling stock.

One fairly basic requirement of a steam railway is to secure a reliable supply of water, but the Great Western relied on drawing water from the nearby Grand Junction Canal. As the needs of the railway grew, the canal was sometimes unwilling or unable to supply as much as they needed. By the evenings, railway staff were often forced to rob the tenders of other locomotives, to give the last services enough water to get out. In the winter of 1839, the canal froze entirely and the company was reduced to sending its fire engine out around the city, in search of unfrozen wells.

The Stockton & Darlington was itself far from complete — and far from solvent — when it opened. It had no engine sheds, almost no sidings, no facilities for the transhipment of coal onto the ships, and many of the promised branches were still unbuilt. But open it had to, since the initial capital raised by the company was more than exhausted. They had under-estimated the cost of compensating the landlords along the route and, like most major construction projects before and since, building costs had spiralled well beyond original estimates. Shortfalls had had to be met by the managing committee raising £60,000 on their own promissory notes, repayment of which was due within six months. On the day of opening, the company actually owned the grand total of one locomotive, one passenger carriage and 150 coal wagons. In the May following the opening, Edward Pease, the railway's original champion, found himself paying the railway employees from his own pocket.

Parliamentary rules... OK?

Some of the rules for the new railways were laid down in the conditions attached to the Acts of Parliament under which they operated, but their parliamentary masters were equally in the dark. In the case of the Stockton & Darlington, some of the regulations had a modicum of logic to them, such as the restriction on night-time operation. Others had the ring of extreme laissez-faire, such as the provision that any landowner within five miles of the land was allowed to attach his own branch line to the main line and run his own trains along it. This reflected the way the turnpikes operated, where the upkeep of the road, the provision of the coaches that ran along it, and the horses that pulled them were all the responsibility of different private individuals, each trying to make a profit. This was seen as the model for most of the earliest railways.

Other rules seem positively perverse to modern eyes. For example, gates had to be provided wherever a railway crossed a road — but to stop the train, not any road traffic. It was the train driver's duty to stop the train, open the gates and close them after passing through. Failure to close them could incur a fine of 40s, half of this sum going to the witness who informed against the driver and half to the poor of the local parish.

However, the Highways Act of 1839 required that all railways should be gated off from the road, in the interest of road safety. Which of these two apparently contradictory pieces of legislation were the companies to obey? The Great Western found the matter vexing enough to justify bringing a test case before the courts, by prosecuting one of their own crossing keepers for not keeping the gate shut across the railway. This established that the railway line did not have to be permanently gated, though the matter was not finally resolved until the Regulation of Railways Act of 1844.

Rules of the road

Most of the line on the Stockton & Darlington and Canterbury & Whitstable Railways was single track with passing loops. The initial absence of any rules of engagement on the Stockton & Darlington led to some angry confrontations, with the drivers of horse-drawn vehicles refusing to reverse. One at least compromised to the extent of getting his passengers to lift his coach off the rails to let the other pass, then lift it back on. It was eventually decided that locomotive-drawn trains would have right of way, unless a slow-moving locomotive found itself overhauled by a horse-drawn vehicle (a distinct possibility where the average running speed of the early locomotives was about 5mph). The locomotive then had to pull into the next loop and let the coach pass, as it was supposed to if a coach was seen approaching from the opposite direction, though this rarely happened in practice. They also tried a system whereby marker posts were put midway between passing points and the first vehicle to pass those midway points had right of way.

They were not alone in lacking operating discipline. For some time after the opening, trains used the twin tracks of the Great Western in a completely arbitrary manner. Not even the practice of having separate 'up' and 'down' lines was observed. Drivers would also sometimes invite numbers of 'guests' to join them on the footplate for the ride, a practice that hardly led to efficient operation. One 'enterprising' driver in 1845 was even found to be using this means to provide a paid taxi service along his branch-line to the junction with the main line, in between the regular services he provided for the railway company. If you were rich and influential, even more ambitious options became possible:

> ***'It was not an uncommon custom, if any important person missed his train, to charter a "special" and start in pursuit. With good luck he might count on overtaking a train which had only had half an hour's "law", before it had got much more than half the distance between London and Brighton. On one occasion the Secretary of the London and Greenwich Railway, having missed the train, mounted an engine, and started in such hot pursuit, that he ran into the tail carriage with sufficient violence to break the legs of one or two passengers.'***
>
> (Quoted in Acworth, W. M.: *The Railways of England*)

One such pursuit, on the Edinburgh to Glasgow line, was reported to have covered the twenty-three miles between Edinburgh and Falkirk at an average of 55mph, around twice the speed of the scheduled service.

The mixed modes of traction on the Stockton & Darlington led to other practices not seen on most modern railways. Much of the early traffic on the line was horse-drawn and the unfortunate animals were asked to do three round trips in six days, pulling a $12^{1}/_{2}$-ton load. The only respite they got was trotting behind the train on downhill sections, and their working life under this regime was a short one. It was realised that a lot more work could be got out of them if the horses were allowed to ride on the downhill sections. Special wagons called 'dandy carts' were developed for this purpose and attached to the rear of the train. The horses were trained to jump onto them at the top of any incline, once they were unharnessed and the rest of the train had rolled by them. A bag of hay was provided on the cart as an incentive for them to do so. So keen were the horses to take a break that, on occasions when the cart was not fitted, the horse might try and climb into the last of the coal wagons on a downhill stretch! With dandy carts, the horses could do four round trips a week and their health was found to improve. At least one driver tried to improve his own health by this means. Robert Sanderson was fined 5 shillings for climbing into the dandy cart for a rest, rather than walking alongside his horse as it hauled the train uphill, leading to a collision with a locomotive.

It was many years before horse traction ceased on the Stockton & Darlington. Even when the company had 19 locomotives in use, there were still some fifty horses operating regularly on the line. But the horses were less of a hazard than many of the independent drivers, who left the points wrongly set, drove at what were then regarded as high speeds across ungated roads and travelled at night without lights. Some thought nothing of leaving their train parked on the single line track while taking refreshment at a local alehouse; one is recorded as having taken a two-hour lunch-break, to the fury of other users of the line. Even the General Manager of the Clarence railway, a Mr Child, saw nothing wrong in stopping his train at his trackside house and taking his guest, George Stephenson, in for breakfast — leaving his other passengers sitting in the train.

One hazard the horses did not pose was that of fire. The concerns of the early opponents of steam locomotion on these grounds were not without foundation. The locomotives on the Stockton & Darlington spewed out hot cinders that set fire to adjoining fields, the passengers' clothes and any merchandise being transported in the train. Passengers looking out of the window at the locomotive in action risked having their eyes burnt. The tarpaulin was eventually developed to protect the merchandise being carried in wagons but, in the meantime, some goods trains would carry a firewatcher to put out any fires. On one occasion in June 1840, a fire broke out in a wagon full of barrels, and a passer-by bravely leapt in to quell it. It was only afterwards that he discovered just how brave he was. The barrels contained highly inflammable spirits and, in one case, gunpowder!

The locomotive drivers also introduced some operating practices that would today be regarded as novel. A driver called George Sunter was able to do the journey between Shildon and Middlesbrough nonstop, despite his locomotive needing two water stops *en route*. He did this by disconnecting the locomotive from the wagons at the brow of a conveniently placed hill and hurrying ahead to the nearest water stop (leaving the wagons to catch up with the aid of gravity and his fireman to control their descent as best he could). By the time they caught up, he had taken on water and was ready for the next stage of the journey. Another used to drop his fireman off at his home in Darlington at the end of the shift and drive the locomotive back to its shed in Shildon single-handed. This may not sound problematic until you realise that his locomotive was of a design whereby you stood at the back of the locomotive to drive it, but at the front (with the coal tender preceding the locomotive) to stoke it.

With the crude engineering of the time, the trains needed frequent lubrication. This was done by the driver regulating the locomotive's speed down to about 2mph, and then walking along the length of the train with an oilcan and brush, applying the lubricant. The problem with this was that the improved lubrication could cause the train to speed up, leaving the driver running to catch up (or leaping on the back of the train and climbing precariously over the wagons to regain the footplate).

Speed bought added problems for goods trains. The Railway Board in 1835 requested that coal trains should not exceed 6mph, since speeds in excess of that were leading to an unacceptable number of wheels breaking. It was also suggested that if goods trains were to exceed that speed, the wagons would need to be fitted with springs, since the cargoes had an alarming tendency to bounce out of the wagons.

Track

The design of a railway track seems so obvious to us today that it is hard to imagine anyone opting for a radically different approach. However, some of the early railways, instead of being mounted on transverse sleepers, had their rails secured to two parallel rows of stone or wooden blocks. The Stockton & Darlington used both, some of their wooden blocks being recycled oak from old Royal Navy warships, dating from the time of Nelson. The Liverpool & Manchester initially followed suit, and *The Times* found the matter of sufficient interest to its readers to justify this lengthy description:

'The structure of the Manchester and Liverpool rail-road is a raised edge rail of rolled iron, two inches broad and one inch thick, in lengths of 25 feet each. These are firmly knitted together and placed upon cast iron chairs or pedestals, and the whole supported at intervals of three feet by stone blocks 20 inches square and 12 inches deep. Into each of the blocks, two holes are drilled and filled up with oak plugs, and to these the pedestals bearing the rail are spiked down. On the embankments, and other places where the foundation may be expected to subside, additional firmness is secured by the introduction of oak sleepers. The whole length of the road is 31 miles, and posts are placed every quarter of a mile to mark the distance.'

(*The Times — 31 August 1833*)

There was some logic to this arrangement for a horse-drawn railway, since it left a clear space between the rails for the horse to walk. But with the greater stresses of a steam railway, this method made it difficult to maintain the correct gauge, unless they were very firmly bedded in. They were also prone to uneven settlement, which was not easy to remedy.

Some of the raw materials for the track-beds of the earliest colliery railways were available locally, in the form of pit waste. Others arrived as a consequence of the coal-transporting business. The ships that carried coals to London and elsewhere made the return journey 'in ballast', carrying stones and gravel for stability. This tended to be dumped near the quayside, until the early railways found a use for it in their track-beds. The term *ballast* had purely nautical associations until the 1830s.

In 1834, Robert Stephenson, working on the London & Birmingham Railway, invited suggestions for the best way of building the permanent way. It produced a host of weird and wonderful ideas, from continuous cast-iron rails set direct into the ballast of the track-bed, to rails supported on slate sleepers by brick arches. It was Joseph Locke, while building the Grand Junction, who was largely responsible for devising the system that was used throughout Britain into the twentieth century — of rails fixed into their chairs by wooden wedges, with the chairs mounted on wooden sleepers running at right-angles to the track.

The track of the Liverpool & Manchester had to be relaid relatively quickly with heavier gauge rails, as a result of the increasing weight and volume of traffic using it. It was built to cater for locomotives of no more than six tons, (the weight limit specified at the Rainhill Trials) but they doubled and trebled in size within a very few years. *Herepath's Railway Magazine* lamented the state of the track in March 1836:

> ***'I should like to see some little improvement of the road. In many places the ballasting and dirt are almost on a level with the edge of the rails, while in others the naked blocks and sleepers present a terrifying aspect, threatening inevitable destruction to engines, carriages and passengers, should the train by any accident run off the rails. Indeed, the toute ensemble looks like some half-finished work, reflecting the features, not of a rich and flourishing company, but of abject, pitiable poverty.'***

Parliament had to approve the cost of completely re-laying the track, replacing the stone blocks that supported the rails with wooden sleepers. Brunel similarly found himself faced in 1843 with re-laying the lines between London and Maidenhead with heavier gauge rails, at a cost of £93,000. There were also problems with the system of longitudinal sleepers that Brunel originally sought to introduce on the Great Western. They were intended to give greater rigidity, but experience showed that rigidity was the last thing a track needed — a degree of give made it much more robust. There was more trial and error: the Liverpool & Manchester found that the gaps they left between the rails for expansion were not enough to cope with an exceptionally hot summer. A section at Parkside buckled badly and had to be replaced.

But the big breakthrough with rails was to result from Sir Henry Bessemer's discovery of a method for making cheap steel in 1856. Within a year, steel rails were starting to be installed and were found to be something like sixteen times more durable than their iron counterparts.

Open to all?

The private users of the Stockton & Darlington Railway provided their own wagons, but at first there was virtually no standard specification for them, beyond the gauge. This meant that they all had buffers at different heights, different types of couplings and were sometimes too insubstantially built to survive the mechanical unloading processes that were eventually installed on the railway. They were also often poorly maintained by their owners, either out of meanness or ignorance, and this added to the frequency of breakdowns of trains.

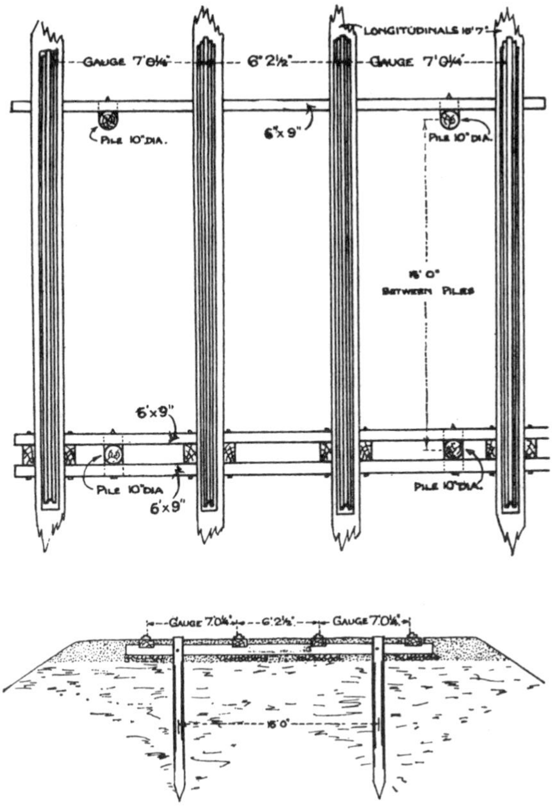

ORIGINAL PERMANENT WAY, 1838

Brunel's original method for fixing the permanent way (from MacDermot).

Similarly, the first passengers to use the railway travelled in the company's horse-drawn coach *Express*. As demand grew, it was met by local independent coach operators and innkeepers introducing their own horse-drawn coaches. They were literally no more than stagecoach bodies on unsprung railway chassis and, apart from the rails beneath them, there was little to distinguish them from the old stagecoaches. Coach horns would be blown to warn of their approach and passengers could sit outside, on top of the coach. Because outside travel was cheaper, you could often find as many as thirteen passengers crowded onto the roof of a coach. It was not uncommon for people to fall off and be injured. The company's response was not to ban outside travel, but to erect nets below the door level of the coaches, to try and catch them when they fell.

The first traffic policemen

Security was a problem from the earliest days. Three hundred railway labourers were engaged to keep the crowds off the track at the Rainhill Trials, and cavalry were stationed at intervals along the track at the opening of the Liverpool & Manchester (though this was probably more to do with the presence of the Duke of Wellington than with concerns about the railway itself). The early lines were patrolled by so-called 'constables' or 'policemen', who combined the jobs of track inspector and signalman, as well as more traditional policing roles of preventing trespass, ensuring gates were kept closed and enforcing the many by-laws. Whilst on railway property, they had all the powers of the newly established conventional police, a uniform modelled on theirs, and even truncheons with which to enforce the by-laws. The London & Birmingham (1833) and Great Western (1835) were the first railways to be given these powers in their enabling Acts. The London & Birmingham officers had their powers extended in 1837 to cover half a mile either side of railway property. They patrolled a 2-3 mile section of track in this capacity, and Brunel described his as 'tolerably useless'. Their value as a human signal was certainly open to question. The Great Western trains of the day needed at least a mile to stop and, by the time they saw the frantic waving of the constable, it was usually too late. Rear-end collisions were commonplace.

The Liverpool & Manchester employed a similar force, described here in a contemporary account:

> ***'The company keep a police establishment who have station-houses at intervals of about a mile along the road. These stations form also depots for passengers and goods from or to any of the intervening places. The duties assigned to these men are to guard the road, — to prevent or give notice of any obstruction, — and to render assistance in the event of any accident occurring; and to do this effectually they keep up a continual line of communication.'***
>
> *('A Tourist' — 1833, pages 23-24)*

The early railways suffered from many of the safety problems that plague their modern counterparts — people wandering onto the track: hooligans putting things on the rails, causing derailments, or throwing stones at trains. In one early case, some workmen put a plank across the rails to form a seat for a picnic. In the crash that followed, the fireman on the locomotive was killed. Horribly all too common were railway employees being crushed between wagons as they tried to connect or disconnect them. The Liverpool & Manchester introduced a Register in 1831, to record all personal accidents and learn the lessons from them. As well as being responsible, this was no more than recognition of the fact that accidents were expensive and bad for the company's reputation. The railways soon became a fruitful arena for the litigious and the downright fraudulent, until an Act of 1846 clarified liability for personal injury and death on the railways.

The Great Western was the first to start installing a trackside telegraph, from May 1838. It cost around £300 a mile to install, so its progress along the line was slow. It got as far as West Drayton by July 1840, but then broke down and was not repaired for three years. It offered a relatively slow but sure way to warn of problems along the line but, oddly enough, nobody at first seemed to think about this application. This may have been something to do with the fact that many of the train guards could not read or write. It was first used to warn of a broken-down train on the line in April 1839, and this application was deemed so unusual that it was reported to the Directors. Not until the 1860s was the telegraph regularly used to forewarn of the arrival of trains on any part of the Great Western.

The demon drink

The train drivers of the day were totally exposed to the elements and it was not uncommon for them to fortify themselves against it with strong liquor. Railway staff were relatively well paid (a Great Western driver in 1838 could earn £2 7s 6d a week, compared with an average wage of £1) and consequently they could afford to do so. More generally, the excesses of the Regency were still fresh in people's minds and drink was strongly associated with the transport traditions of the coaching industry. Drunkenness in charge of a vehicle was far more tolerated than it would be today.

Cases involving the Great Western seem to be particularly well documented, though there is no reason for believing that they suffered more than any other early railway (except, perhaps, the sternly Quaker management of the Stockton & Darlington). One Great Western driver, named John Chicken, found guilty of being drunk in charge of a train, was let off a fine as a result of the following less than ringing testimonial from a colleague: 'I was drinking with driver Chicken in the refreshment room at Maidenhead Station. He drank no more than usual and his presence of mind was not impaired.'

But sometimes the offence was too striking to avoid punishment. One driver on a Slough–Paddington run in May 1842 was seen to clamber along the roofs of the moving train to the rearmost carriage, entering through the window and leaving his fireman in charge of the footplate. There, in front of the amazed passengers, he, the guard and the conductor set about emptying the contents of a gallon jar of ale. Only as the train approached Paddington did he clamber rather less steadily back along the roofs to the footplate. Outraged complaints from the passengers led to the driver being fined £1.

But it was not just the drivers who were prone to this problem. There were specialised constables, known as switchmen, whose job it was to operate the points. It was not unknown for them to go for a pint or six before the next train arrived. Unfortunately, on one occasion the switchmen left some of the main line points set for the carriage shed. When the next train arrived somewhat earlier than they had expected, it went careering off the main line into the carriage shed, where it shunted the carriages through the shed wall and into another locomotive. In this case, the two miscreant switchmen were dismissed. Another of their number was a Mr Broomhead, a habitué of licensed premises and of any grassy bank suitable for a snooze. He had a series of mishaps, involving a train driving through a farm gate and a crash between two trains going the opposite ways along the same line, prior to losing his job.

The Mint public house, near Paddington station, became a favourite haunt for railway staff, so much so that the company was forced to station a policeman outside to prevent them entering. As a compromise, the pub was allowed to send supplies of beer — but not spirits — over to the railway staff. Even so, drunkenness remained so rife at the station that the company was eventually forced to buy the lease of the pub and turn it into a coffee shop.

Some would-be employees did not require strong drink to addle their wits. As one son of an official on the Stockton & Darlington Railway observed:

> ***'Between the years 1830 to 1840 the locomotive engine had a great attraction for men of weak intellect who were often wanting to be employed as firemen, and regularly came every month to see my father from all parts of the surrounding country... They were generally men who were not in work, and were quite harmless. There were not so many police or lunatic asylums in those days.'***

(*Notes of incidents connected with the Stockton & Darlington Railway — Stockton Reference Library*)

A note of warning

The stagecoach era had been marked by the use of a bugle, for both warning and greeting other road-users. This tradition continued for a number of years at both terminals of the Liverpool & Manchester Railway. Trains were 'played out of the terminal stations by a lively tune performed by a trumpeter at the end of the platform'. The *Tyne,* a locomotive on the Newcastle & Carlisle Railway, went a stage further. It was fitted (under the influence of a local vicar) with a steam pipe organ. It could thus presumably both run you down and accompany the funeral service that followed the accident. Whilst on the subject of organ pipes, a tube was laid between Lime Street and Edge Hill on the Liverpool & Manchester, which enabled a code of signals to be transmitted by means of a strong blast of air sounding an organ pipe.

The lack of adequate braking was a major problem on the early trains. The tenders may have had brakes (albeit with ineffective wooden brake-blocks) but without any substantial braking under their control, the drivers relied heavily on those fitted to the rest of the train, operated by the guard. Many of the earliest locomotives had steam whistles (or 'steam trumpets', as they were called on the Leicester & Swannington, the first railway to fit them, in 1833). Whistle codes were developed to distinguish between warning of the train's approach and telling the guard at the rear of the train to apply his brakes. In October 1841, Brunel proposed that all GWR locomotives should be fitted with two whistles — one high-pitched for normal use and another deeper one to tell the guard to apply the brakes.

A stroll on the tracks

Passengers lacked any discipline in their approach to the railways. Like the legislators, they regarded the railway as no different to the lane outside their house, in what were much more traffic-free days. They felt at liberty to wander on the track or, if overcome with fatigue on the way home from licensed premises, fall asleep on it. Trespass onto the line by the general public was also a problem — the Newcastle & Carlisle found it necessary to threaten trespassers with seven years' transportation. This early report from the Liverpool & Manchester showed that the railway could not be treated in such a cavalier manner:

> **'Liverpool — shocking accident on the railroad:** ***We have to record a calamitous accident on the railway, occasioning the loss of three lives, and, in all probability, a fourth. It appears that, as the second-class train, which leaves Liverpool at 3.00 p.m., was***

proceeding over Parr Moss, a little on the other side of Newton, on Friday afternoon, one of the tubes that passes longitudinally through the boiler burst. The consequence was that a quantity of water fell into the fire, steam was generated in abundance, and the engine (the Ajax) stopped. Several of the passengers alighted to see what was the matter, and they incautiously got on the line of railway taken by the trains going to Liverpool, the contrary to that on which the disabled engine stood. While they were in this situation, a train of wagons from Bolton, proceeding to Liverpool, came up. The persons who had alighted did not see the advancing train, being enveloped in a dense cloud of vapour, and from the same cause they were by the conductor also unseen. They accordingly came upon them with fearful violence; several were knocked down and the wheels of the train passed over four of them. Three of the unfortunate party were killed on the spot, their bodies being dreadfully crushed; the fourth survived and was taken forward to the infirmary, but his recovery is considered hopeless... This latter accident shows the necessity of passengers attending to the caution so repeatedly urged, to sit still when the train stops otherwise than at the regular stations.'

(*The Times — 4 February 1833*)

At the inquest following this accident, one of the drivers involved told the court: *'To stop an engine like the Liverpool, it would require the breaks (sic) to be applied at least three hundred yards before it could be stopped, when going at the rate of 14-15 miles an hour, and with twelve or sixteen wagons.'*

One way of stopping passengers climbing randomly out of trains was to lock them into their carriages for the duration of the journey. But this practice became hotly controversial from May 1842, after 53 passengers in a French railway train burned to death near Versailles, trapped in their carriages after an accident. A press campaign led to a Board of Trade Circular, requiring that one door of each carriage be left unlocked.

'Head came into contact with a bridge, being allowed to ride outside.

Jumped out after his hat.

Strolling on the line in the night without authority.

Run over at night, trespassing, in a state of intoxication.'

(Some causes of death from the first annual accident reports of the Railway Department)

The number of serious accidents on the railways increased substantially in 1840 and 1841. Those two years alone saw 29 people killed, compared with just five for the whole of the previous decade. A major cause for this was thought to be the fact that the railways were now becoming a network, rather than a series of individual lines, and that through running was proving significantly more dangerous. One consequence of this was the Regulation of Railways Act 1844, which required the reporting of all railway accidents — whether or not injury was caused — and gave Inspectors powers to prevent the opening of new lines unless they were satisfied with the safety of their operating procedures.

In the event of a fatal accident in these early days, one consequence might be that the courts placed a deodand on the locomotive involved. This was a mediaeval practice, and was supposed to atone for the souls of those who suffered a violent death. Any object causing that death, or its cash equivalent, was forfeit to the state. There were cases of locomotives having sums of between £500 and £1,400 levied against them, until the abolition of the practice in 1846. But one man who might have felt hard done by was one Donald McDonald, who was killed when hit by a locomotive. The judge placed a deodand on the offending locomotive — of one shilling (5p).

Chapter 5:
The Railway Experience

'Those rattling pig pens upon wheels, misnamed third-class carriages, are despicable affairs...a species of horizontal shower bath...'

(*Illustrated London News*, quoted in Phillips, page 25)

'The red hot cinders every now and then dropping from the grate, and the immense volume of steam issuing from the chimney, together with the black faces of the men, and the flying velocity of the engine, I could not help observing to the guard who attended me, looked as if his Satanic Majesty had just sent two of his imps with the instrument of torture, vomiting with fire and smoke, to bring back some spirits escaped from his grasp; to which the deep grunting of our engine, now distinctly audible from our slow motion, seemed to typify the moans of despair.'

(*Herepath's Railway Magazine, 1836, describing a trip on the Liverpool & Manchester Railway*)

Queen class to pig class — the first railway carriages

The passenger carriages on the first railways tended to be closely modelled on — and were sometimes actually made from — the only example they had to go by: the stagecoach. The coaches of the Oystermouth Railway of 1807 were based on the American stagecoach, with the only concession to the train concept being some padding on the underframe, in lieu of buffers, where one stagecoach came into contact with the next during the journey. Spring buffers appeared only from the 1830s. (They were not universally and instantly accepted. One of the more bizarre proposals to be put to the South Western Railway in 1841 was to suspend large bales of wool from the front and rear of trains, and between individual carriages, to absorb the impact of any collisions.)

A seat with a view

Early rail passengers continued to travel on top of the carriages, stagecoach-style. The very earliest first-class carriages on the Liverpool & Manchester even had rooftop seats for those who preferred to travel in the open air. This was not to be recommended for any railway that had tunnels or low bridges, and the practice was stopped. But railway employees continued to frequent the roof, even after passengers were removed, and would make their perilous way from one end of the moving train to the other, picking their way along the carriage roofs among the baggage stowed there. The ride in these early four-wheeled coaches, with a short wheelbase (seven feet was not uncommon and third class on the Bodmin & Wadebridge Railway (1834) had a wheelbase of just four feet) and running on a rudimentary permanent way, must have been very choppy indeed, making rooftop journeys particularly dangerous.

The upper classes — luxury travel

The word 'class' did not feature in the pre-railway travel vocabulary, but there were, in effect, four classes of road travel at that time — 'mail-coach', 'stage-coach (inside and outside)' and 'goods wagon'. The steamships divided passengers into 'cabin' and 'deck'. The Liverpool & Manchester Railway was the first to use the term 'class', but they did so initially simply to distinguish fast and slow trains.

One early carriage that went considerably beyond the stagecoach, and was perhaps the grandest item of rolling stock of its time, was that provided for the Duke of Wellington at the opening of the Liverpool & Manchester Railway. It was the first eight-wheeler carriage of the railway age:

> ***'It is 32 feet in length by eight in width, and is supported by eight wheels. The sides were splendidly ornamented. A canopy twenty-four feet long was placed upon gilded pillars, and so contrived as to be lowered when passing into the tunnel. The drapery was of rich crimson cloth, and the whole surmounted by a ducal coronet.'***
>
> (*Morning Post — 18 September 1830*)

Royal patronage led to further superlatives in coach building. Queen Victoria first travelled on the Great Western in June 1842; she was said to prefer her royal trains to the royal yacht, being a very bad sailor, though it took much encouragement from Prince Albert to get her to use rail. She was a nervous rail passenger — she disliked travelling at more than 40mph, and her itinerary had to be planned with this in mind. She was beaten to the rail age by Queen Adelaide, the widow of King William IV. The carriage built for her by the London & Birmingham Railway was the first to have steam heating and boasted 8-foot headroom. The royal saloon carriage for the London & South Western Railway, dating from 1844, was notable mainly for the riot of elaborate drapery in it. They unleashed a Mr Herring, described as the 'Fleet Street Draper', on it, with apparently spectacular results. But, no matter how exquisitely draped, these early four-wheeled carriages would not have given a particularly smooth ride, even at 40mph.

Moving slightly down the social ladder, the fledgling Great Western, true to its tradition of concentrating on its first-class passengers, introduced something called the posting carriage. This was a form of super-first-class accommodation, seating just 18 people in (what was for the day) drawing room luxury. The *Reading Mercury* said that they reminded them more:

> ***'... of the comfortable state cabins of one of our first-class river steamers than almost anything we can liken it to. It is fitted up along the sides with large plate-glass windows, commanding a most extensive view of the surrounding country...Here are luxurious couches, cushions and sofas, upon which one may recline at full length — nay, even tables, at which those whose appetites are too much excited to await the expiration of a three-hours transit from London to Bristol, may enjoy themselves, or read or play chess.'***

Despite these warm words, they proved to be of little practical use and were phased out by 1856. Even more exclusive were the private carriage trucks, where the super-rich could drive their own coaches onto special trucks on the train, enabling them to travel without any risk — as the Duke of Wellington put it — of a journey in 'a public conveyance in which one may be quite certain of having worse company than in any stage coach, without the chance of relief at short distance'. The Great Western had 161 of these carriage trucks by 1845, and most stations had provision for loading them. This was the Duke's preferred form of rail travel (if rail journeys he had to make) until August 1843, when attendance upon the Queen required him to share her carriage to Southampton. His views on the company on that occasion are not recorded.

An interesting variation on the carriage truck theme was this custom-built example of containerisation for people, from Manchester coachbuilders Carr & Yates, described in the *Manchester Mercury* of 14 August 1830:

> ***'This vehicle has been constructed so that it may be drawn on its own wheels from the residence of any gentleman to the railway, and the body of the carriage may then be raised from the wheels by means of a crane and placed upon a frame or wagon having wheels adapted for the railway. It is then conveyed along the line and at the end of the journey may be replaced upon a set of ordinary wheels and driven along the streets to the final destination of the passenger and family, for whose exclusive use it may be devoted... The present carriage has been ordered merely by way of experiment and it is not yet certain whether this novel mode of conveyance will be finally adopted.'***

Even the ordinary first-class carriages of the early railways could be works of art. Built by the same coachbuilders that constructed the stagecoaches (they were one highway interest who actually made a lot of money from the railways) they were elaborately painted — those of the Liverpool & Manchester were individually named, like their coaching forebears, and the London & Birmingham and London & Southampton had their companies' armorial bearings hand painted on their doors.

Brunel took a minute interest in the design of his Great Western carriages, as with every other aspect of the railways. He developed long-wheelbase six-wheeled carriages for high-speed running, and painstakingly tracked down the minor engineering faults that caused them to make violent lateral movements at speed. The problem was felt to be so serious that it was instrumental in the establishment of a separate carriage and wagon department at the Swindon works.

Other ranks

More representative of the full range of conditions variously enjoyed or endured by ordinary passengers is this early account of the different classes of carriage on the Liverpool & Manchester Railway. It covers the whole gamut of early rail travel, from the exclusivity and luxury of the private carriage to what we may with some justification describe as pig class:

'The passage-carriages are divided into three classes; and are made to resemble four coach bodies joined together on one frame. Those of the first class contain seats for 18 passengers, three abreast, each seat being separated by arms and numbered. Those of the second class carry twenty-four passengers, four abreast, and have the seats likewise separated and numbered. The third class are open carriages, containing seats for twenty-four passengers. Each train of carriages is attended by one or more guards, who have seats on the outside. To enable private carriages to travel along the railway, flat frames are provided, upon which the carriage is raised and its wheels firmly secured upon the platform by moveable grooves.

'The cattle-carriages are covered and fenced around with a light grating. Some of them, for the conveyance of pigs, are quite open; and it is no small difficulty for the poor Irishman, who may be thus travelling, to keep his stock from rebellion.'

(*'A Tourist' — 1833, page 25*)

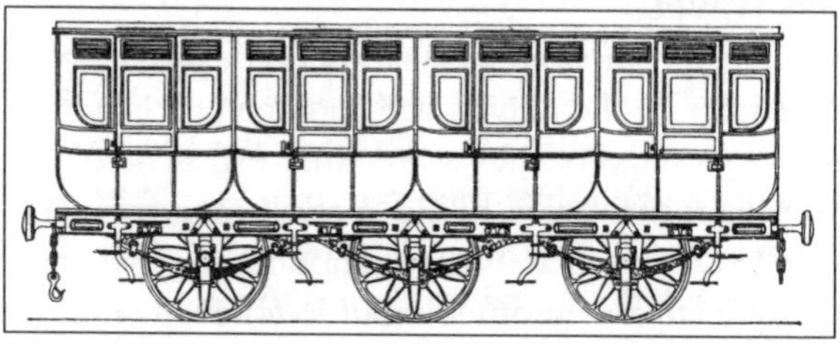

The Great Western first-class carriage, which was from the outset a six-wheeler (from MacDermot).

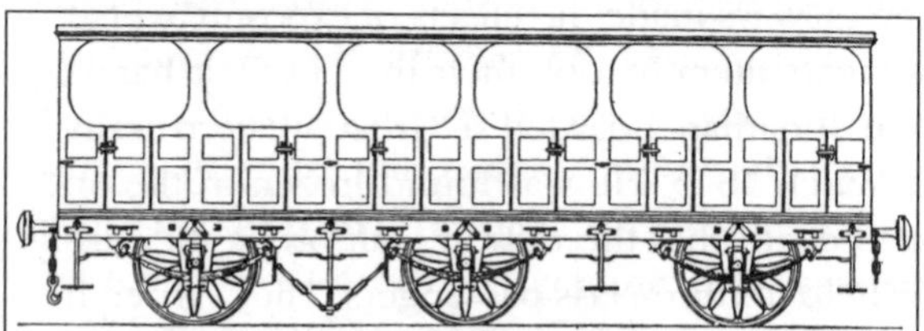

Second Class carriage

The Great Western second-class carriage (from MacDermot).

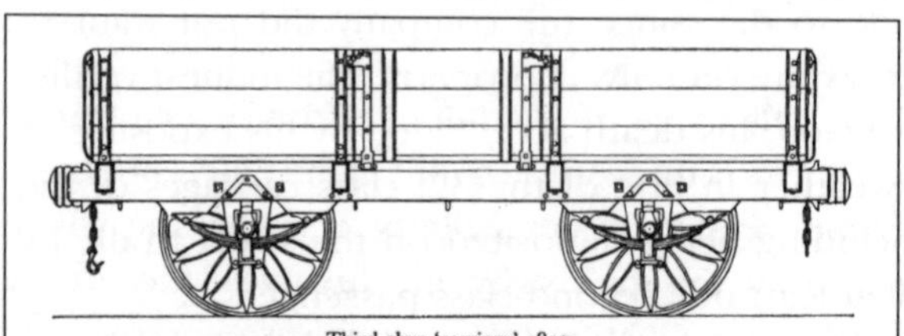

Third class 'carriage' 1840

The Great Western third-class 'carriage' or 'common wagon' of 1840. It was these that were involved in the Sonning accident of December 1841, leading to the parliamentary reforms to improve conditions for third-class passengers (from MacDermot).

In marked contrast to their first-class accommodation were the Great Western's earliest second-class carriages — open to the elements at the sides (to save weight, claimed the company) with seats just 15 inches wide and with the guard sitting in among the passengers. Second-class coaches on the Great Western initially travelled immediately behind the locomotive, where they were showered with cinders and soot in dry weather and by rain, driven in by the speed of the train, in the wet. Any umbrellas raised by the hapless passengers immediately blew inside out and, in heavy rain, they were forced to sit, soaking wet and ankle deep in water. A letter to *The Times* condemned these carriages as 'barbarous structures, disgraceful to our times and country'. It was said that the company made conditions for their second-class passengers well nigh intolerable in the hope of persuading them to travel first-class next time. In similar vein, Sir Edward Watkin of the South Eastern Railway openly admitted to a policy of employing inhumane conditions to drive third-class passengers into second-class. But even some of the Liverpool & Manchester's earliest first-class accommodation was open at the sides. However, they did at least have adjoining compartments, charged at second-class rates, in which the servants of first-class travellers could ride.

The joys of third-class travel

But even this was relative luxury, compared to what third-class passengers faced. Travelling on a budget before the railway age had been no laughing matter. Outside passengers on stagecoaches were fully exposed to the elements, and deaths from exposure were by no means unknown. The Bath mail-coach of 3 March 1812 arrived at its destination to find two of its outside passengers frozen to death and another about to follow them. But the increased speed of the railways made the effects of exposure worse.

In bad weather, passengers literally took their lives in their hands. A wire worker named John Jonathan boarded a Great Western train at Bristol, one cold day in March 1845. He was found frozen in the open wagon at Bath, so close to death that the railway staff broke their usual rule about not giving any help to third-class passengers. They carried him from the train — but only to get him off the station premises, leaving him on the pavement outside to die, since the company did not want to encourage passengers to expire on railway property. The inquest verdict was 'died by visitation of God, his death accelerated by his exposure to the inclemency of the weather in one of the 3rd class carriages of the GWR'. A similar fate (including being deposited on the street to die by railway staff) even befell at least one second-class passenger.

But it was not just the passengers who were at risk of death from exposure. The Great Western posted travelling guards on the back of the locomotive tenders, to keep an eye open for problems on the train. They were exposed to the elements, apart from the upturned bathtub arrangement in which they were seated, affectionately known to the staff as 'iron coffins'. Not for nothing was this job regarded as the most dangerous on the railways: even under normal conditions, it was all too easy to fall from their precarious perch. In the coldest weather, they sometimes were literally frozen to their seats and had to be cut out of them. As staff, they were at least carried to the refreshment room to recover, rather than out into the street to die. This unsatisfactory arrangement persisted until 1864, when the invention of the communication cord rendered their job superfluous.

Another great disadvantage of third-class travel was its extreme slowness. As we will see, legislation from 1844 required that so-called Parliamentary trains should travel at a minimum of 12mph, but this was not universally observed on all third-class services. Also, the provision in the Act that required trains benefiting from the tax break it offered to stop at every station limited the scope for third-class passengers to enjoy both a civilised minimum standard of travel and a reasonable speed of travel. The provision about stopping everywhere would not be relaxed until the 1860s. The regular service from London to Liverpool took about six hours; but the earliest third-class train took nine hours just to get from London to Birmingham. Having got there at 3pm, the unfortunate passengers then had to wait until 6am the following morning to begin the second half of their journey. At least there was little chance of them missing their connection.

The *Quarterly Review* of 1844 supported the view that there should be a 'relation between fares and velocity, between the value received and the price paid'. In their view, it cost twice as much to run a train twice as fast, due in part to the additional wear and tear on track and rolling stock, so faster trains should be more expensive. But the idea of having different classes of accommodation on the same train had already been introduced, by both the Leeds & Selby and Newcastle & Carlisle Railways in 1835/36.

The slowness of third-class services was compounded on the Great Western by the strict order of precedence that their early Rule Book gave to different classes of trains. Express trains took precedence over ordinary trains, which in turn went before goods services. An ordinary train could be held back for up to 15 minutes to let a late-running express through, a third-class train would wait up to twenty minutes and a goods train half an hour — and, in most cases, nobody knew how late the offending train was running.

As if all this were not enough, the combination of four-wheeled coaches with a short wheelbase and primitive springing, along with chain couplings that jerked the carriages about and crashed them together, and lightly built tracks, produced a thoroughly uncomfortable pitching motion. Travelling on the Brandling Junction Railway in the early 1840s was said to give the passengers a sensation 'precisely similar to that of a boat on a somewhat troubled sea', with the same end result if you were a bad sailor. An early — and less than satisfactory — solution to this on the Liverpool & Manchester was to ring a bell just before the train was about to depart, so that passengers could at least brace themselves. A more effective answer came with the invention by Henry Booth of screw couplings for the carriages.

The view among many railway companies — and large sections of the general public — was that travel for the poor was provided as a concession, and that they should be grateful for whatever they were given. As the *Railway Times* of the day put it:

> ***'We do not feel disposed to attach much weight to the argument in favour of third-class carriages with seats. On a short line, little physical inconvenience can result from their absence.'***
>
> *(Quoted in Acworth)*

The *Liverpool Times* even described the pig wagons provided on the Liverpool & Manchester as:

> ***'A vehicle constructed for the accommodation of the latter respectable class of quadrupeds, which certainly is a much handsomer and more commodious vehicle than those in which His Majesty's liege subjects were accustomed to travel fifty years ago.'***
>
> *(Quoted in Ferneyhough, page 93)*

Attitudes among carriers to third-class passengers varied enormously. The Great Western barely tolerated them. The Liverpool & Manchester initially made no provision for them whatsoever. When they were forced to do so by Parliament, the demand was such that they had to double the service within months. By contrast, no less than 68.9% of the passengers on the Manchester & Leeds in 1844 (notwithstanding the rudimentary nature of their carriages) were 'persons in the lower stations of life'. Or, at least, they were people travelling third-class. It came to the notice of the Great Western that a number of rich merchants and others from the higher stations of life were skimping on costs by travelling third-class. This so outraged the ironmaster William Crawshay that he called upon the company to teach these cheapskates a lesson, by hiring chimney sweeps to go and sit beside them and ensure that they received some grimy mementos of their cut-price journey.

The mind-set of almost wishing to punish the third-class passenger comes through in this 1838 description by the Manchester & Leeds Railway of their three classes of carriage:

'First class: *six inside — complete with everything which can conduce to comfort.*

Second class: *to carry twenty-four passengers — divisions chair high — windows in door but none in panels — and no cushions.*

Third class: *open boxes — no roofs, nor buffer springs.'*

But few railway companies were less sympathetic to the needs of their third-class passengers than the Great Western. They too did not even take third-class passengers at first. Charles Saunders, the Company Secretary, was asked in 1839 about the railway's policy towards third-class passengers. He replied:

> ***'There has been no decision of the Directors on that subject, but I think they will probably send carriages once a day, perhaps with merchandise: carriages of an inferior description, at a very slow speed for the accommodation of those persons, and at a very low price; perhaps, too, it may only be done at night.'***

In 1839 they allowed a private contractor, a Mr Dibbin, to carry some third-class passengers as part of his goods trains and the following year started running some services of their own. Third-class passengers were relegated to open wagons immediately behind the tenders of good trains, often travelling during the hours of darkness. Their luggage allowance was limited to 14 lbs and specific instructions were given that 'no member of staff may give assistance to third-class passengers'. The only third-class train for the West Country set out from London at 6.00am, and was referred to derisively by the railway staff as the *Plymouth Cheap.*

The Liverpool & Manchester similarly resisted third-class travel, when it was first proposed to them before their opening, on the grounds that it would encourage all the other passengers to downgrade their class of travel. All sorts of means were found by different railway companies to make the travelling experience of third-class passengers uncomfortable; in the Midland Railway third class, the headroom was just 5 feet 4 inches. The seating on the South East and Brighton companies' third class was just 12 inches wide, with an uncompromising upright back.

But at least these companies were making some provision for third-class travel, and the economic case for cheap fares was recognised early on:

> ***'Although we do not complain that the fares on our railway (the Great Western) are high, taking speed and accommodation into account, we think a reduction, when the line is finished to Reading would operate advantageously both to the Company and the public. On the Manchester and Leeds Railway they have a low class of fares, and on their 13 miles they carry more passengers than the Manchester and Liverpool (sic) on their 31. And the cheap passengers pay a greater profit per ton than those of the first class. The carriages are lighter, cheaper, and hold 90 to 100 passengers. They can thus carry passengers at a less expense of power, and with less wear and tear, than by the heavy first-class carriages with few passengers.'***
>
> (*Berkshire Chronicle — 19 October 1839*)

The great achievement of the so-called Gladstone Act of 1844 (discussed in detail later) was to provide minimum standards for at least some third-class travel, in terms of cost, minimum speed and weather protection. However, it did not mean an end to the miseries of such travel. The Act required that a specified number of Parliamentary trains were provided, offering weather protection 'as far as consistent with the necessary admission of light and air' — whatever that meant, and offering as it did a major loophole to the railway companies. But, provided this rather unclear provision was met (often at some ungodly hour), it was still open to the railway company to run additional third-class services at whatever standards they could get away with. Excursions, in particular, were often subject to the absolute minimum levels of passenger comfort and safety.

But even the Parliamentary trains were hardly bywords for luxury. Ventilation on the Great Western third-class carriages was via louvres;

any kind of view out was denied to all but the most determined, but at least you could not fall out of them. Indeed, it was difficult to get out of them at all. The early models — in use until 1856 — were potential death traps, with only one opening door on each side for 59 passengers to scramble through in an emergency. The first ones also had no spring buffers. The London & South Western third-class accommodation had tarpaulin curtains to protect their passengers from the weather (and also the daylight). After dark, any lighting in the carriages was initially whatever the passengers themselves provided. After 1834, one oil lamp was provided in one compartment of each first-class coach on the Liverpool & Manchester. The other classes continued to fend for themselves. For fresh-air fiends, the London & Greenwich Railway in 1836-8 offered outdoor seats at either end of their second-class carriages, even after the rest of their second-class passengers had full weather protection. But there was also such a thing as too little ventilation. First-class passengers on the Newcastle & Carlisle Railway had no opening ventilation at all. In hot weather, they had to rely on opening the doors and gasping for air while the trains were in the stations.

But let it not be said that the open third-class carriages were entirely without amenities. The wagons of the South Staffordshire Railway had hundreds of holes drilled into their floors. Not only, was it claimed, did these drain the rainwater in wet conditions; when it was hot, they provided a useful updraft that helped to cool the nether regions of the passengers. Over the years, the GWR had a continuing track record of converting goods wagons into passenger accommodation for the lower orders. Not until the 1870s did their practice of using open wagons for third-class passengers cease entirely.

In the vehicles known as Stanhopes, run by the Manchester & Leeds and others, the passengers actually had to stand up. The Glasgow, Paisley & Kilmarnock Railway went one further in April 1840, and decided that, where seats had been fitted for third-class passengers, they should be removed.

Some railway companies, such as the Great Northern in Lincolnshire and the Edinburgh & Glasgow, offered the unimaginable amenities of fourth–class travel, at rates below the penny a mile required by the Gladstone Act. This was particularly the case where coastal railways were in direct competition with steamers. For example, the Glasgow, Paisley & Greenock Railway, competing with the Clyde steamers, was in 1841 offering standing-room only fourth-class travel at just 0.27 pence a mile. This meant that some railways were offering five different classes of travel (including the Parliamentary trains — this became six in the 1860s, when special early workmen's trains were introduced). The narrow distinction between third-class passengers and animals was finally removed by the Sheffield, Ashton & Manchester Railway in their 1845 specification for cattle trucks. These had 'to be fitted with spring buffers and drawbars, to answer occasionally for passengers'.

Despite the perils of third-class travel, the Gladstone Act ensured that it was this sector of the passenger market that enjoyed a dramatic boom throughout the rest of the century, while the volume of first- and second-class passengers remained roughly constant. In the year ending June 1843 (which was admittedly a poor year for passenger travel) just under 6.9 million third-class rail journeys were made, representing some 29% of traffic in volume terms. By June 1848, the figure had more than quadrupled, to over 29 million, and represented over a half of all rail passengers.

Thus were the fine distinctions of the class system reflected in the early railways. But it went far beyond the accommodation provided in carriages. The natural tendency for railway stations to produce a mingling of the classes was restricted by the provision not just of separate classes of carriage, but also separate station entrances, staircases, booking halls, waiting rooms and places of refreshment for the different classes of traveller. In Manchester's Hunts Bank station, third-class passengers wishing to eat had to make their way to the basement. Some stations also had separate waiting rooms for women and saloons for men. Even your choice of overnight accommodation could be affected. The London & Birmingham Railway built two hotels at the entrance to their London terminus — the *Victoria* and the *Euston.* The latter was exclusively for first-class passengers, and was described as being 'more a respectable club-house than an ordinary hotel'.

As an aside, whilst on the subject of hotels, it is worth noting that the railway interests did not always get their own way. When contractor Samuel Peto built Colchester station about a mile from the town, he assumed the town would grow out to meet it, and built a large hotel next to the station. However, the established hoteliers fought back by running a fleet of omnibuses from the station to their establishments. After fighting a losing battle for seven years, Peto sold his white elephant to the Metropolitan Idiot Asylum.

For all the shortcomings of third-class travel, the greatest impact of the railways was felt by those on lower incomes. The *Illustrated London News* summed up in 1850 the transformation the railways had effected for them:

'The working classes of thirty years ago did not know their own country. Very few travelled for pleasure beyond a small circle beyond the places which they inhabited... Now travelling bids fair to become not only the necessity of the rich, but the luxury of the poor.'

Next of kin? The first tickets

Train tickets, such an indispensable part of railway travel today, did not appear in their modern form until 1837. Many early railways followed the practice of the stagecoaches and got passengers to book seats in advance. These were recorded on paper tickets torn from a book containing counterfoils (from which comes the term 'booking'). In the case of the Newcastle & Carlisle Railway, they recorded the number, date, time of departure and destination. The Liverpool & Manchester went one better. There, the passengers had to book twenty-four hours before travelling, filling out a form giving name, address, place of birth, age, occupation and reason for travelling. One of the confidence-building reasons given for collecting this short biography was to help trace next of kin in the event of a disaster. Other companies, like the London & Greenwich and Leicester & Swannington, issued their passengers with reusable metal tokens.

It was Thomas Edmondson, an employee of the Newcastle & Carlisle Railway, who came up with the idea of pre-printed tickets. They originally took the form of tickets with pre-printed destinations, onto which he would stamp the date with another machine of his own invention. Within a year, machinery for printing the tickets entirely to order had been introduced. When the Newcastle & Carlisle showed no interest in his idea, Edmondson moved to the Liverpool & Manchester and introduced it there. For the benefit of illiterate railway staff, the tickets had a symbol for the destination printed on the back. When the Railway Clearing House was set up, its members were required to use the Edmondson system, for which he received a royalty of ten shillings (50 pence) per mile of track per year.

Season tickets were available on some railways from the 1830s. The Stockton & Darlington called them 'freedom tickets' (denoting freedom of use). For many years, they were available only to first- and second-class passengers; third-class passengers had to buy theirs on a daily basis. They became generally available on the Liverpool & Manchester from 1845, who also introduced cut-price day return tickets in the early 1840s, had free travel for the under-threes from 1831 and half-fares for the under-twelves from the early 1840s.

Abandon hope — the birth of railway food

In the days of the stagecoach, passengers would arrive at staging posts at regular intervals, where they could take their refreshment while the horses were being changed. They also travelled in manageably small numbers. The railways presented entirely new catering problems, with huge numbers of people descending on a station at once, with very little time to eat and drink. The solution to this problem, the travelling refreshment carriage, was mooted (if only in *Punch*) as early as 1845, but it would not be until 1868 that George Pullman in America introduced the first railway dining car.

The problem was seen as an opportunity by many an enterprising caterer, and very soon every platform was thronged with waiters bearing trays of sandwiches and home-brewed ale. This frequently led to chaos, as passengers disembarked to go food shopping, and caused serious delay to the services. Not infrequently, the amount of strong drink they consumed led to violence and disorder. Thus a meeting of the Board of the Liverpool & Manchester Railway in 1837 could be heard complaining about:

> ***'... the inconvenience and nuisance of the existing practice of hawking about Eccles cakes and Ale and Spirit to railway passengers at almost every stopping place between Warrington Junction and Manchester.'***

Other, more up-market, suppliers would limit their approach to first-class passengers, offering them a more select range of liquor and cigars. Whatever the market, the company banned it, as did the Grand Junction in the same year, the latter publishing this announcement in its timetable:

> ***'No person will be allowed to sell eatables of any kind upon the Line. The Company earnestly hope that the public will cooperate with them in enforcing this regulation as it will be the means of removing a cause of delay.'***

The first reference to a place of refreshment provided by a railway company appears to be the Garnkirk & Glasgow Railway, which was opened in 1831 mainly to take coal the ten miles between Airdrie and Glasgow. They discovered that large numbers of people were waiting for trains at the rural end of the line, and decided to cater for their needs by constructing the Gartsherrie Inn nearby. This survived until 1843, when it was converted into a house.

As lines grew longer, the need to refresh the passengers grew greater. The London & Birmingham Railway, which opened in 1838, was planned with refreshment rooms and other facilities at either end, and one in the approximate middle of the line at Wolverton. Predictably, existing licensees objected to the competition:

> ***'The lower part of the magnificent station house in Birmingham has recently been licensed as an hotel to Mr Dee, Mine Host of the Royal, so that passengers, if they think proper, may be accommodated with every good thing without leaving the Company's premises. The innkeepers of the town complain of this establishment, in company with the station house, as a monopoly; but we presume that the immense influx of passengers into Birmingham, as evidenced this day, which will be occasioned by the entire opening of the railway, will speedily render these complaints uncalled for.'***
>
> (*The Times — 18 September 1838*)

The appalling reputation of railway catering started early. The Wolverton refreshment rooms opened in March 1839, but by November of that year the complaints had reached such a pitch that the caterer was removed. A large part of the problem appeared to be an ignorance of the concept of fast food, with basic mistakes being made like serving scalding hot soup to passengers who had just three minutes to consume it.

Or was it a mistake? It was said that passengers arriving at Tonbridge rushed out and purchased hot coffee, only to be called back to their train before they had had time to drink it. The train then sat in the station for several more minutes, giving the passengers the galling opportunity to see their coffee being poured back into the urn, ready to be served to the next set of passengers. Stories of this kind abounded around the country, sometimes with tea or soup substituted as the offending beverage.

But possibly the biggest blunder in railway catering was perpetrated by the Great Western. In 1841, as a cost-saving measure, they engaged a builder called Rigby to construct the refreshment rooms and other buildings at Swindon at his own expense. In return, he got an effective 99-year monopoly on refreshments on the Great Western, for a peppercorn rent. Under the agreement, no other facility was to be constructed between London and Bristol and it was guaranteed that all trains would stop to use them for at least ten minutes. This last part of the agreement would later return the haunt the GWR when they were striving for faster express services in the run-up to the report of the Gauge Commissioners. They reduced the stops of express trains at Swindon to one minute, and tried to get the courts to define express trains as being 'for special purposes', and thus outside the terms of the agreement — but the courts would only allow this definition to be applied to mail trains. Rigby sold on the remaining years of his lease for the healthy sum of £20,000 in 1848, but the arrangement became so ruinous for the Great Western that they eventually bought out the outstanding lease for less than half that period in 1895, for £100,000.

These refreshment rooms quickly became notorious for both price and quality (there were separate ones for first- and second-class passengers — third-class and workmen, as usual, had to go to a separate establishment across a courtyard from the station). But this did not stop the catering manager complaining in December 1842 about derogatory remarks made about their coffee by no less than the Railway's Chief Engineer. Brunel responded in acerbic manner:

> ***'I assure you, Mr Player is quite wrong in supposing that I thought you purchased inferior coffee. I thought I said to him that I had never tasted such bad roasted corn. I did not think you had such a thing as coffee in the place. I am certain that I never tasted any. I have long since ceased to make complaints at Swindon. I avoid taking anything there when I can help it.'***
>
> *(Quoted in MacDermot, page 75)*

The Directors of the GWR inclined to Brunel's point of view:

> ***'The charges and management of the Swindon Refreshment Rooms were most objectionable in every respect and gave notice to (*****the head lessee*****) that the quality and prices of provisions are so unsatisfactory that they must make an immediate alteration.'***
>
> *(Ibid, page 75)*

By the middle of the century, railway food had firmly established its position as a byword for awfulness. Charles Dickens wrote a short piece, *Mugby Junction*, which parodied a railway refreshment room and

Anthony Trollope produced this devastating critique of that cornerstone of the travellers' diet, the railway sandwich:

> ***'The real disgrace of England is the railway sandwich — that whitened sepulchre, fair enough outside, but so meagre, poor and spiritless within, such a thing of shreds and parings, with a dab of food, telling us that the poor bone whence it was scraped had been made utterly bare before it was sent to the kitchen for the soup pot.'***
>
> (Anthony Trollope: *He Knew He Was Right — 1868*)

A good read

Before the railways, there was no such thing as a national newspaper, since no paper could be distributed nationwide quickly enough for its news to remain current. The provincial newspapers of 1830 have been described as 'late echoes of the London press'. Fast stagecoaches were used to maximise the area that could be covered by newspapers, and 'specials' would be chartered in the event of earth-shattering news breaking. In 1838, the newspaper distributor W. H. Smith negotiated with the Grand Junction Railway to have newspapers delivered from Birmingham to Liverpool and Manchester. Within seven years, he was chartering nine express trains daily to deliver papers to all three cities. By 1851, one could for example buy London newspapers in Bristol by 11am and the Isle of Wight by 11.30am.

This initially threatened the provincial papers, since the London news could reach them no more quickly than did the London papers carrying that news. Their saving grace was that the London papers were more expensive than the local product and carried no local news. By 1847, London newspapers were still selling only 1,500 copies in Manchester, compared with the 9,000 circulation of the *Manchester Guardian.* But, by the following year, some 3,500 miles of telegraph were in place, and news could henceforth be transmitted almost instantaneously around the kingdom.

Railway passengers were themselves a prime market for newspapers. Initially, men and boys would sell them off the platform but the first record of a station shop for the sale of newspapers was in 1841, let to a William Marshall at Fenchurch Street station. The London & North Western let one at Euston to a Mr Gibbs, until they discovered that he was making £1,200 a year for a rental of £60. The contract was terminated, and W. H. Smith paid £1,500 a year for exclusive rights to sell newspapers, books and other material from all the stations of the London & North Western Railway. Many of the early independent station traders, who were often employees of the railway invalided out of their other jobs, specialised in material that was salacious in some way — dealing with subjects like sex, religion and politics in sensational terms. Smith, who came to be known as *Old Morality*, did much to clean up the standard of literature available on the platforms, and Matthew Arnold's poetry, Macauly's *History of England* and self-improvement works by the likes of Samuel Smiles were soon being made available to the traveller. Enterprising publishers also saw the market for cheap paperback versions of books for the railway traveller. *Routledge's Railway Library*, begun in 1848, was one of a number of series launched with this market in mind. *Murray's Railway Reading* promised 'cheap and healthy literature', but the expression 'railway literature' itself soon became a term of abuse among the literary élite.

Timetables....

> ***'We have twenty stopping places... but if we are to be limited to a timetable, we must be stopping at every one of the twenty stations...'***
>
> ***'Do you keep a record of actual departure times from the intermediate stations?'***
>
> ***'No, it is hardly desirable with the number of stations on our line. The man merely has to open and shut the gate; the train stops, takes up the passengers, and goes on.'***
>
> *Henry Booth, Secretary of the Liverpool & Manchester Railway, giving evidence to a parliamentary Select Committee in 1841.*

George Bradshaw was a Quaker mapmaker from Manchester who diversified into railway timetables in 1838. The earliest surviving example, dating from the following year, consisted of just eight pages of railway times and cab fares, and five pages of maps and plans. The document grew with the railway network. The following year, it was 32 pages, by 1845, 89 pages. By the end of the century it was approaching a thousand pages in length, and *Bradshaw* (or, to give it its original name, *Bradshaw's Railway Timetables and Assistant to Travelling*) had become the generic term for a railway timetable. Its price never changed from 6d all through the 19th century. A continental edition first appeared in 1847.

Great Western Railway.

READING, STEVENTON, AND THE FARINGDON ROAD.

TEN MILES FROM OXFORD.

EXTENSION OF THE LINE TO THE FARINGDON ROAD.

SIXTY-THREE MILES FROM LONDON.

The LINE is now OPEN to the FARINGDON ROAD, for the Conveyance of Passengers, Carriages, Horses, Goods, and Parcels.
This Station, which is on a Turnpike Road, is distant from CHELTENHAM, 38 Miles; GLOUCESTER, 41 Miles; BATH, 48 Miles.
The MOULSFORD and PANGBOURNE Stations are now Opened for Carriages, Horses, and Goods.
HORSES and CARRIAGES being at the under-mentioned Stations, 10 minutes before the time specified for the departure of a Train, will be conveyed on this Railway, at the following Charges:—

BETWEEN	Carriages. 4-Wheel.	2-Wheel.	Horses. Each.	Per Pair, being the same Property.
PADDINGTON and FARINGDON ROAD	36s.	27s.	32s.	56s.
" and STEVENTON	32s.	24s.	28s.	48.
" and MOULSFORD	28s.	21s.	24s.	40s.
" and PANGBOURNE	24s.	18s.	20s.	32s.
" and READING	20s.	15s.	16s.	28s.
" and TWYFORD	16s.	12s.	14s.	24s.
" and MAIDENHEAD	12s.	9s.	10s.	16s.
" and SLOUGH	11s.	8s.	9s.	16s.

POST HORSES are kept in readiness at the above Stations; and upon sufficient notice being given at Paddington, or the Bull and Mouth Office, St. Martin's-le-Grand, would be sent to bring Carriages from any part of London, to the Station, at a charge of 9s. west of St. Martin's Lane, and 10s. 6d. beyond it, both including Post-boy.

TRAINS, (Daily, excepting Sundays,)

DOWN TO	Hour. a.m.	CALLING AT												
Faringdon Road	8	. .	. . .	. .	. . .	Slough	Maidenhead	. .	Reading	Pangbourne	. .	. . .	Steventon	Faringdon Road
Slough	8.30	Ealing	Hanwell	Southall	West Drayton	Slough								
Faringdon Road	9	. .	. .	. .	. . . .	Slough	. . . .	Twyford	Reading	. . .	. .	Moulsford	Steventon	Faringdon Road
Faringdon Road	10	. .	. .	. .	. . . .	Slough	Maidenhead	. .	Reading	Pangbourne	Goring	. . .	Steventon	Faringdon Road
Maidenhead	10.30	Ealing	Hanwell	Southall	West Drayton	Slough	Maidenhead							
Faringdon Road	12	. .	. .	. .	West Drayton	Slough	Maidenhead	Twyford	Reading	Pangbourne	. .	Moulsford	Steventon	Faringdon Road
Slough	1.30	Ealing	Hanwell	Southall	West Drayton	Slough								
Faringdon Road	2	. .	. .	. .	. . .	Slough	Maidenhead	Twyford	Reading	. . .	Goring	. . .	Steventon	Faringdon Road
Slough	3.30	Ealing	Hanwell	Southall	West Drayton	Slough								
Faringdon Road	4	. .	. .	. .	. . . .	Slough	Maidenhead	Twyford	Reading	Pangbourne	. .	Moulsford	Steventon	Faringdon Road
Maidenhead	4.30	Ealing	Hanwell	Southall	West Drayton	Slough	Maidenhead							
Reading	5	. .	Hanwell	. .	West Drayton	Slough	Maidenhead	Twyford	Reading					
Slough	5.30	Ealing	Hanwell	Southall	West Drayton	Slough								
Maidenhead	6	Ealing	. .	Southall	West Drayton	Slough	Maidenhead							
Faringdon Road	7	. .	. .	. .	. . .	Slough	. . . .	. .	Reading	Pangbourne	Goring	Moulsford	Steventon	Faringdon Road
Reading	8	Ealing	Hanwell	Southall	West Drayton	Slough	Maidenhead	Twyford	Reading					
(Mail.) Faringdon Road	8.55	. .	. .	. .	West Drayton	Slough	Maidenhead	. .	Reading	. . .	. .	Moulsford	Steventon	Faringdon Road
GOODS.														
Faringdon Road	4 A.M.	. .	.	. .	West Drayton	Slough	Maidenhead	Twyford	Reading	Pangbourne	. .	. . .	Steventon	Faringdon Road
Faringdon Road	9 P.M.	. .	. .	. .	. . . .	Slough	Maidenhead	. .	Reading	. . .	. .	Moulsford	Steventon	Faringdon Road

UP FROM	Hour. a.m.	CALLING AT												
(Mail.) Faringdon Road	3	Steventon	Moulsford	. .	. . .	Reading	. .	Maidenhead	Slough	West Drayton	. .	. .	. .	Paddington
Reading	7.30	. . .	. . .	. .	. . .	Reading	Twyford	Maidenhead	Slough	West Drayton	Southall	Hanwell	Ealing	Paddington
Faringdon Road	8	Steventon	Moulsford	. .	Pangbourne	Reading	Twyford	Maidenhead	Slough	. . .	. .	. .	. .	Paddington
Slough	9								Slough	West Drayton	Southall	Hanwell	Ealing	Paddington
Faringdon Road	9	Steventon	. . . .	Goring	. . .	Reading	. .	Maidenhead	Slough	. . .	. .	. .	. .	Paddington
Slough	10								Slough	West Drayton	Southall	Hanwell	Ealing	Paddington
Reading	10.30	. . .	. . .	. .	. . .	Reading	Twyford	Maidenhead	Slough	West Drayton	Southall	Hanwell	Ealing	Paddington
Faringdon Road	11	Steventon	Moulsford	. .	Pangbourne	Reading	. .	. . .	Slough	. . .	. .	. .	. .	Paddington
Maidenhead	12							Maidenhead	Slough	West Drayton	Southall	Hanwell	Ealing	Paddington
Faringdon Road	1	Steventon	. . . .	Goring	. . .	Reading	Twyford	Maidenhead	Slough	West Drayton	. .	. .	. .	Paddington
Faringdon Road	3	Steventon	Moulsford	. .	Pangbourne	Reading	. .	Maidenhead	Slough	. . .	. .	. .	. .	Paddington
Slough	4								Slough	West Drayton	Southall	Hanwell	Ealing	Paddington
Faringdon Road	5	Steventon	. . . .	Goring	Pangbourne	Reading	Twyford	. . . .	. .	. . .	. .	. .	. .	Paddington
Maidenhead	6							Maidenhead	Slough	West Drayton	Southall	. .	Ealing	Paddington
Slough	7								Slough	West Drayton	Southall	Hanwell	Ealing	Paddington
Faringdon Road	7	Steventon	Moulsford	. .	Pangbourne	Reading	Twyford	Maidenhead	Slough	. . .	. .	. .	. .	Paddington
Maidenhead	9.30							Maidenhead	Slough	West Drayton	. .	Hanwell	. .	Paddington
GOODS.														
Faringdon Road	4 A.M.	Steventon	Moulsford	. .	. . .	Reading	. .	Maidenhead	Slough	West Drayton	Southall on Wednesdays only			Paddington
Faringdon Road (Except on Saturdays)	8 P.M.	Steventon	Moulsford		Pangbourne	Reading	Twyford	Maidenhead	Slough	. . .	. .	. .	. .	Paddington

ON SUNDAYS,

DOWN TO	Hour. a.m.	CALLING AT												
Faringdon Road	8	. .	. .	. .	. . .	Slough	Maidenhead	Twyford	Reading	Pangbourne	. .	Moulsford	Steventon	Faringdon Road
Slough	8.30	Ealing	Hanwell	Southall	West Drayton	Slough								
Reading	9	. .	. . .	Southall	West Drayton	Slough	Maidenhead	Twyford	Reading					
Slough	9.30	Ealing	Hanwell	. .	West Drayton	Slough								
Reading	5	Ealing	Hanwell	Southall	West Drayton	Slough	Maidenhead	Twyford	Reading					
Slough	6	Ealing	Hanwell	Southall	West Drayton	Slough								
Faringdon Road	7	. .	. .	. .	. . .	Slough	Maidenhead	. .	Reading	Pangbourne	Goring	Moulsford	Steventon	Faringdon Road
Maidenhead	8	Ealing	Hanwell	Southall	West Drayton	Slough	Maidenhead							
(Mail.) Faringdon Road	8.56	. .	. .	. .	West Drayton	Slough	Maidenhead	. .	Reading		. .	Moulsford	Steventon	Faringdon Road
Goods. Faringdon Road	4 A.M.	. .	. .	. .	West Drayton	Slough	Maidenhead	Twyford	Reading	Pangbourne	. .	. . .	Steventon	Faringdon Road

UP FROM	Hour. a.m.	CALLING AT												
(Mail.) Faringdon Road	3	Steventon	Moulsford	. .	. . .	Reading	. .	Maidenhead	Slough	West Drayton	. .	. .	. .	Paddington
Reading	7.30	. . .	. . .	. .	. . .	Reading	Twyford	Maidenhead	Slough	West Drayton	Southall	Hanwell	Ealing	Paddington
Faringdon Road	8	Steventon	Moulsford	Goring	Pangbourne	Reading	Twyford	Maidenhead	Slough	. . .	. .	. .	. .	Paddington
Slough	9								Slough	West Drayton	Southall	Hanwell	Ealing	Paddington
Slough	5								Slough	West Drayton	Southall	Hanwell	Ealing	Paddington
Faringdon Road	5	Steventon	Moulsford	Goring	Pangbourne	Reading	Twyford	Maidenhead	Slough	. . .	. .	. .	. .	Paddington
Slough	7								Slough	West Drayton	. .	Hanwell	. .	Paddington
Reading	7	. . .	. . .	. .	. . .	Reading	Twyford	Maidenhead	Slough	West Drayton	Southall	Hanwell	Ealing	Paddington
Maidenhead	9.30							Maidenhead	Slough	West Drayton	Southall	Hanwell	Ealing	Paddington
GOODS.														
Faringdon Road	4 A.M.	Steventon	Moulsford	. .	. . .	Reading	. .	Maidenhead	Slough	West Drayton	. .	. .	. .	Paddington
Faringdon Road	8 P.M.	Steventon	Moulsford	. .	Pangbourne	Reading	Twyford	Maidenhead	Slough	. . .	. .	. .	. .	Paddington

Passengers and Parcels between the long and short Stations, can proceed in either direction to Slough and be taken on by the succeeding Train.
The Goods' Train, which leaves Faringdon Road at 4 o'clock in the Morning, will, for the present, start from Reading at 6 o'clock, by which Train, Passengers, Carriages, &c., &c., will be conveyed to Paddington and other Stations.

FARES.

Paddington	1st Class.	2nd Class. Open Carriage.	Goods' Train.
To Ealing	1 6	0 9	. .
" Hanwell	2 0	1 0	. .
" Southall	2 6	1 3	0 9
" West Drayton	3 0	1 6	1 0
" Slough	4 6	2 6	1 6
" Maidenhead	5 6	3 6	2 0
" Twyford	7 0	5 0	2 6
" Reading	8 0	5 6	3 0
" Pangbourne	9 6	6 6	3 6
" Goring	10 6	7 0	. .
" Moulsford	11 6	8 0	4 6
" Steventon	12 6	8 6	5 0
" Faringdon Road	14 0	10 0	6 0

Reading	1st Class.	2nd Class. Open Carriage.	Goods' Train.
To Paddington	8 0	5 6	3 0
" Ealing	7 6	5 0	. .
" Hanwell	6 6	4 6	. .
" Southall	6 6	4 6	2 9
" West Drayton	5 6	4 0	2 6
" Slough	4 6	3 0	2 0
" Maidenhead	3 0	2 0	1 6
" Twyford	1 6	1 0	0 9
" Pangbourne	1 6	1 0	0 9
" Goring	2 6	1 6	. .
" Moulsford	3 6	2 6	1 6
" Steventon	4 6	3 0	2 0
" Faringdon Road	6 0	4 6	3 0

Faringdon Road	1st Class.	2nd Class. Open Carriage.	Goods' Train.
To Paddington	14 0	10 0	6 0
" Ealing	13 6	9 6	. .
" Hanwell	12 6	9 0	. .
" Southall	12 6	9 0	5 9
" West Drayton	11 6	8 6	5 6
" Slough	10 6	7 6	5 0
" Maidenhead	9 0	6 6	4 6
" Twyford	7 6	5 6	4 0
" Reading	6 0	4 6	3 0
" Pangbourne	5 0	4 0	2 6
" Goring	4 0	3 0	. .
" Moulsford	3 0	2 0	1 6
" Steventon	2 0	1 6	1 0

The Goods' Train Passengers will be conveyed in uncovered Trucks by the Goods' Trains only, and 14-lbs. of Luggage allowed for each.

The Charge for Goods between Paddington and the Faringdon Road Station, will be 18s. per Ton; and between Paddington and Reading, 12s. per Ton, including loading and unloading. The Charge to the other Stations in proportion. Sheep, Beasts, &c., are conveyed by the Goods' Trains.

Conveyances will run between the FARINGDON ROAD Station and Cheltenham; STEVENTON Station and Oxford, through Abingdon; between the TWYFORD Station and Henley; the MAIDENHEAD Station and Marlow and Wycombe; the WEST DRAYTON Station and Uxbridge; and Windsor Omnibuses meet every Train at Slough.

OMNIBUSES start from Princes Street, Bank, one hour before the departure of each Train, calling at the Angel Inn, Islington; Bull Inn, Holborn; Moore's Green Man and Still, Griffin's Green Man and Still, Oxford Street; Golden Cross, Charing Cross; Chaplin's Universal Office, and Bull and Mouth, Regent Circus; and Gloucester Warehouse, Oxford Street, to the Paddington Station. **Fare Sixpence,** without Luggage.

Parcels may be booked at the Railway Office, Princes Street, Bank; all the London Parcels Delivery Company's Receiving Houses, and the above established Booking Offices; for Cheltenham, Gloucester, Witney, Burford, Cirencester, Cricklade; Oxford, Abingdon, Reading, Newbury, Windsor, &c., at which places, and all the Railway Stations, they will be received for conveyance. FOUR Daily Deliveries will be made at all parts of London, and in the Country.

W. SNELL, Printer, 9a, Newcastle Place, Edgware Road, London.

Train Bill, August 1840

The Great Western timetable for August 1840. It was very coy about times of arrival. A first-class fare from London to Reading was 8s (40p) or 3s if you were prepared to travel in an open truck behind a goods train (from MacDermot).

It purported to be 'a correct account of the hours of arrival and departure of the trains of every railway in Great Britain', though many railways were much more accurate about the time of their trains' departures than their arrivals, and some, like the Liverpool & Manchester up to 1843, issued a 'schedule of departures', which did not even begin to speculate as to when the traveller might get there. The South Yorkshire Railway 'timetable' of 1851 went one better, giving neither arrival nor departure times and stating, rather superfluously, that 'no guarantee of punctuality' could be given. Charles Saunders, Company Secretary of the Great Western, explained the situation to an 1841 Parliamentary Committee on Railways, with perhaps more candour than wisdom:

> ***'At the opening in 1838 we found the engines were so inefficient that timetable working was hopeless; one or two engines might keep time, the other eight or ten were always out of time. So we suspended timetables till the locomotive power became sufficient.'***

Bradshaw, invaluable though it was, was also a byword for impenetrability, lampooned by everyone from *Punch* and music hall comedians to Charles Dickens. It was printed in a tiny typeface on poor paper, with a wealth of arcane symbols and codes that only its greatest devotees could unravel. Anthony Trollope complained that he lacked the strength and mental ability to fathom it out and *Punch* called for reading railway timetables to be made part of the school curriculum.

Some railways initially refused to supply Bradshaw with the information he required. As one railway director put it:

> ***'We are asked, gentlemen, to supply Bradshaw's Railway Guide with particulars of our trains. I most strongly object to our complying with this request. I believe it would tend to make punctuality a sort of obligation, and that failure to keep the time announced would bring penalties.'***
>
> (*Blythe — Chapter 4*)

Some proprietors had a different, but no less cavalier, attitude towards timetables. When George Hudson was criticised for the number of his trains that were late, he would simply produce statistics for the number of his trains that were early, showing that, in net terms, his railway ran virtually on time! But timetables at least enforced punctuality on the passengers, even on those who were accustomed to having others await their convenience. The London & Birmingham Railway advised in 1839 that 'Gentlemen's carriages and horses must be at the station at least a quarter of an hour before the time of departure', to enable them to be loaded onto the flat wagons on which they and their carriages could travel in privacy.

The last Bradshaw appeared in 1961.

...and time...

One thing a timetable needs is general agreement on what the time is. From the introduction of the first mail coaches in 1784, differences in local timekeeping became evident. Were you to have made the journey between Yarmouth and Penzance in those days, you would have found a difference of almost half an hour in local time, but these discrepancies were tolerated by the coach operators. The earliest railways were also relaxed about time — the Liverpool & Manchester's first timetables had the trains timetabled to run half hourly and the local time difference between the two ends of the line was only about three minutes. The Great Western had bigger time differences, but their 1841 timetable gave the following helpful information:

> ***'London time is about four minutes earlier than Reading time, seven and a half minutes before Cirencester and fourteen minutes before Bridgewater.'***

Things gradually began to change as the railway network spread, journeys got longer and there were more connections to be made. Trains then had to be timetabled to the minute.

The earliest timetables of the Great Western and the London & North Eastern, among others, were based on local time. They showed Birmingham seven minutes behind London, Manchester nine, Bath and Bristol both eleven and Liverpool twelve minutes behind. Different operators applied different policies, leading to anomalies. At Rugby, the London & North Western kept to local time, while the branch from that same station to Leeds on the Midland line worked from London time. These problems were resolved by the Great Western and the South Western from 1840, when they applied London time in all their stations. Elsewhere, these vagaries of timekeeping led to frequent complaints, and sometimes even lawsuits, from irate passengers who had been left stranded.

From 1845, there was lobbying in Parliament for standardisation, but the anomalies continued. The Chester & Holyhead line set its clocks by the Craig-y-Don gun, which was fired daily, $16^{1}/2$ minutes out of kilter with Greenwich, but their most important duty as a railway was to carry the new Irish mail train, which worked off Greenwich Mean Time. Elsewhere, the Lancashire & Yorkshire Railway won a significant victory in 1847, when the Corporation of Manchester agreed that all its clocks should be adjusted by nine minutes to comply with Greenwich Mean Time. As the telegraph system spread around the country, so too did the ability to transmit GMT time checks instantaneously, and resistance to the new system began to crumble. Among the last to concede was the Dean of Exeter, who in 1852 allowed his clock to be advanced by 14 minutes, the day after the time signals began to arrive from Greenwich. Only with the Statutes (Definition of Time) Act of 1880 did Greenwich Mean Time legally become the nation's standard. Four years later, British railway time became the world's standard, when twenty-five nations at the Prime Meridian Conference in Washington signed up to GMT as an international convention.

...and time out: leisure travel

'The succession of romantic and picturesque scenery along the line will bear comparison with the views from any railway in the kingdom.'

(*What seems today an improbable claim from the 1838 Prospectus for the railway linking those well-known beauty spots of Manchester, Bolton and Bury*)

Every major form of leisure excursion that was catered for by the early railways had a history that pre-dated the railway era. For example, the arrival of steamships in the earliest years of the 19th century greatly increased the volume of seaside tourism — Margate, for example, received 17,000 visitors by sailing ship in 1812/13. Steamship services were introduced in 1815 and, by 1820/21, Margate's visitor numbers had reached 44,000. John Constable referred to the crowded Brighton seafront as 'Piccadilly by the Sea'.

Railway excursions could attract huge numbers. During Whit Week 1845 the *Manchester Guardian* claimed that 150,000 people left the city on railway excursion trips. The claim for the largest single excursion in this period consisted of nine locomotives pulling 240 carriages with 6,600 passengers from Leeds to Hull in 1844, though it is likely that this was in fact split into several trains. One that did happen was the first railway excursion to Brighton at Easter 1844, which required six locomotives to pull the train's 57 carriages, the journey taking 4½ hours. Fares to Brighton began at 5s for a round trip of just over a hundred miles and, by 1849, had been reduced to 3s 6d. By 1860, the town could receive up to 150,000 excursionists in a single day. In addition to increasing the town's attractions as a tourist venue, the railways also turned it into part of London's commuter belt.

The various seaside resorts served by the railways soon developed their own pecking order of status. Gravesend and Southend were for clerks and artisans, Margate for tradespeople, Ramsgate for a rather nicer class of person but, if you were really select (or ambitious), it had to be Broadstairs. Blackpool, from the start, had a strongly working-class clientele and, by 1850, they could already boast over ten thousand visiting artisans on a warm weekend.

One unexpected bonus of the tourist trade, according to the Metropolitan Police, was that these excursions to Brighton 'greatly diminished' the level of crime in London. What they did for crime in Brighton is not recorded. In similar vein, the residents of Windsor were warned that the railway would attract to the town 'to behold the seat of Royalty, all the ladies of St Giles and the Seven Dials, with the gentlemen their paramours, and others of the same grade from Old Drury, Field Lane, Billingsgate, Rag Fair, etc... to the very great annoyance of the people of Windsor'.

By contrast, a dramatic upturn in fortunes occurred in the case of Folkestone. In the early 1840s, both the town and its port were in a steep decline. Then the South Eastern Railway decided to acquire the port as a base for running a steamship service to Boulogne. As well as benefiting from the direct boost to the local economy, the town was rapidly transformed into a rather superior resort, almost doubling its population in the twenty years from 1841.

Some seaside resorts were virtually the creation of the railways. As early as 1829, the Kilmarnock & Troon Railway was credited with making Troon a 'fashionable sea-bathing town'. By 1840 the Preston & Wyre Railway ran to a new port of Fleetwood, which numbered sea bathing among its amenities, Weston-super Mare got its branch line in 1841, and the residents of York could enjoy a trip to Scarborough from 1845. Other examples of rail-based seaside towns (whose growth, however, post-dates the period of our interest) include Saltburn in Yorkshire, Hunstanton in Norfolk and the Lincolnshire resorts of Cleethorpes and Skegness (the latter immortalised in the LNER poster by John Hassall — *Skegness is so bracing*).

Entrepreneurs like Joseph Crisp in Liverpool and Thomas Cook in Leicester soon began providing joint train/boat holidays. By 1845, Crisp was running excursions offering a fortnight in London or 20 days in Paris, while Cook was providing tours from Leicester to Liverpool and thence by boat to North Wales. Cook's interest in the travel industry stemmed from his Baptist background, trying to lure the people of Leicester away from the temptations of the flesh that that town had to offer. His trip for 510 Leicester temperance workers to a rally in Loughborough in July 1841 is sometimes claimed as the first excursion. Certainly, it had a bargain fare of one shilling (5p) for the 12-mile return trip and included ham sandwiches, tea, cricket and other sports in the price.

However, there are various other trips which pre-date this and which appear to meet the criteria of an excursion. One of the earliest of these was a return trip to Liverpool by 120 Sunday School teachers from Manchester in June 1831. For all his convictions, Cook (a part-time temperance lecturer) was at least more tolerant of the sins of his clients than another of his competitors. John Frame would allow only those who had signed the pledge of temperance to go on his excursions. But perhaps the most bizarre claim for the first excursion is the following:

> ***'The first special excursion train in Britain at really cheap fares appears to have been run by the little Bodmin and Wadebridge Railway in Cornwall on 14 June 1836. The "attraction" was a public hanging in Bodmin.'***
>
> *(MacDermot — page 353)*

This particular tourist attraction was snuffed out, so to speak, by the abolition of public hangings in 1867. But these were not the only types of excursion run for less than uplifting purposes in those early days. On 12 July 1842, a large number of 'swells, nobs and fancy men', apparently accompanied by a quantity of pickpockets and 'the sweepings of St Giles and Whitechapel' boarded a train from Paddington to Twyford. There, in the station yard, an illegal bare-knuckle prizefight was being staged, offering a purse of £50 to the last man standing. This brutal event lasted just over two hours and the loser, known to history as 'Tom the Greek', later died from his injuries. Rail excursions to prizefights became a minor industry. They were often accompanied by riotous behaviour on the part of the crowd and, if magistrates got wind of them, police or even troops would be dispatched to break them up. Promoters would therefore hold them close to county boundaries, so that if one lot of magistrates broke them up, they could move into the next county and conclude their entertainment before the new magistrates got wind of it. A Regulation of Railways Act of 1868 forbade the running of prizefight specials and offered rewards to informers reporting planned events. This helped to kill the so-called sport.

From the start, horse racing became a popular destination for rail travellers. The Stockton & Darlington would have punters hanging from the sides of its passenger coaches on Darlington race days; the racecourse at Newton, close to the Liverpool & Manchester Railway, got its own dedicated branch line in 1832; the Great Northern Railway transformed the St Leger meeting at Doncaster from a small-scale exclusive gathering to a major popular festival; and over 25,000 people made the rail journey to the races in Paisley over the two days of its 1840 meeting. The Ascot races were the destination for one of the Great Western's first excursions in 1839, and the return journey gave them an early taste of sports-fan hooliganism. When the train became overloaded, a number of disgruntled passengers climbed onto the carriage roofs, stagecoach-style, and refused to be talked down for half an hour.

Some of the early excursions had rather more adventure in them than the passengers might have wished. Simmons cites the case of one trial excursion to the Continent in July 1846. On the way back, the crew of the ship got drunk, the ship got blown off course and the train that eventually came to meet them suffered a boiler explosion, leaving the long-suffering passengers to walk the final $1^1/2$ miles into Ely. Apparently, the experiment was not repeated. Other trips were a more straightforward shambles. One, from Oxford to London, only reached the capital at 4.00pm — and had to turn around and return immediately!

There were also trips organised by employers or local communities. One of the earliest excursions along the newly-completed Great Western Railway took place on 23 September 1841, when almost a thousand people travelled from Cirencester to London at a cost of 13s 6d (67p) a head, to see the wonders of the capital. Further north, the Newcastle locomotive builder R. & W. Hawthorn set a trend by hiring a train in 1840 to take some 320 of their workers, their families and friends to Carlisle at half price.

Liverpool was also a favourite venue for early excursionists — over 6,000 travelled there from Manchester, Bolton and Oldham on a single day in July 1845. The quality of the rolling stock in which they travelled may be judged by their nickname — 'wagon trains'. The low standards applied to excursion trains soon became a more general cause for concern. The Great Western, in line with its tradition of minimal customer care for cut-price passengers, kept all its worst rolling stock for such excursion trips. Other companies did the same, and standards were relaxed to the point where the Board of Trade was forced to intervene. They specified the minimum number of guards to be provided; ordered that lumbering excursions should not delay scheduled services, and that the dangerous practice of locomotives pushing excursion trains from the rear should be abolished. This Inspector's report into an accident on a Manchester to Scarborough excursion in 1860, suggests their legislation did not solve all the problems at a stroke:

> ***'The impropriety of running excursion trains at all is manifest, if a railway company has not the means of putting efficient men in charge of them, as they frequently become, from the low fares at which the public is enabled to travel in them, exceedingly heavy and unmanageable, and they are, in consequence, much more difficult to drive... this excursion train had only one brake van to eight vehicles, which is quite insufficient.'***
>
> *(Quoted in Simmons, 1986 — pages 266-267)*

The one event that introduced the idea of travel to more people than any other was to be the Great Exhibition of 1851. This attracted six million paying visitors, averaging 43,000 and reaching a peak of 110,000 in a day. About five million of these are thought to have travelled there by train. Passengers from Leeds could do the 400-mile round trip for just 5s. The London & North Western Railway alone took around 775,000 people to the exhibition and Thomas Cook organised excursions for 150,000 people. It boosted the traffic of railways serving London by between 22 and 38%.

Holy Sunday

> ***'Trips to hell, at seven shillings and sixpence per head.'***
>
> *(One York clergyman's view of Sunday railway services, c1840)*

One major limiting factor to tourism was the observance of the Sabbath. The 1851 census showed that half the nation's population attended at least one church service on a Sunday, and during the so-called 'church interval', between 10am and 4pm, many railway companies observed a break in rail services while people were attending the church variety.

Often this was enforced by religious fundamentalists on the board of the railways concerned. However, the Post Office had a legal right to be provided with mail trains on a Sunday, a day on which mail was then both collected and delivered, and most railway companies combined these with a passenger service to make them more viable. The Liverpool & Manchester operated Sunday services but were embarrassed by the revenues. Their solution, arrived at in the severe winter of 1838, was to donate the profits from Sunday working to charitable causes.

Sabbatarianism was strongest in Scotland, where Sunday stagecoaches did not run and even the mail-coaches were being challenged. One particularly enthusiastic Scottish Member of Parliament made four attempts to ban all forms of Sunday labour between 1834 and 1837. He was particularly opposed to the operation of the railways, which he saw as 'the threatened invasion of Sabbath breaking customs from England'.

Despite his efforts, Parliament considered the restoration of a full Sunday service throughout the land. The argument was made that this form of Sabbatarianism was a class-based luxury, an easy option for the wealthy who had their own coaches and could therefore travel where and when they pleased. When the Regulation of Railways Bill of 1844 raised the possibility of providing the cheap Parliamentary trains on Sundays, support came from the surprising quarter of the 75-year-old Duke of Wellington. Not noted as a champion of either the railways or the poor, he nonetheless wrote to Gladstone, arguing that: 'it would be scarcely fair to prevent the travelling of the third-class trains. The people conveyed by them, the poorest, would be stopped on their journey, obliged to incur a day's expense, which would probably amount to more than the whole cost of the journey.'

This from the man who had once condemned railways on the grounds that 'they encourage the lower classes to travel about'. However, his efforts were successful. By 1847, only 2.6% of the railway network of England and Wales was closed to passengers on a Sunday. Nevertheless, Sabbatarianism enjoyed something of a revival in the latter part of the century: by 1914, 22% of the railway lines in England, and almost 60% of those in Scotland, were closed on Sundays.

Consume your own smoke

The early locomotives were not allowed to smoke, and neither were many of their passengers. The Liverpool & Manchester introduced a smoking ban in the earliest days of its operation:

'No smoking will be allowed in any of the First Class Carriages, even with the general consent of the Passengers present, as the annoyance would be experienced in a still greater degree by those who may occupy the same coach on the succeeding journey.'

The same policy did not apply in their rather well-ventilated second- and (eventually) third-class carriages, where, in any event, their customers often preferred to chew their tobacco. Great Western operated a strict policy of no smoking throughout its operation — understandable in first-class to prevent a nuisance, but less easy to comprehend in an open third-class carriage. Nobody was exempt from the rule. In one case, a barrister named Bagley was marched off to the police cells for flagrantly ignoring the rules. Enraged, he demanded the sacking of the guard responsible and an apology from the Board of Directors but, when he appeared before them, he instead received a lecture about how someone in his position should know better than to flout the law.

In contrast, the Eastern Counties Railway became the first to provide a smoking carriage in 1846, and an Act of Parliament in the 1860s would eventually even make their provision obligatory.

Customer relations

The Liverpool & Manchester may have been one of the first railway practitioners of the black art of public relations. Very early into their operation, the company set up a Passengers' Diary at their Liverpool and Manchester termini. Passengers were invited to record 'complaints on account of incivility on the part of the Company's servants, or with reference to the charge for luggage, or the loss of any parcel or package or the delay in forwarding the same'. They were safe from the wrath of most of their passengers, on the grounds that most of them could not read or write.

One little victory

Last and by no means least in the field of leisure, taking the term in its very widest sense, reference must be made to a little-trumpeted victory, resulting from the railways setting an example. In 1846, Manchester Borough Council's Public Parks Committee resolved the immediate provision of 'the requisite conveniences for persons frequenting the parks, which have been so judiciously provided by the railway companies'.

Chapter 6:
A wholesome absence of interference: State regulation and the railways

'Laissez-faire, in short, should be the general practice: every departure from it, unless required by some great good, is a certain evil.'

(John Stuart Mill: *Principles of Political Economy — 1848*)

'Competition is more efficient as an instrument of injury to existing companies than a means of guaranteeing cheapness of travelling... The public have never permanently benefited from competition between different lines of railway.'

(*Samuel Laing, Secretary to the Board of Trade, to the 1844 Parliamentary Committee on Railways*)

'There is a wholesome absence of interference in this country in all those matters which experience has shown might wisely be left to private individuals stimulated by the love of gain and the desire to administer to the wants and comforts of their fellow men.'

(*John Bright MP — Hansard 1844 xxvi,* quoted in Stevens, C: *English railways and their relation to the State — London 1915, page 25*).

A free market and laissez-faire were the ethical cornerstones of the Victorian manufacturing classes. The turnpike principle for operating the first railways reflected in microcosm the almost religious belief in the free market that prevailed at the time. Its advocates had absolute faith that competition would provide sufficient regulation, and state control was correspondingly frowned upon, as restricting the individual's pursuit of wealth and happiness.

Britain was almost unique among industrialised nations in leaving the development of its national railway system almost entirely to private enterprise. Unfortunately, as we shall see, the model did not always work for railways. Others had a different approach. The French Government decided upon the route for a railway and invited capitalists to invest in it. Their investment would be protected against competition but their profits would be capped. After a fixed period, by when they would be deemed to have made a sufficient return on their investment, the ownership of the line would revert to the state. In Belgium, the Government decided where the main railway lines would go, paid for their construction and controlled them thereafter. Private sector involvement was limited to building branch lines off them.

Laissez-faire and the Stockton & Darlington

The proprietors of the Stockton & Darlington were strong advocates of free trade. They applied it to what seems a ludicrous extent in the management principles of the railway, though their ideological commitment may have been reinforced to some degree by the fact that they were severely strapped for cash in their early years. Everything that could be sub-contracted was sub-contracted — the maintenance of the rails, the provision of wagons and locomotives, the warehouses, the horse-operated shunting. To compound the managerial problems associated with this, the contracts were sub-divided into the smallest possible penny packets, resulting in dozens of small businessmen trying to make a living on the knife-edge of tiny profit margins, and tripping over each other in the process.

In one typically absurd example, the provision and operation of a stationary steam engine was sub-let to one interest — the engineer Timothy Hackworth and his partner William Lister — whilst the provision of the ropes they used to haul the wagons along that length of line was let on a different contract to one John Grimshaw. Grimshaw's profit margin depended upon his ropes being used with great care, whilst the imperative for the other contractor, to maximise throughput, meant that the ropes were rapidly tested to destruction. Grimshaw ended up making a loss, and a claim against the railway company. This was but one example of what Vaughan calls 'a mass of complications and conflicting interests' in the affairs of the Railway, and claims against them from failing small contractors were commonplace.

There were also claims from disappointed colliery owners, who had been promised their own branch lines. In March 1829 the company still had not built the Hagger Leases branch to the Stockton & Darlington, and the Revd Luke Prattman, one of the coal-owners ill-served by this delay, successfully claimed £610 compensation from the company. When his branch line was eventually built, in 1830, it was so insubstantial that it was suitable only for horse-drawn traffic.

The company's passion for sub-contracting led to other problems, such as fraudulent contractors. Messrs Mischamp & Harris were brought in to run the Weardale Extension to the Stockton & Darlington. An investigation in 1847 found that they had been using second-hand materials and charging for new; or using no materials at all and charging for new; or even using no materials at all and **over**charging for them, to the total tune of £2,675 10s 9d.

As more and more branch lines were joined to the main railway, either by the company itself or through private initiatives, congestion on the single main line grew ever worse. The company could not take the number of wagons the proprietors wished to be moved each day, and the chaos of unregulated movement along the railway made it difficult to return them to the owners as quickly as they wanted. This in turn exacerbated other problems — creating a need for more sidings and marshalling space to store and manage the wagons awaiting transhipment; more horses, locomotives and staff to move them around; and causing more unscheduled chaos on the main line, as private interests exerted their right to move their own wagons to and from their destination.

A further example of the competition ethos can be seen in the company's treatment of its locomotive drivers and their horse-drawn equivalents. Initially, these were salaried staff and the company provided food for the horses, fuel for the locomotives and all other necessary materials. By February 1826 the company extended its sub-contracting principles to this aspect of railway management. The drivers became self-employed contractors, operating the Company's horses or locomotives. Horse leaders got 1/2d and locomotive-men 1/4d per ton moved, from which they had to supply their own feed or fuel, as appropriate, the wages of their firemen and engine cleaners, and any other materials required. The result was that they skimped on the maintenance of the company's locomotives and the feeding of their horses, and stole coal from the loads they were carrying from the collieries to fuel their locomotives.

The men did so well out of the new system that the Quaker management of the company were concerned that they would spend their new-found wealth recklessly and to the detriment of their morals. Various formulae were tried over the years, which either gave the men more income than the company felt was good for their immortal souls, or not enough to ensure the proper maintenance of the company's assets. By March 1837, the company reverted to putting the men back onto a salaried status, though they went back once more to the contracted-out system in 1840.

The railways and competition

The nature of railways, with their high capital costs, always gave them a tendency to become an effective monopoly. Once a route was established between two towns, no other operator could ever compete in the market for that traffic on equally favourable terms. Parliament relied instead upon the precedent of the canals, setting maximum tolls in their enabling Bills and working on the premise that the railway would operate like a public highway, accommodating a variety of competing independent carriers. This form of competition, it was hoped, would be the guardian of the public interest.

But the tolls were more complicated than the Railway Acts anticipated. Charges for rail transport were made up of three components — payments for use of the track, payments for providing steam haulage and a payment, per unit of weight, for the movement of goods along the line. When the railway company became the sole haulier on the line, this made it easy for them, by combining these charges, to evade the maximum tolls set by Parliament. As early as 1836, James Morrison, the MP for Ipswich, raised the concern that their parliamentary Acts were giving the companies 'what was really equivalent to a monopoly'. He called for Parliament to limit railway dividends and to review each company's charges after twenty years.

This pressure culminated in a Select Committee of Inquiry in 1839 under the chairmanship of Sir Robert Peel. It had a wide remit to look at the special problems of the railways. They recognised that, for practicality and safety reasons, a free-for-all arrangement was not viable:

> ***'It does not appear to have been the intention of Parliament to give a railway company the complete monopoly of their line (but) the intention of Parliament cannot be carried out in the way contemplated for it is obvious that the payment of tolls is only a small part of the arrangement which is necessary to open a railroad to public competition. The safety of the public requires one supervising authority which should have the power of making and enforcing all regulations necessary. On this account it is necessary that the company should possess complete control over their road although***

> ***they acquire an entire monopoly of the means of communication. But if these extensive powers are granted to private companies it becomes most important that they should be controlled so as to secure the public as far as possible from any abuse which might arise from irresponsible authority.'***
>
> *(Parliamentary Papers 1839 X)*

Thereafter, Parliament gave all new railways a monopoly of haulage rights. This was a major departure from the free market principles that governed previous systems of transport, such as the turnpikes and canals. The turnpike model of free access to the railways was incompatible with the relatively high entry costs of steam-hauled traction, and with the need for centralised management in the interests of safety and efficiency. Even so, Section 42 of the Railway Clauses (Consolidation) Bill of 1845 still allowed for at least the possibility of the turnpike principle being incorporated into new railway Bills.

The work of the Select Committee culminated in the Railway Regulation Act of 1840. This set up a Railway Department at the Board of Trade, with power to collect statistics, approve by-laws and carry out inspections of new lines and other matters. The resources initially devoted to this were tiny — the head of the Board of Trade's statistical department ran it, alongside his other duties, aided by a legal clerk and a junior. If an Inspector were required, an officer from the Royal Engineers would be called in. In their first three months, they were swamped with more than 25 fatal accident reports and a full-time RE officer was soon appointed to their Department. Initially the Department did not even have the power to prevent a dangerously constructed railway from opening — this was only obtained in a separate Act the following year.

One of the Department's first duties in this respect concerned the opening of the final section of the Great Western Railway between London and Bristol, set for 30 June 1841. It was almost delayed, because the Board of Trade's Inspector found so much work incomplete that he refused at first to sanction the opening. Much last-minute negotiation (and, no doubt, arm-twisting) followed and the opening finally proceeded on schedule. The Inspector's concerns proved to be well-founded when, following much frantic signalling by workmen, the inaugural train was stopped just feet short of a stretch of incomplete track inside the Box Tunnel. It was only after four hours (when an improvised set of points had been constructed inside the tunnel) that the train was able to emerge safely.

If the Board could do relatively little at first about safety, they could do virtually nothing about wasteful and destructive competition. As Vaughan explains:

> ***'There was... much confusion in the minds of the railway Directors. The representatives of the existing companies said they did not want 'dangerous meddling' from the Government — and then complained bitterly that the Government did not prevent the construction of competitive lines which 'destroyed' the capital of the original lines. Then again, when railway companies amalgamated to reduce competition and improve their efficiency, they were accused of 'monopoly' by Parliament and public.'***
>
> *(Vaughan, 1997 — page 94)*

On Christmas Eve 1841, an accident occurred which was to have a major impact on the operation of the railways. The 4.30am goods train from Paddington was passing through Sonning cutting, just outside Reading. It was about 6.40am and pitch dark. Between the locomotive and seventeen goods wagons were sandwiched two open third-class trucks, full of passengers. The locomotive ran into a landslip, which had covered the track to a depth of about two feet, bringing the train to a shuddering halt. The weight of the goods wagons crushed the passenger wagons against the tender, killing eight of the thirty-eight passengers and injuring seventeen others. The local newspaper described the scene in lurid terms:

> ***'The spectacle presented at this time must have been most awful. The dreadful mutilation of the dead bodies, the groans and shrieks of the wounded, and the terror inspired by so tremendous a crash of carriages and machinery, overcame the stoutest nerves and harrowed the feelings of the most rugged of spectators...'***
>
> *(Quoted in Phillips, page 25)*

The inquest brought in a verdict of accidental death, but *The Times* accused the Great Western Railway of negligence and attacked the practices of putting passenger wagons immediately behind the locomotive, and of making cheap travel of this kind available only at night. This led to an inquiry into the services provided for third-class passengers. Their findings in turn resulted in the Regulation of Railways

Act of 1844 (or, as the railway companies called it, before Parliament watered it down, the Railway Plunder Bill).

Railway mania and regulation

Some of the economic consequences of railway mania are discussed elsewhere in the book. Here, we look at the Government's part in it, or rather their failure to regulate the speculative madness that seized the nation. In 1834 there had been an early hint that the free market might not be an adequate regulator, when a bout of railway mania hit the nation. Harvests had been good, the cotton industry was buoyant and confidence knew no bounds. A new law of 1826 had permitted the creation of joint stock banks and provided a new source of credit for investment. Parliament found itself swamped by the number of railway Bills coming before it, and was forced to try and limit the pressure by introducing higher hurdles, in terms of the quality of the planning of the scheme and its financial soundness, before it could even be considered by Parliament. A collapse of the economy the following year ensured that this particular outbreak of railway mania was short-lived.

Up until then, railway building had largely been promoted by communities and, in particular, their business leaders. The business case for them was based upon the benefits a railway would bring to the local economy. During the railway manias of the 1830s and 1840s, the driving force became speculation.

The network had grown rapidly; in 1836, it totalled just 400 miles. By 1840, some 1,500 miles of track were opened, and this grew to 2,148 miles in 1844. By this time, the largest outbreak of railway mania was well under way and hundreds of new schemes were coming before Parliament. In just thirty days leading up to the deadline for submission in November 1845, 412 schemes were deposited. Surveying this motley assortment of often hastily assembled and ill-conceived schemes, the Member for Salford, a Mr Brotherton, spoke of 'more fraud and felony than I have ever seen in public works'. Had they all been built, they would have more than doubled the size of the network.

Many contemporary observers were convinced that all the viable railway lines had already been approved. It was said of the Lancaster & Carlisle line that it would get no passengers 'unless the crows were to contract with the railway people to be conveyed at low fares'. (In this case, the sceptics were wrong, but many of the schemes were of very uncertain viability.)

The *Athenaeum* magazine of May 1843 gave a long list of the duplication that had already taken place in rail services around the country. It was one of a number of publications that argued the case for more effective state control. But Parliament's detailed (if not necessarily strategic) processes for vetting railway schemes were totally overwhelmed by the volume of applications. In 1844 Gladstone set up a Board under the Chairmanship of Lord Dalhousie, to provide a preliminary sieve of the submitted schemes and to make recommendations to Parliament. The job of this advisory committee — nicknamed 'the five kings' — was to bring forward only those of genuine public benefit, with able and honest promoters and some possibility of being profitable. Even so, the 1845 parliamentary session saw the passage of 121 railway Acts, 94 of them for new railways, rather than just amendments to existing ones. Although Parliament tended to follow the recommendations of the Board more often than not, they were not in tune with what Lewin called 'the spirit of unreasoning optimism' that was in the air. Some powerful interests were mobilised against them, some key decisions went against them, they lost the support of the Prime Minister and, in July 1845, the Board was wound up. Its functions passed to a Railway Commission, independent of the Board of Trade (eventually returning to the Board in 1851). It would be a further century before railways came under effective public control. The result of all this, as the President of the Board of Trade later put it in 1854, was that railways had 'grown up haphazard rather than upon any system of well-devised legislation'.

Speculation grew even more frantic in the two following years. 1846 saw 219 new lines approved and 1847 a further 425. Their total proposed share capital was over £231 million, equivalent to two-thirds of the value of all exports for 1846 and almost fourteen times the value of all the gold held by the Bank of England. In the absence of solid collateral to secure loans, advances were made against future harvests, imports and a host of more or less speculative propositions. A vast new group of people — many of them very naïve in matters of speculation — were drawn to the stock market, in many cases by extravagant claims or barefaced fraud. One consequence of this frantic activity was vast inflation in the cost of all those materials and labour associated with railway construction. In 1846 Brunel complained to a parliamentary Select Committee that his costs had increased by 50% in the past year alone and Robert Stephenson begged Parliament to intervene to prevent 'violent competition'.

Nature — and events overseas — intervened to bring this round of speculation to an end. 1847 saw the second year of the Irish potato famine and a poor harvest in the rest of Britain (confounding all those whose investment in railways was secured on the promise of a bumper crop). Raw materials from overseas also increased in cost, sucking more money out of the country. Share prices crashed and a financial crisis loomed, as the Bank of England no longer had enough reserves of gold to cover the value of banknotes in circulation. This was contrary to the Bank Act of 1844 and the Bank of England was forced to stop trading on 25 October 1847. There were riots in the City and the Government had to suspend the Bank Act as one means of restoring calm. Many blamed the railway industry for the crisis, but railway interests rounded on the incompetence of the Government for failing to control such rampant speculation. Robert Stephenson cited the failure of Parliament to impose any limits, quoting one case with no fewer than 19 proposals competing for the same destination. The collapse knocked the bottom out of the market in railway shares, and brought railway promotion itself to a virtual halt. 1295 miles of new railway were authorised in 1847. The new mileage for 1850 was 6¾.

State regulation and state empowerment

Parliament had allowed the railways a free market in the hope that competition would prevent the creation of monopolies, such as those that had been seen on some of the canals. There had been some safeguards built into their enabling Acts, for example limiting the maximum rates per ton-mile or the size of dividend that could be paid without reducing freight rates. But these provisions were sometimes not enforceable or, where they were enforceable, not enforced. As the downfall of George Hudson would later demonstrate in spectacular fashion, the railways were subject to little or no effective scrutiny. The Select Committee on Railway Communication (1839-40) recommended that companies should make regular returns of their traffic and finances to the new Railway Department of the Board of Trade, but these provisions were watered down in the later legislation.

But even if the early railways were regulated (however badly) by Acts of Parliament, the law also empowered them, for as one contemporary put it:

> ***'Powers of an unusually extensive and durable character were readily granted to all railway companies in this country.'***
>
> (*Dionysius Lardner, 1850*)

The Acts determined the route of the railway (but also gave the company powers to compulsorily purchase the land needed, in what one writer called 'the most dramatic infringement of private property rights since the Civil War'); they laid down how much capital could be borrowed or raised by share issues (but also gave the investors the comfort of limited liability); and specified the maximum the company could charge for the passage of freight along them (though generally not to an extent that interfered with the commercial freedom of the company). They also attempted, with greater or lesser success, to prevent the railways operating against the public interest in other ways. For example, the 1826 Act authorising the Liverpool & Manchester Railway, mindful of the massive dividends the local canal companies had been paying to its shareholders, required the company to cut its freight rates by 5% for every percentage point that their dividend to shareholders exceeded ten. They also sought to look after the individual interests of property owners affected by the line, and to compensate them for any damage.

Virtually all railway schemes were opposed by a small army of petitioners and were subjected to minute scrutiny by committees of the Lords and the Commons. The evidence submitted to the Commons between 1835 and 1899 survives, in the form of 3,500 volumes of up to 2,000 pages each, and serves as an illustration of the cumbersome nature of the procedure. The MPs and Lords making up the membership of the committees usually had local connections. This helped them to understand the local issues and to debunk the inflated claims of the promoters, but also made them susceptible to pressure from powerful interests within their community. More fundamentally, the system was simply unable to cope with the volume of schemes submitted during the periods of railway mania.

The responsibility for the cost and delay of this process rested clearly with Parliament and its failure to set a clear direction for the railway system, and some unlikely supporters for greater state intervention emerged. Even the Duke of Wellington complained in 1838 of 'the improvident manner in which the Legislature had passed the railway Bills without any guard against their monopoly and mismanagement'. He tried, unsuccessfully, to introduce a clause whereby any new company was bound by any general measure introduced by the Government in the succeeding year.

But whilst the individual merits of a scheme might be minutely scrutinised, no similar consideration was given to wider national interests. As Macaulay was later to put it to the House in 1846: 'That the whole society was interested in having a good system of internal communications seemed to be forgotten... ...nobody applied to be heard on behalf of the community.'

A young William Gladstone had also recognised this shortcoming, whilst President of the Board of Trade. As we have seen, their Railways Department became a Railway Board in August 1844, presided over by Gladstone's successor at the Board of Trade, Lord Dalhousie. One of the criteria by which they evaluated railway proposals was in terms of their wider public interest. Their position was that 'each line should be viewed as a member of a great system of communications binding together the various districts'.

One characteristic of Gladstone's approach to the railways was the concept of 'equivalents'. He saw that two competing lines, not being used to capacity and costing twice as much to build, offered fewer prospects of low fares than a single line used to full capacity. Gladstone would therefore encourage the building of a single line between two destinations, with the promise of freedom from competition, in return for lower fares. At least eight major railway proposals in the 1845 session were approved on this basis.

The absence of well-devised legislation was not for want of trying. Among the other powers Gladstone sought, through his Bill for a Regulation of Railways Act 1844, was the ability for the Government to revise the fares of any railway which paid a dividend of more than 10% a year over a three-year period, and to purchase any railway fifteen years after its incorporation. Among its more miscellaneous provisions, it also provided for the cut-price transport of troops, the poor and the insane. Such a radical and wide-ranging set of proposals predictably attracted huge opposition from the railway companies, and was out of temper with the prevailing mood of the country, which was in the grip of a huge speculative bubble of railway mania promising easy, risk-free profits.

The Bill was savaged in Parliament (and, in private, by the Prime Minister, Sir Robert Peel) and emerged in a much watered-down form. This gave the Government powers to acquire railways and to reduce fares, but only applied to those railways incorporated after 31 December 1844, and then only after they had been in private ownership for 21 years. The company also had to have paid a dividend of 10% a year or more for the three preceding years. In the years following the great railway mania, virtually no company met those criteria.

But by far the greatest achievement of the Act was the Parliamentary train, discussed earlier, which revolutionised travel for the poor. This required every railway to run at least one train a day, along the full extent of its lines in each direction and stopping at every station, on which the fares would be no more than a penny a mile. Passengers were to be allowed free carriage of up to 56lb of luggage and the train had to average at least 12mph, including stops. They were also to have seats and weather protection. As an incentive to comply, the Government waived its normal 5 per cent ticket tax. In their first full year, Parliamentary trains carried four million passengers and, by 1850, over 55% of all railway passenger journeys were made under the provisions of this Act.

But the 1844 Act was by no means a passport to luxury for the third-class passenger. The Great Western's response, illustrated earlier, was a form of cattle truck, with seating for sixty people, no windows and the only light or air coming from louvres or a tiny ventilator on the roof. But, by offering a degree of weather protection to third-class passengers, the Act did at least make the Great Western's open-sided second-class carriages obsolete. Moreover, as we have also seen, provided they ran the two Parliamentary trains a day, there was still nothing to stop the companies running other third-class services with standards as low as they dared to make them.

The 1844 Act failed for a number of reasons: it could be claimed that it discriminated unfairly against the railways and, with a large railway interest in Parliament, this case was certainly argued; it appeared to go against the accepted wisdom of the day, that competition was the greatest protection of the public interest; it was somewhat premature, since amalgamation had not yet gone far enough for its problems to become clear; it also suffered from a backlash against the centralisation of central Government powers that had grown out of the recent Factory Acts and the changes to the Poor Law. In practice, the Parliamentary train was one of the very few positive outcomes of this Bill, and it would be almost a quarter of a century before any significant further controls were introduced.

Independent freight

Although they were originally conceived as carriers of freight, the greatest success of the early railways was in capturing passenger traffic from the roads. Their initial impact on freight was measured more in terms of getting the canal operators to lower their costs and improve their services. The 1842 parliamentary returns for railways show them carrying a relatively modest 5 million tons of freight in the previous year (of which 4 million were coal).

It was still possible in the early days that the independent carriers might have had a wider role in the delivery of goods by rail. The earliest railways did not have a holistic approach to through traffic, and the shipment of goods along a route involving several railway companies could be almost as much of a bureaucratic nightmare as with the canals. By contrast, a carrier like Pickfords had already been in business for almost a hundred years, and had a track record of running a scheduled service between 340 towns, using the roads and canals. That expertise, it was claimed, could produce unity of management and could potentially lead to cost savings for the railway.

However, the arrangement was not without its problems. In practice, the final cost to the end-user often ended up considerably higher; in 1844 the average cost per ton of freight on the London & Birmingham Railway (which used independent carriers) was £2 10s. On the Great Western (which made its own arrangements) it was £1 10s 6d. There were also operational problems. There was a good deal of litigation between the railway companies and the carriers, relating to forged invoices and other frauds; and employees of the carriers fought pitched battles for the use of rolling stock, where this was in short supply.

Railway companies like the Liverpool & Manchester, whose Act allowed them to operate as carriers, made it their aim to become the sole carrier on their line. Others set out to make life as uncomfortable as possible for the independent operators using their line. In one case, which was referred to the courts in 1842, the Grand Junction Railway tried to prevent Pickfords filling a wagon with parcels and paying a wholesale rate per ton for its carriage. Instead, they sought to charge them a (higher) rate per pound for each individual parcel. The court ruled that this particular practice was monopolistic and unacceptable.

By the mid-1840s, amalgamations of the railways began to produce huge and powerful companies like the Midland and the London & North Western. They were able to negotiate away the rights of the independent companies, who henceforth became purely the delivery agents, fetching goods to and from the railways. The completion of this arrangement enabled freight rates to fall by at least 25%.

The problems of the independent carrier were compounded by the lack of co-ordination for through traffic between the railway companies themselves. Some companies would not accept the rolling stock of adjoining railways on their lines; others had different designs of rolling stock, leading to compatibility problems; some accepted independent carriers, others did not; there were no standard rates for the carriage of goods and not even a standard classification of types of goods; no generally accepted tables of the mileage between stations, on which to base the division of receipts; no common signalling practices; and some railways simply did not accept through booking.

Privately owned wagons, which were a problem from the earliest days of the Stockton & Darlington, were to remain so for much longer. As late as 1914, around a half of all railway wagons were still privately owned, and represented an obstacle to the railway companies introducing larger and more efficient rolling stock. There were constraints on the railway companies being able to move them around freely, and poor maintenance of the 'private owner' stock also caused difficulties for the railways, right up until the practice was abolished in 1948.

The Railway Clearing House (RCH) was established in 1842, in imitation of the unified systems operated nationally by the big independent carriers and of that of the banks, to try and address some of these problems. Initiated by the London & Birmingham and with nine founder members, the RCH had five objectives:

- to organise the through booking of passengers;
- to organise the through booking of personally owned carriages and horses;
- to share out passenger receipts, based on the mileage covered on each railway;
- to encourage the through transport of goods on a rate by mile basis;
- to settle debts between member companies.

From 1847, they also employed staff to check the numbers of wagons travelling on other companies' lines, and their contents. The RCH was a force for the standardisation of operating practices more widely; they introduced a standard classification for charging for goods; required member companies to use Edmondson's patented ticketing system; and from 1847 they agreed that they would all operate on Greenwich Mean Time.

This was a truly massive piece of accounting for a pre-computer age. Not only did they have to keep track of all the different companies' rolling stock going onto 'foreign' rails, making charges for its use if it was not returned within a given time; they even had to monitor the whereabouts of the tarpaulins used to cover the open goods wagons. By the end of the century, they would employ some 2,000 central staff and thousands more local inspectors to deal with over 20 million transactions per year.

...and some positive Government intervention

One area where the Government was not shy in intervening was taxation. From 1832, it taxed railway companies on the number of carriages they dispatched, whether they were full or empty. Following protests by the railway companies, it modified it to a tax based on total passenger miles, until it was replaced in 1842 by a 5% tax on total passenger revenues.

Chapter 7:
Changing the landscape of Britain

'In thirty years the railway engineers built more than 25,000 bridges alone, and this was more than all the bridges which had previously existed in the country.'

(Bryan Morgan: *The Railway Lover's Companion*)

'The Victorians who created the railway look like a race imbued with some demonic energy.'

(Michael Robbins: *The Railway Age in Britain and Its Impact on the world*)

The early railways had a major impact on the landscape of Britain. As well as their physical presence in town and countryside, they created whole new communities and what was arguably the 19th century's most characteristic contribution to world architecture. But, before that, the construction of the railways is itself a story of human endeavour that is at once magnificent and squalid.

At the height of the railway boom, in 1847, some 210,000 people were employed in the construction of the railways. It was the largest category of employment in the nation, apart from textiles and agriculture. They were called 'navvies' — a shortened form of 'navigators', the term used for their canal-building forebears from about 1775. The relative decline in canal building after about 1820 meant that there was a core of available labour to build the new railways. These were supplemented by local recruits — often poorly paid or displaced agricultural workers — or by immigrants fleeing famine, particularly in Ireland.

Britain's railway network was made by human labour. Mechanical diggers were used in the United States from about 1842, but mechanisation did not feature on a large scale in Britain until the building of the Grand Central Railway in the last years of the 19th century. Contractors would even use horses to remove spoil along tracks specifically laid for steam locomotives. This meant that the navvies shifted prodigious amounts of material by hand. For example, the navvies on the London & Birmingham Railway moved more material in five years than did the army of slaves building the Great Pyramid of Egypt in twenty, using not dissimilar technology. The best of the navvies could in a single day dig sixteen cubic yards of earth and throw it, above their heads, into a wagon. That represents a hole three feet deep, three feet wide and 45 feet long. These were men of iron.

The need for such massive feats of engineering stems in part from the nature of railways. They are much more susceptible to gradients than a road. On a macadamised turnpike, a slope of 1:100 requires an additional force of one-third to pull a given load up it, compared with pulling it along a level section of road. With rail, whilst a given force could pull a heavier weight on the flat on rails than on the road, a 1:100 slope on a railway requires not a third more, but four times more force to pull that same load up it. This meant, given the relative lack of power of the earliest locomotives, that the lines had to be very conservatively engineered. On the majority of the Great Western line, known for its flatness as 'Brunel's billiard table', the gradient is no more than 1:1,320 (or four feet in a mile) and nowhere does it exceed 1:660. This also has its effect on the length of the route — Brunel's GWR line to Bristol was also nicknamed the Great Way Round, because of its alleged tendency to go round some of the greatest obstacles to find a flat route.

Statistics from two short sections of line illustrate the scale of these early railway works. The Box Tunnel on the Great Western consumed over 100 tons of gunpowder and 150 tons of candles, and took up to 300 horses and 4,000 men (a hundred of whom died on the project) to shift 250,000 cubic yards of soil and rock, and lay 30 million bricks. At Tring cutting, they dug out 1.4 million cubic metres of chalk — enough to make a bank 10 yards wide, 10 yards high and *eight miles* long.

The demand for railway contractors also grew hugely during this period. Before 1835, it was rare for more than 200 miles of railway to be authorised in a year. In 1836 there were 1,500 miles permitted or under construction. This drew a lot more entrepreneurs into the industry, many of whom had no experience in the industry and many of whom failed.

The contractors

The building of the railways was not normally undertaken by the railway companies themselves, but was left to contractors. These ranged from the smallest of sub-contractors, labourers struggling in a precarious hand-to-mouth manner to make the first faltering steps to a higher station in life, to some of the largest and wealthiest employers in the land. One of the greatest, Sir Samuel Morton Peto (1809–89), had a payroll of 14,000 in 1850. Peto had started life as a bricklayer, before inheriting a share in the family building business in 1830. The firm carried out some important contracts, including Nelson's Column and work on the Houses of Parliament, before Peto formed a new partnership in 1846 with Edward Betts to specialise in railway work. In the years that followed he built railways throughout Britain and across the world. He was also (with some breaks) a Member of Parliament from 1847 to 1868, and was one of the main benefactors of the Great Exhibition of 1851, underwriting it with a guarantee of £50,000.

But possibly pre-eminent among all the contractors was Thomas Brassey (1805–70). Between 1844 and 1861 he was the sole or joint contractor for some 1,940 miles of railway — about a sixth of all the network built up to that time. Railway companies generally preferred to employ a large, solvent and competent contractor but, in the early days of the railways, this was an exceedingly rare breed. Given the uncertainties of this new type of work, it was said that no contractor could estimate his costs to within less than 25%, and many consequently went under. A third of the thirty main contractors on the London & Birmingham Railway failed completely.

Some of the most successful contractors were also those who were most strongly committed to the decent treatment of their labourers by the sub-contractors they employed. Peto, for example, insisted upon his sub-contractors paying their men 'every Saturday afternoon in the current coin of the realm'. Irregular payment, or the use of the truck system, discussed below, guaranteed that the sub-contractor would be sacked. In this way, Peto recruited and retained the best men. He was equally strict over the conduct of the labourers themselves, and absence due to drink could earn a man the sack.

Thomas Brassey started his career as an assistant surveyor on the Holyhead road and was spotted in 1834 by George Stephenson, when the latter was seeking suitable stone for the Sankey Viaduct. Stephenson quickly recognised Brassey's special qualities of judgement and trustworthiness, and encouraged him into the railway industry, where his first contract was the construction of the Penkridge Viaduct on the Grand Junction Railway. There he worked with another of the great early engineers, Joseph Locke, with whom he developed a long and close working relationship.

The key to Brassey's approach was to find good men, then to trust them and to leave them to get on with their work. Unlike some contractors, who would enforce the letter of a contract, even to the point of seeing the sub-contractor go under, Brassey was conscious of the problems that factors like unforeseeable ground conditions could

The interior of the Farringdon Street station on the Metropolitan Railway giving a rather exaggerated depiction of the broad gauge rolling stock, running on mixed gauge track, some time before 1848.

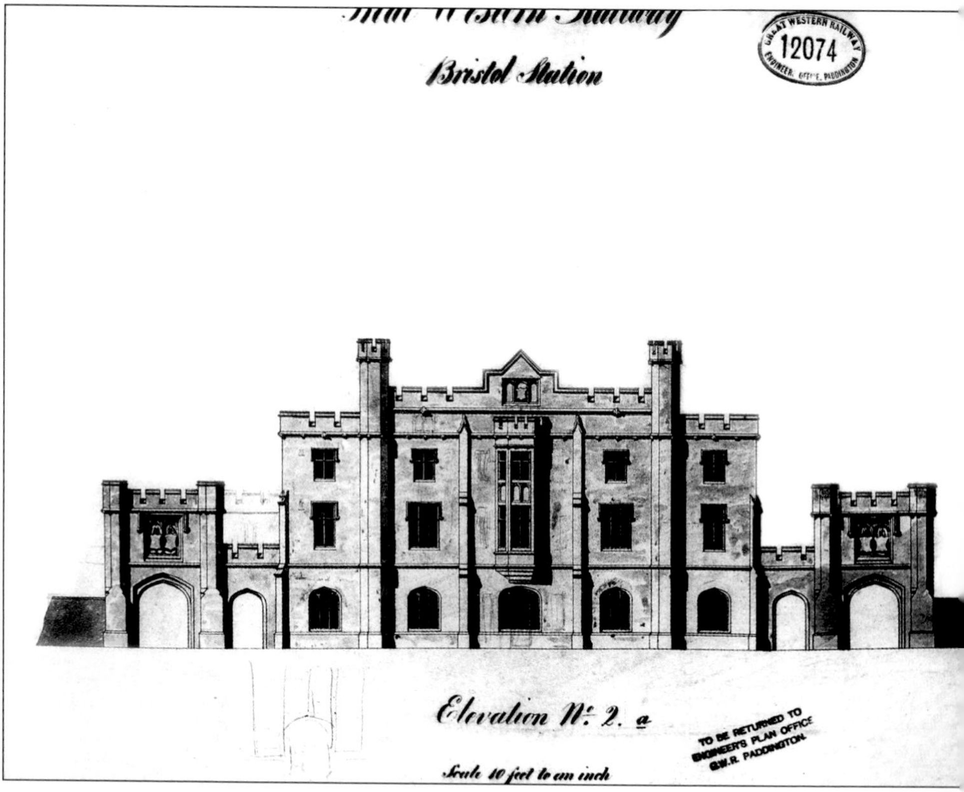

Above: One of the castle-like elevations of the Great Western station at Bristol.

Left: George Stephenson. (p118)

Above right: An interestingly faked photograph, purporting to be of George Stephenson and *Rocket* around the time of the opening of the Liverpo & Manchester Railway. The fact that the event took place a decade before the invention of photography may have made the forgery easier to spot… (810/CR)

Right: George Hudson. (p119)

Far right: Isambard Kingdom Brunel (1806–1859), pictured in the last year of his life. *From L. T. C. Rolt: Isambard Kingdom Brunel (Longman 1957). Picture opposite p257.*

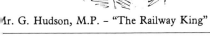

Mr. G. Hudson, M.P. – "The Railway King"

Alfred Croquis del.
Dion. Lardner
THE EDITOR OF "THE CABINET CYCLOPEDIA".
Published by James Fraser 215 Regent Street London

Left: Dr Dionysius Lardner, the would-be nemesis of Brunel, who was so often proved wrong by him.

Below: Concerns at the aesthetic impact of the chimneys on atmospheric railway pumping stations led to some elaborate attempts to disguise them. This was one of the stations on the Croydon and Epsom line.

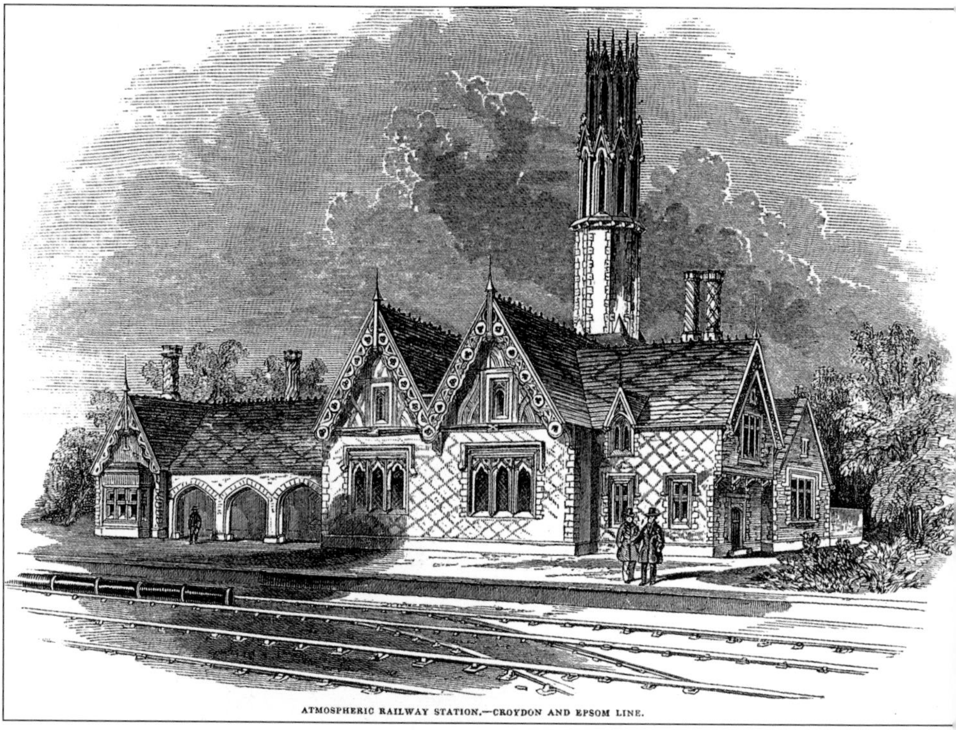

Left: Brunel's final masterpiece, the Royal Albert Bridge at Saltash. Brunel was wheeled over it in 1859, a dying man, to see the fruits of his labours.

ɔove: A dandy cart and chaldron from the Stockton &
arlington Railway, now at the National Railway Museum.
·74/2733/60)

ft: Brunel's bridge-building feats were not limited to brick
ıd stone. This is an oblique wooden bridge he built at Bath.

ɘlow: An early railway policeman signals that the train may
ıter the tunnel. *Illustrated London News*

·low right: The signalman's Christmas dinner. Although
'awn much later in the 19th century, this well illustrates
.e miserable lot of the railway signalman in bad weather.
'ustrated London News (p120)

Above and below: These two pictures show the different classes of carriage used by the Bodmin & Wadebridge Railway in Cornwall, from around 1834. Their very short wheelbase must have given them an extremely uncomfortable, pitching ride.

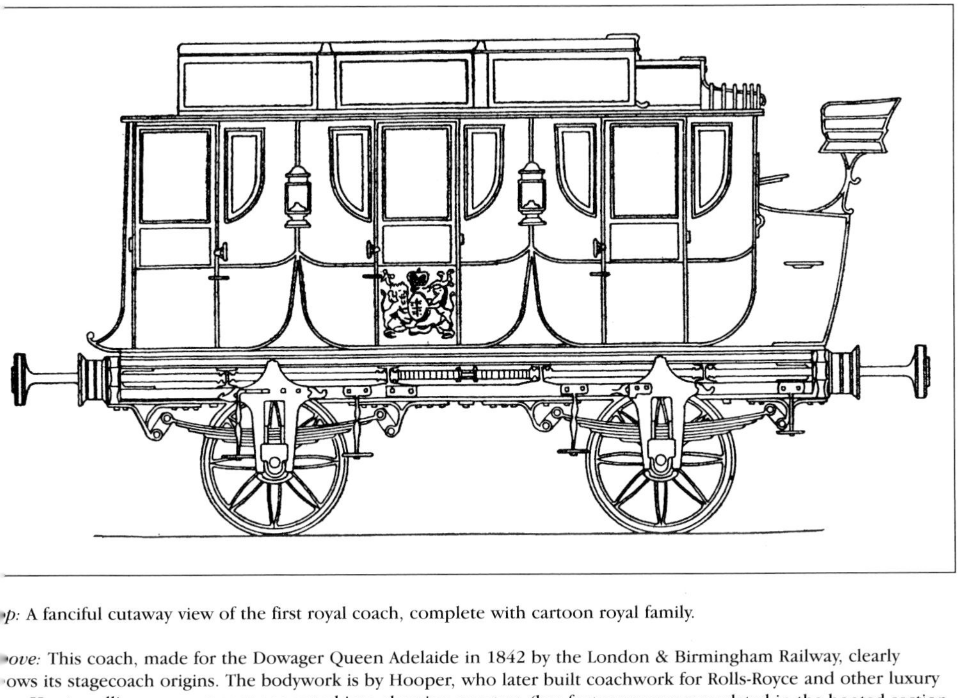

p: A fanciful cutaway view of the first royal coach, complete with cartoon royal family.

ove: This coach, made for the Dowager Queen Adelaide in 1842 by the London & Birmingham Railway, clearly ows its stagecoach origins. The bodywork is by Hooper, who later built coachwork for Rolls-Royce and other luxury rs. Her travelling compartment converted into sleeping quarters (her feet were accommodated in the booted section, low the outdoor seat). Luggage was carried on the roof. The design was also used as a mail-coach. The original can seen in the National Railway Museum in York (from Ellis).

The Royal Railway Carriage and Engine

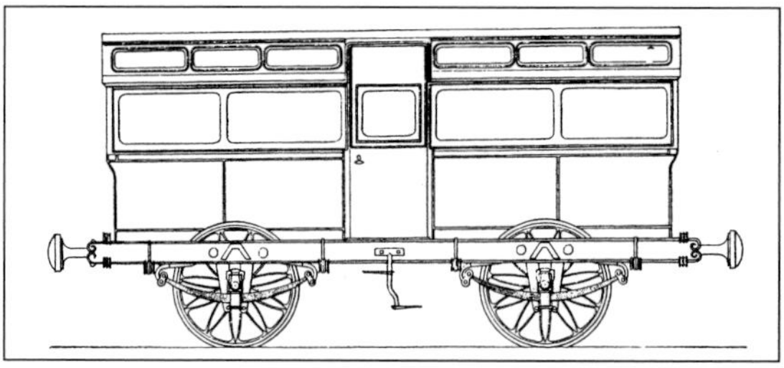

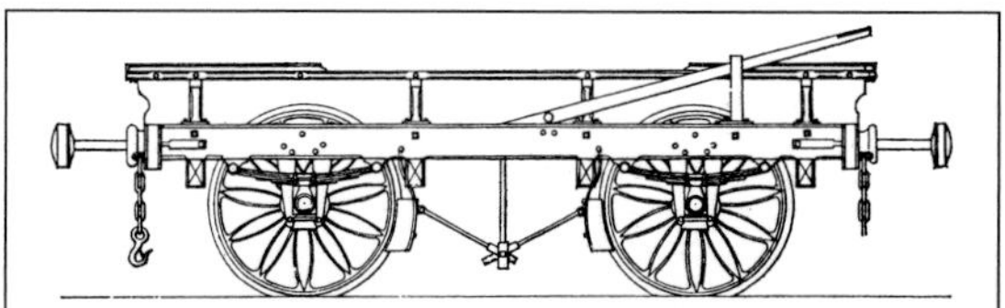

Top: A Royal passenger carriage and locomotiv provided by the London & Birmingham Railwa in 1843. It is thought to be the first carriage to be heated by steam. (p95)

Above: The interior of the first royal carriage, built for the Dowager Queen Adelaide in 1842/43.

Left: The Great Western posting (or saloon) carriage (from MacDermot).

Below left: The Great Western carriage truck, onto which the affluent traveller could have his own private carriage secured (from MacDermot).

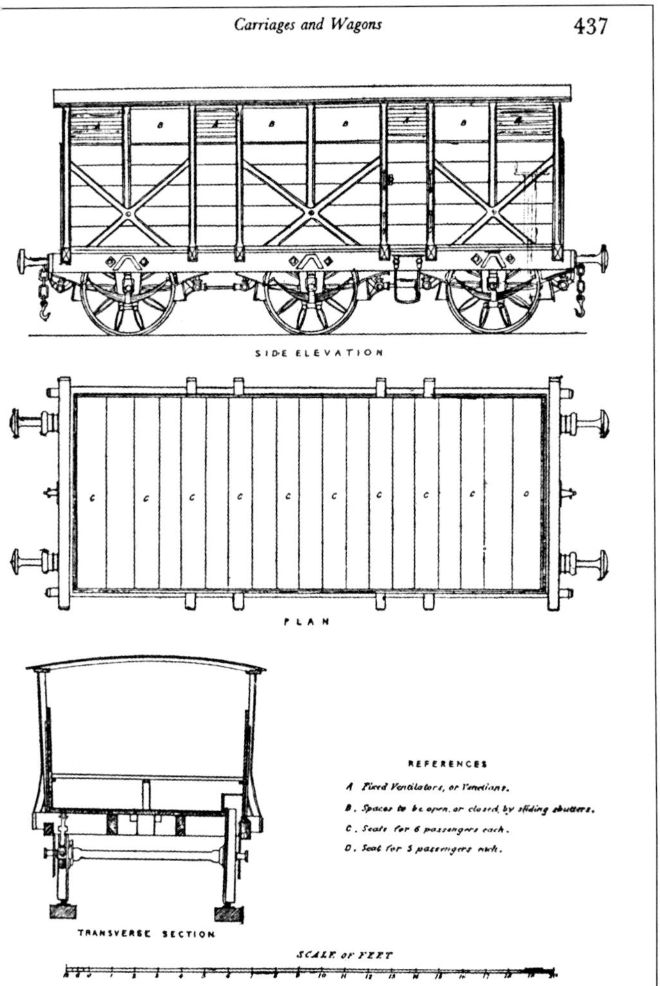

Above: An early composite Stockton & Darlington Railway coach, photographed during the railway's 150th birthday celebrations.

Left: The Great Western 'carriage' of 1844 — the company's response to the legislation of that year, seating 59 passengers in conditions of considerable intimacy (from MacDermot).

ft: This view of the Great Western ilway near Bath shows a farmhand :velling with his animals.

ght: The Great Western Railway's rsebox, the construction of which ars a considerable resemblance to eir improved third-class carriage for mans. This odd-looking vehicle is wider than it was long (from acDermot).

low: Stanhopes offered the cheapest rm of rail transport in the days after e Gladstone Act. These examples rom Ellis) were operated by the South affordshire Railway from about 1847.

ttom: The workman's Penny Train sembarks at London's Victoria station. ustrated London News (p 109)

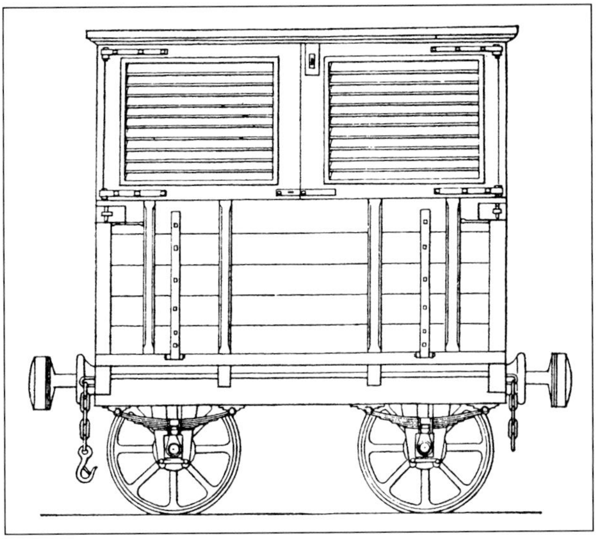

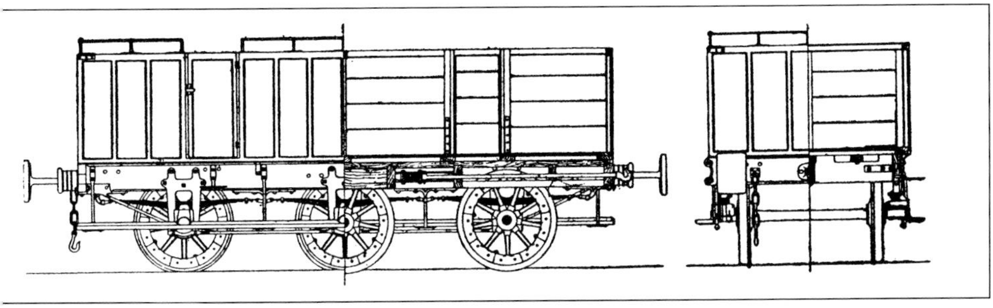

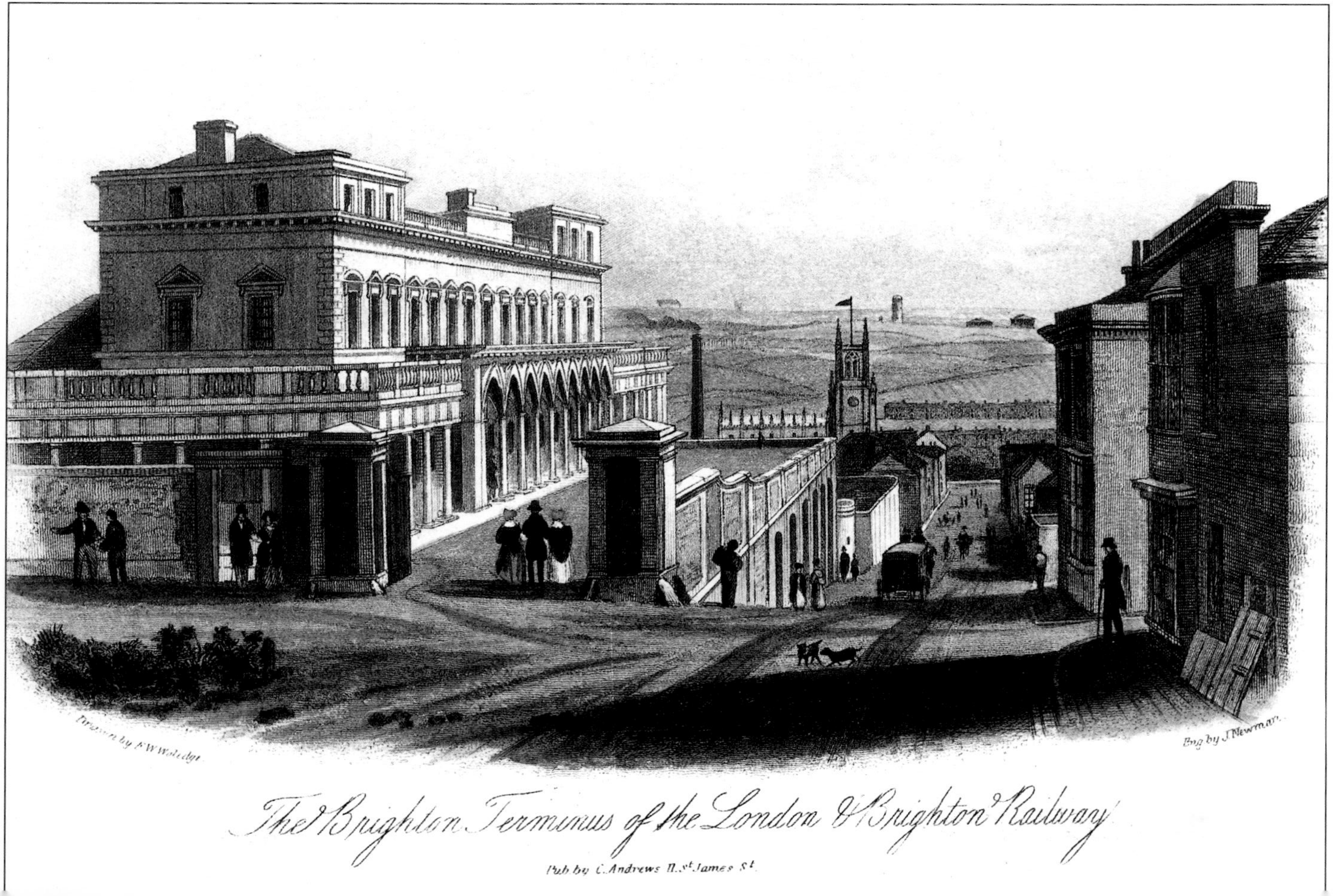

Drawn by F.W.Woledge
Eng by J. Newman
The Brighton Terminus of the London & Brighton Railway
Pub by C. Andrews 11 St James St

Left: The Brighton terminus of the London & Brighton Railway, a sight familiar to thousands of day-trippers from the 1840s onwards.

bove: Railway companies vied with each other
o gain royal patronage by building a branch line
o Windsor. This shows the route across the
Iome Park.

bove: The station at Ramsgate Harbour,
n early destination for railway tourists.
757/711/1/63)

First Class

Second Class

Left: First-, second- and third-class passengers travelling to The Derby in 1842. *Illustrated London News* (p112)

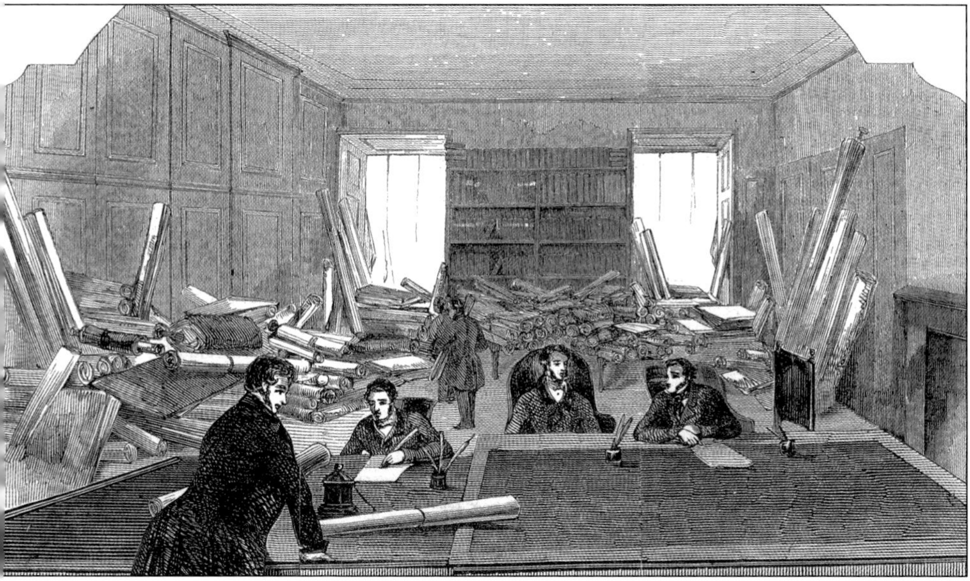

Top: The Railway Room at the offices of the Board of Trade, as they struggled to cope with the mountain of deposited plans during the rush of railway mania in 1845. *Illustrated London News*

Above: Constructing the embankment across the Wolverton Valley on the London & Birmingham line. A further impression of some of the vast works undertaken by the armies of navvies.

Above: The construction in 1839 of the part of the London & Birmingham Railway cutting through Camden Town. These were the works whose disruptive qualities were later described by Charles Dickens in *Dombey and Son*.

Left: This illustration of the Tring cutting under construction on the London & Birmingham Railway gives an indication of the scale of the works, carried out almost entirely without mechanical aid.

Above: Samuel Peto, (1809–89) one of the greatest of the early railway contractors. (698/2576/52)

Left: The imposing entrance to the Box Tunnel on the Great Western — a fitting monument to the many men who lost their lives in its construction. (from Measom)

:eft: Swindon railway station in 1845, which :he *Illustrated London News* described in 1845 as 'perhaps second to none in the <ingdom'. They particularly singled out for praise 'the magnificent refreshment rooms'. The reality was to prove very different.

Top: Swindon station, as illustrated by Measom in 1852.

Above: A view of the new Swindon works and workers' housing from the gallery of Swindon station. (one of several illustrations :aken from Measom's *Guide to the Great Western Railway*, published in 1852)

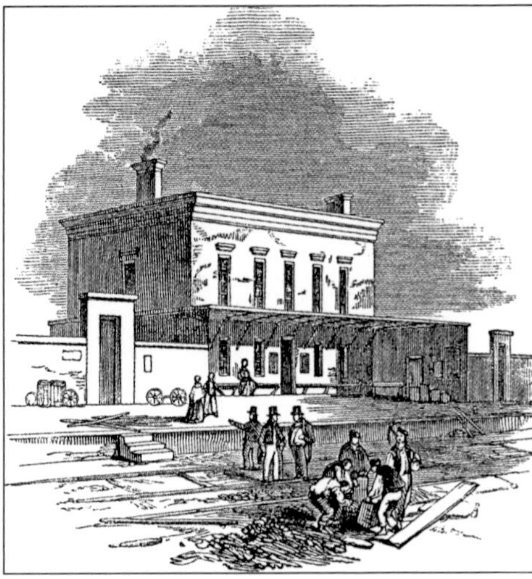

This spread and opposite: The *Illustrated London News* carried detailed accounts of the opening of new railway lines. In August 1845 they covered the opening of the Eastern Counties Railway to Cambridge and Ely, and showed how the original stations ranged from the grand classical edifice at Cambridge, through the more domestic scale and style of those at (left) Elsenham, (above) Chesterford and Wendon (below), to (below right) what was little more than the hut which formed Ickleton station.

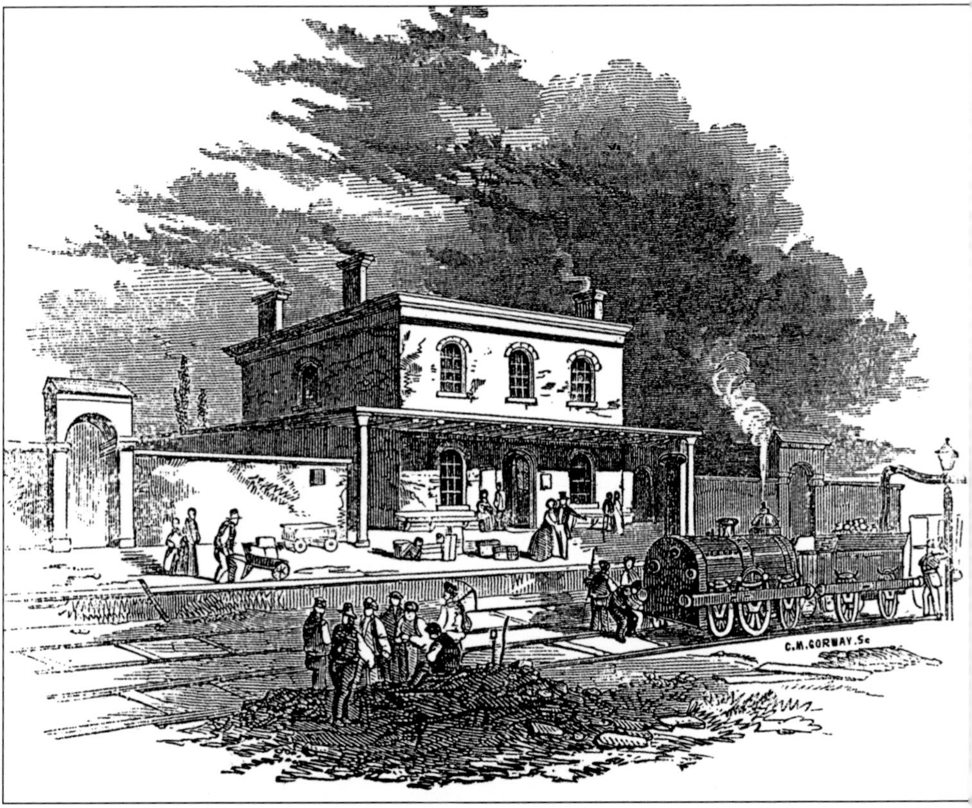

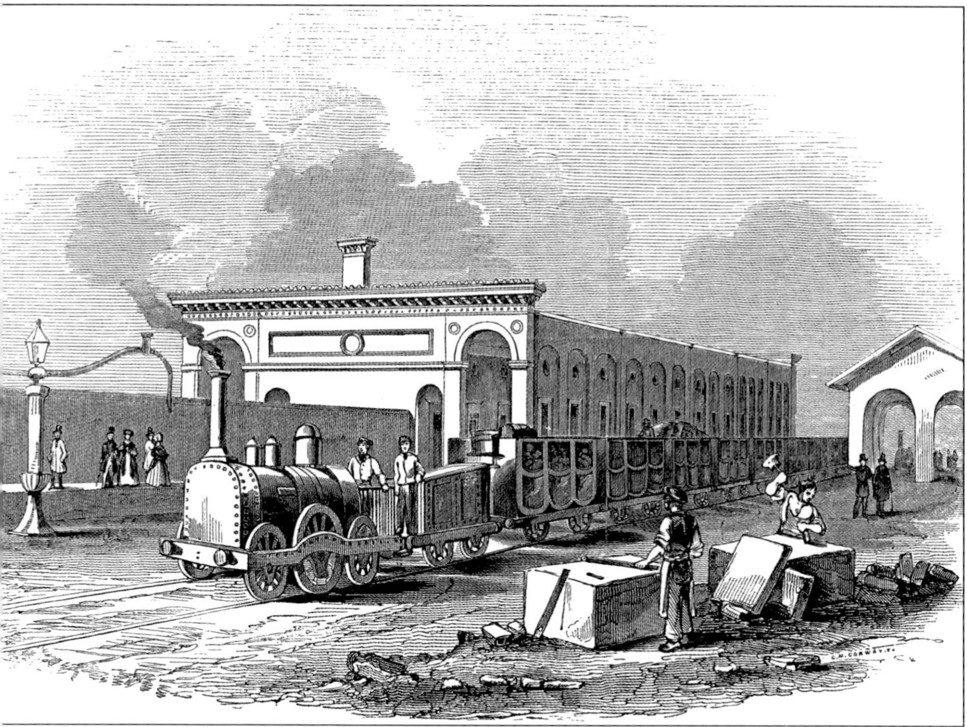

Above: Thrapston Station. *Illustrated London News*

Above: Oundle Station. *Illustrated London News*

An *Illustrated London News* view of the emerging new settlement at Swindon in 1845, showing the Great Western Railway works, the workers' cottages and other amenities, such as the church. The old town of Swindon stood some distance away.

Top: Gloucester station — another of Measom's illustrations.

Above: Measom's illustration of the new railway terminus at Bristol.

Top right: Didcot was an important junction on the Great Western and its station is correspondingly impressive. (from Measom)

Above right: The one-sided station at Reading proved to be difficult to operate, and there was soon pressure to change it to a more conventional layout. (from Measom)

Right: Oxford's station, as it is shown in 1852, seems surprisingly modest for a city of its importance. This is the station that replaced distant Steventon as Oxford's link with the railway in 1844. (from Measom)

The imposing entrance to Euston station, the terminus of the London & Birmingham Railway, shown in an Ackermann print dating from about 1838.

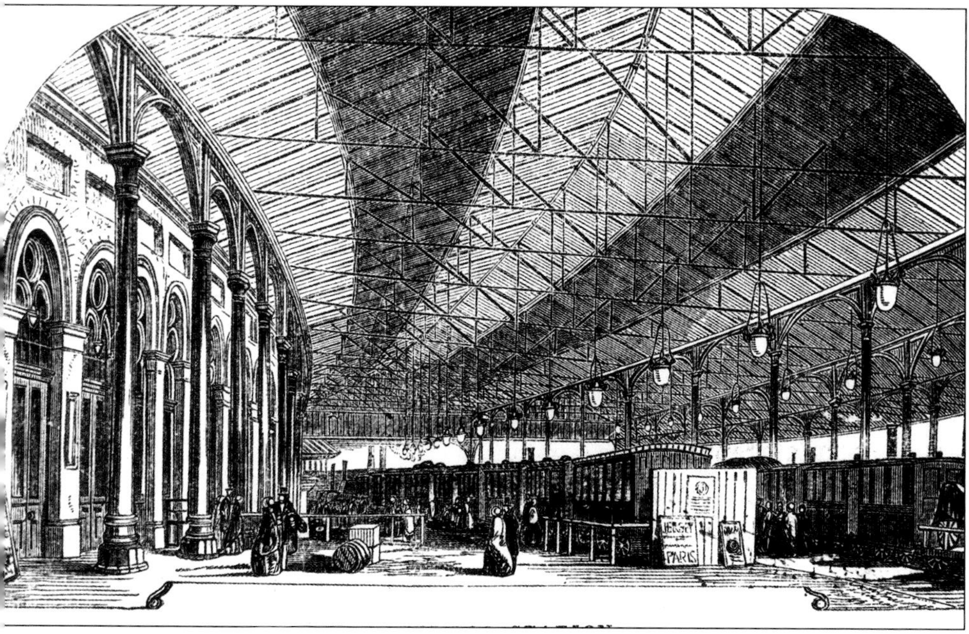

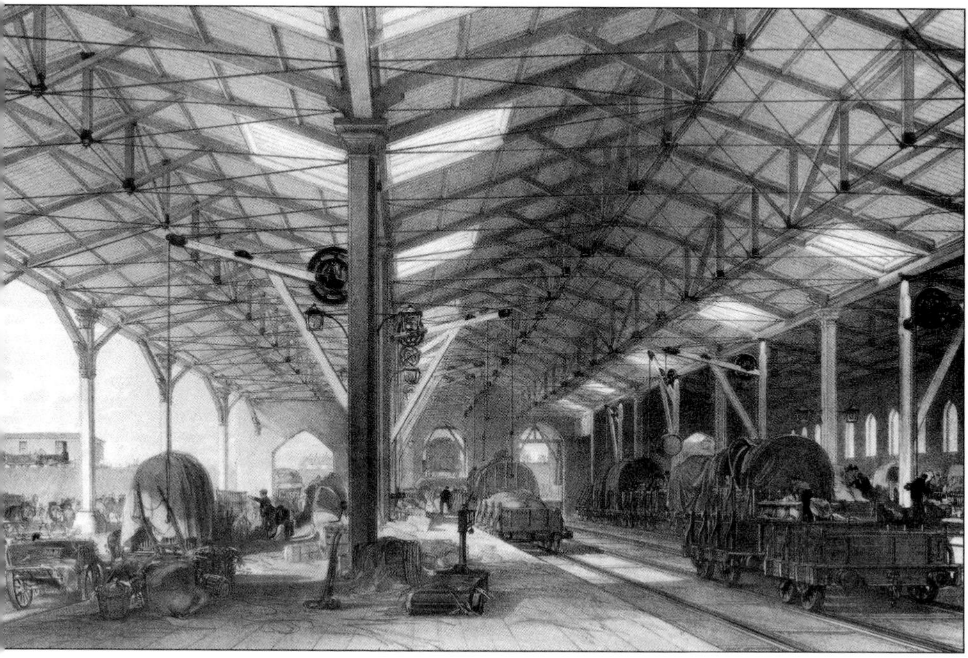

op: The interior of Waterloo station,
aken from Measom's 1856 guide to
he South Western Railway.

bove: Unlike some of Brunel's
assenger stations, the goods shed
: Bristol was a distinctly utilitarian
tructure.

The Springwell Colliery Engine No 2, built by Robert Stephenson in 1826. (595/DAR1181)

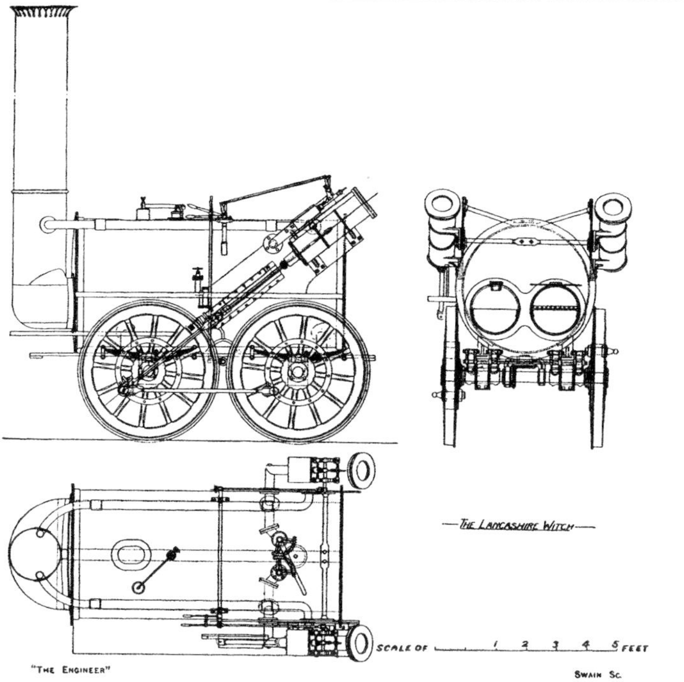

FIG. 4—BOLTON AND LEIGH RAILWAY "LANCASHIRE WITCH," 1828
From "A Century of Locomotive Building," by permission of Robert Stephenson & Co., Ltd.

Above: The pleasures of the railroad — showing the inconvenience of a blow-up. A cartoon by Hugh Hughes from 1831. (AE185.777)

Left: The *Lancashire Witch*, built by Robert Stephenson for the Bolton & Leigh Railway in 1828, was the first of his locomotives to use inclined, rather than vertical, cylinders.

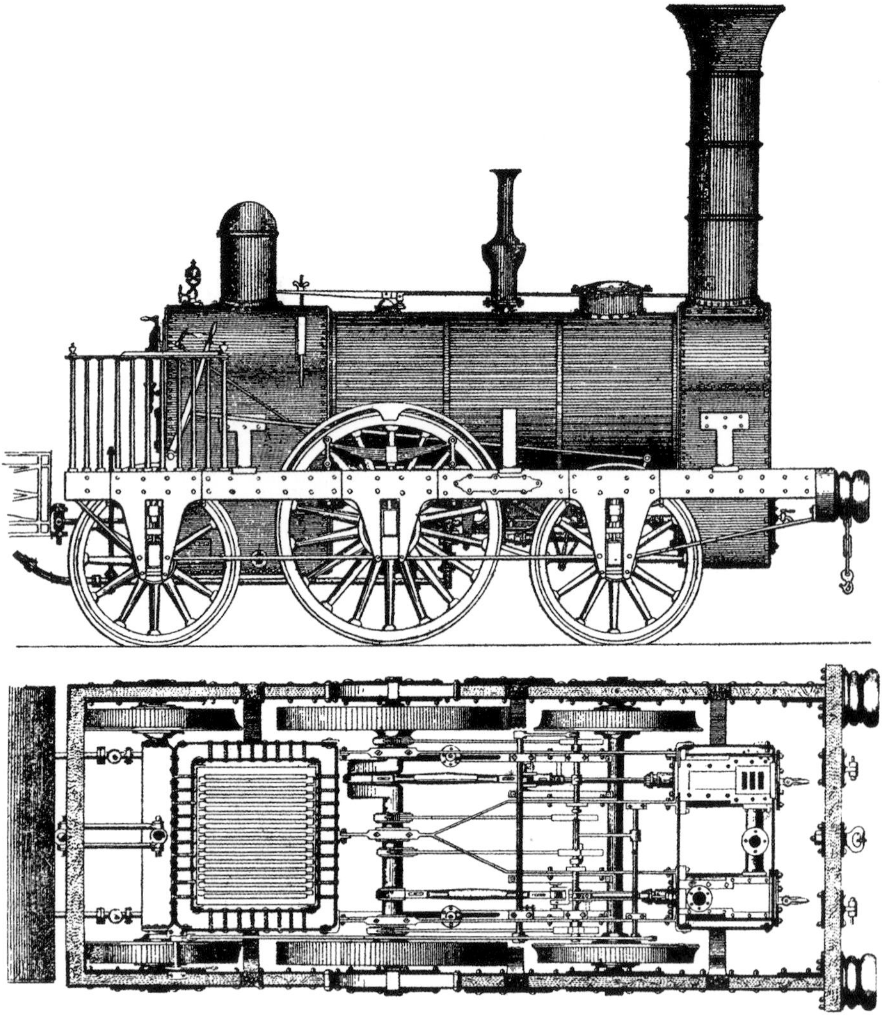

FIG. 17—STEPHENSON'S 2-2-2 PATENT ENGINE OF 1837

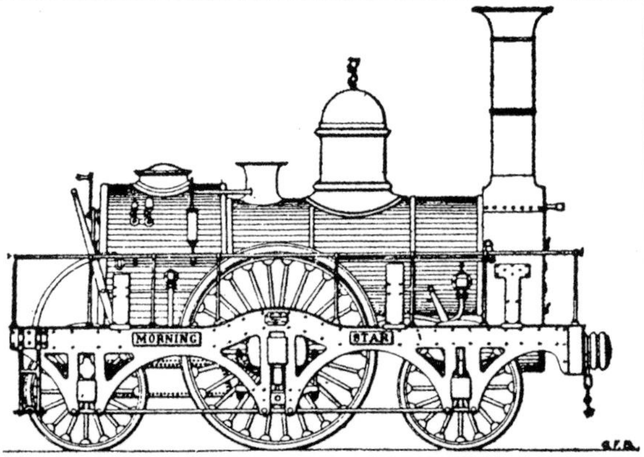

Above: A Stephenson locomotive from the middle of our period. This is his 2-2-2 Patent engine of 1837 (from a drawing originally published in *The Engineer.*

Left: Morning Star of 1838. One of two locomotives ordered from Stephensons by the New Orleans Railway, and then cancelled. They were converted from 5ft 6in to 7ft 0in for the Great Western, and were the company's salvation, being virtually their only reliable and sufficiently powerful locomotives at that time. (From MacDermot).

present. Where this happened, he would sometimes meet the loss himself, rather than see a good man fail. His reputation, and his epitaph, was for 'unfailing courtesy and kindness, and scrupulous honesty'. One of his biographers describes him as 'a man almost without faults'.

Sometimes a large contractor would also be the main source of finance for a scheme. On the Stourbridge Railway, for example, Peto was paid just £9,400 in cash for a scheme costing £71,000, taking the balance in shares in the company, bonds and mortgages. If they picked the right scheme, this could be exceedingly profitable for the contractor, but they needed to have a keen eye for a railway's profitability.

'Rough alike in morals and manners': the navvies

The contractors employed a rootless breed of men from many nations to do this work. They could earn three times the wage of an agricultural worker. This contemporary description of them reflects their traditional image:

> ***'Rough alike in morals and manners, collected from the wild hills of Yorkshire and Lancashire, coming in troops from the fens of Lincolnshire, and afterwards pouring from every country in the Empire; displaying an unbending vigour and an independent bearing; mostly dwelling apart from the villagers near whom they worked; with all the propensities of an untaught undisciplined nature; unable to read and unwilling to be taught; impetuous, impulsive and brute-like, regarded as the pariahs of private life, herding together like beasts of the field, owning no moral law and feeling no social tie, they increased with an increasing demand, and from thousands grew to hundreds of thousands. They lived but for the present; they cared not for the past, they were indifferent to the future.'***
>
> (J. R. Francis: *A History of the British Railway — 1851, Volume 2 page 67*)

In practice, many of them were probably no more rough and ready than the people who were flocking into the cities to work in the mills and the factories, but their transient status added an extra dimension of menace to them. It was probably also the case that the relative anonymity of a nomadic labour camp was attractive to some fugitive law-breakers. Having said this, their lawlessness as a group could sometimes take on epic proportions. In 1839, one of the contractors building the Chester & Birkenhead Railway absconded with the workers' wages. When his appointed successor refused to compensate the men for their losses, it led to a strike that rapidly escalated into anarchy, according to this report:

> ***'One story has it that forthwith a gang of Irishmen sallied in a body to a place in which a number of English labourers were at work, mutilated the hands, arms and bodies of those who refused to strike... The labourers in a formidable band mustering upwards of two thousand men, armed with bludgeons and pickaxes, traversed the country; and after perpetrating sundry petty outrages on the inhabitants, possessed themselves of the entire village of Lutton, pillaged the inn, at which, to their great joy, a harvest dinner was preparing, stopped a postchaise and robbed its passengers, and indicated a disposition to proceed to the commission of more daring acts. On Thursday, a detachment of soldiery was despatched from Liverpool, and another, to which a piece of ordnance and a few cavalry were attached, were sent from Chester to the scene of the disorder. They mustered upwards of two hundred men.'***
>
> (*Berkshire Chronicle — 19 October 1839*)

The lawlessness was eventually stopped and over twenty of the ringleaders were sent to prison. In a similar manner, fighting on a large scale broke out at Ealing between Anglo/Scots and Irish labourers over the allocation of work on the Great Western in April 1838. The Anglo/Scots feared that the Irish were about to undercut their rates. *The Times* described the affair as 'a desperate and alarming affray with atrocities on both sides, brutal and unmanly'. It reached such a scale that, once again, the 12th Lancers were brought in to break it up with cavalry charges. This provoked a strike among those navvies still at work, so the Lancers — just to display even-handedness — arrested twenty-four of the protesters from each side, chosen largely at random, and handed them over to the police.

This disorder apparently in turn inspired a pitched battle at the Bristol end of the Great Western, between some three hundred men in rival groups from Gloucester and Devon. Once again this required the attention of the army. In Bangor in 1845, a group of Welsh brick-workers attacked a band of Irishmen working on the Chester & Holyhead Railway. On this occasion, the army left the railway company with a £30 bill for their services in restoring order.

The disorder in Preston in 1838, between workers on the North Union Railway and local weavers, took on fatal proportions. The trouble began when some Irish navvies were refused credit in a local shop. They eventually retired in high dudgeon to a local pub, which was occupied by some similarly ill-disposed local weavers, who had been laid off. The inevitable fighting gradually escalated until about twenty of the Irishmen had been seriously injured and several Englishmen shot, some fatally. A party of the 86th Regiment of Foot was summoned from Blackburn but, by the time they arrived (presumably on foot), the trouble was over.

Even when they were not responsible, the navvies were blamed (rather like travellers today) for every local wrongdoing. An outbreak of sheep stealing was laid at the door of the navvies excavating the nearby Bramhope Tunnel, until the real, local criminals were unearthed by the authorities.

Payday presented the greatest threat to public order. As Thomas Beggs of the Scottish Temperance League put it:

> ***'All my observations of the habits of the working classes, and the influences operating upon them would tell me this, that it is always bad policy to let working men, particularly of the lower classes of operatives, have large sums of money in their possession at one time.'***
>
> (*Evidence to a Parliamentary Committee 1846*)

The longer payday was delayed, the worse its consequences. The Caledonian Railway paid its workers only monthly, and this tended to be followed by a binge lasting anything up to five days. Those working on the Woodhead Tunnel were paid only once every nine weeks ('to preclude their indulgence in hebdomadal excesses', as the plain English of their paymasters put it).

Certainly, the alcohol intake of the navvies appears to have been as prodigious as their work-rate. A Revd Barrett, one of the clergymen who did missionary work among them, estimated that a typical seven-man hut would get through between 30 and 60 gallons of beer and half a gallon of spirits a week. Many a brewer made a good living from the building of the railways. Their consumption of food was no less extreme: one writer summarised it as 'Two pounds of meat, two pounds of bread and five quarts of ale a day'.

A number of the leading railway figures of the day, including Samuel Peto and Brunel himself, disputed the conventional image of the navvies, and there seems to be some evidence that they were as much sinned against as sinning. Some contractors provided their navvies and their families with decent accommodation — sometimes at a rental level below cost. Peto, for example, provided barracks for the single men, where they slept in hammocks and had a superintendent for the premises and someone to cook for them. Separate arrangements were made for the married men. Another contractor, Peter Thompson, devised the *Labourers' Moral Cottage* — moral because it was laid out internally to keep the sexes apart. It was also prefabricated, portable and cost just £65 including internal fittings — but there were few takers for it. Peto even provided teaching in basic literacy for his employees and, in line with his Baptist principles, tried to steer them away from the demon drink. There was significantly less lawlessness among the labourers employed by Peto.

However, other contractors left their men to live in complete squalor. Irish labourers in Edinburgh in 1846 were housed (if that is the word) in wooden shacks roofed with turf. Within one of these 20 foot by 12 foot buildings, some 20 to 30 men and their families might live, sleeping in tiered beds, two or three to a bed. The filth was indescribable and disease rife. Worse still were the most rudimentary of dwellings, either with walls made of piled-up sods of earth, or simply holes scooped out of a clay bank with a rough tarpaulin awning suspended over them on pieces of timber. Elsewhere, an influx of railway workers could compound the poverty of the resident population. The 1851 Census in Knaresborough coincided with a period of railway construction, and shows an example of a farm labourer's cottage, already quite snugly occupied by a couple and their four children, also being home to 19 navvies and their dependants, including four married couples and three children. Elsewhere in the town, an Irish widow provided a roof for 17 lodgers.

Under such circumstances, it was hardly surprising that they were not always fastidious in their morals. Burton reports one surgeon as describing the navvies as being '*excessively drunken and dissolute*'. They would, he continued, sell their wife's favours to a neighbour for a gallon of beer and claimed that more than half of them suffered from venereal diseases. During the construction of the Box Tunnel, up to some 4,000 navvies were employed, lodging in neighbouring villages where every spare bed was occupied on a 24-hour hot-bedding system. MacDermot records that:

> ***'Drunkenness and fighting were very bad, and on Sundays the foremen were employed in endeavouring to keep the peace in the villages, there being of course no regular police force in those days. Altogether, it is not surprising to read that there was much rejoicing among***

the inhabitants of the countryside when the tunnel was at last finished and the visitors took their departure.'

One railway that appeared not to have suffered so much from the habitual problem of drunkenness was the Stockton & Darlington. There, the Quaker principles of the proprietors made themselves firmly felt. Edward Pease is said to have checked out all of the contractors, to ensure that none of them was 'a friend of publicans'. One contractor, Thomas Close, had written into his contract that 'the first time he is seen intoxicated, he will be dismissed and the sum due to him as wages shall be forfeited'. Even during the opening day celebrations, the company insisted upon strict sobriety:

'The Company takes this opportunity of enjoining on all their work people that attention to Sobriety and decorum which they have hitherto had the pleasure of observing.'

A common malpractice among employers was the use of 'tommy' or 'truck' shops. Under this system, not unique to the railways, the navvies received part or all of their pay in the form of tokens, which they could exchange only at the company shop. Its prices were, of course, between 20 and 50% above the market level, and some unscrupulous contractors could make more from the shop than they did from actually building the railway. The practice was banned in factories under the Truck Act of 1831, but its provisions did not extend to the railways, since contractors could get round it by having an accomplice run the shop. Peto — and even George Hudson — banned them in their contracts. Instead Peto sought out local suppliers to provide good produce at fair prices; Robert Stephenson banned the tommy shops selling alcohol, but did not otherwise prevent the practice. Where tommy shops did not exist, and the likes of Peto did not provide, the navvies' needs were often met by bands of itinerant traders, who followed the route of the railway construction.

Apologists for the system claimed that it provided a means of giving a loan to a penniless navvy arriving on a job, which assured that he did not abscond with the cash before paying it back; that it provided continuity of labour, by tying workers to the project; that it helped contractors provide the essentials of life to their workers in remote locations; and that it prevented the men from starving when, as so often happened, the smaller contractors encountered cash-flow problems. But these are mostly just rationalisations of an iniquitous practice.

Disraeli's novel *Sybil* (1845) gives a scathing satire of a tommy shop, which ends in it being burnt to the ground by a justly outraged mob.

One other possible argument for the tommy shop was that when the navvies passed one of their Saturday nights of excess — known as 'randies' — at the tommy shop, at least they were not out terrorising the nearest community. Some enterprising contractors even went so far as to arrange brothels in the navvy camps — also operated on the tommy shop system. One can only pity the poor missionaries who were also sent to the navvy camps, as to some land of benighted savages, in an attempt to save their souls.

If the navvies' living conditions were sometimes appalling, their working conditions could be worse. Railway companies drove the cost of their contracts down to the absolute minimum, forcing the contractors to cut corners on health and safety if they were to make any kind of profit from them. Vertical banks of rock and earth were undermined to bring them down, the navvies' chances of survival depending upon their ability to spot them collapsing and their speed in running when they did so. Safety fuses were discarded on the grounds that they caused delay. Cheap iron 'stemmers' were used, instead of the safer copper ones, to ram home explosive charges. The iron ones could make sparks and set the charges off prematurely. In one particularly horrifying accident, a navvy called William Jackson had a stemmer shot through his head like a rocket-propelled javelin, killing him instantly.

Someone made the striking calculation that the mortality rate among the navvies building the Woodhead Tunnel (3%) was worse than that of the British army who fought in the Peninsular War and at the Battle of Waterloo. But the contractors generally made little contribution to the cost of the injuries suffered by their workers. During a spell of railway building nearby, the Northampton Infirmary treated 124 rail-related injuries, at a total cost of £590. The contractors' contribution to all this was just £15 1s 0d.

The reformer Edwin Chadwick called on the 1846 Select Committee on Railway Labourers to require contractors to pay compensation for those employees who were killed or injured, even if it appeared that they had been the architects of their own misfortune. He pointed out that, in France, where such a law had been enacted, the accident rate had been greatly reduced. The Committee was unfortunately not persuaded.

Legislation passed that same year obliged railway companies to pay compensation to passengers (but not staff) injured or killed in accidents. To take one example, the South Eastern Railway found itself paying out a total of £61,897 to passengers between 1848 and 1857 under the provisions of this Act. But it was a fleabite; no company ever paid out more than 1% of its total expenditure in compensation. With regard to staff, the North Eastern Railway was regarded as one of the better employers of the day. But, even as late as 1870, its general policy in the event of a member of staff being killed was to pay the bereaved family 'a small gratuity' of, say, £10, and to offer the children of the deceased employment with the railway. Even this small comfort would not generally have been available to those who built the railways. They had to rely on their own, self-financed, sickness funds. Peto was one of the few contractors who contributed, anonymously, to them.

In many people's eyes, the navvies were less than human and, when reports of railway accidents spoke of the deaths of three men and a navvy, their champions were forced to protest that 'Yes, really, navvies are MEN!' Some of the navvies at least would eventually become national heroes, after Peto and Brassey volunteered the services of their men in 1854 to build a railway to feed the starving British troops at Sebastopol, during the Crimean War. This they did in short order under the entrepreneurs' management, despite the best efforts of a bumbling British Army bureaucracy to frustrate them.

But the early railways did not just draw lines across the landscape. They were a major factor in shaping 19th century urban development.

Railway towns

Middlesbrough could be described as the first railway town. Stockton had proved unsatisfactory as a port, due to problems with navigating the Tees, and in 1830, a branch of the Stockton & Darlington was opened to give an alternative outlet to the sea at a small village of four hundred people, called Middlesbrough. Extensive new docks were to be built there, and a company called the Middlesbrough Owners was formed, initially to develop 32 acres of wasteland. Many of the owners were Quakers, including Joseph Pease, son of Edward, along with others involved in the Stockton & Darlington Railway. The venture was immediately successful, and by the end of 1832 the port was substantially outstripping Stockton as an exporter of coal. A smelting works was also provided, using raw materials from the recently discovered Cleveland iron mines. A new town was laid out on a grid pattern covering 500 acres and, by 1851, its population had already reached 8,000. It was the start of what would eventually become a town of 150,000 people.

However, as Middlesbrough grew, it also diversified, and so was not a railway town in the sense of a place that owed its entire being to the presence of the railway. According to Simmons, only six towns properly fit this definition — Crewe, Eastleigh, Horwich, Shildon, Swindon and

Wolverton. There were others, which started from a larger base and which had the railway as a dominant employer, but we will look at two of the early examples of his pure railway towns.

In 1837, the Cheshire parish of Monks Coppenhall had just a primitive wayside station on the Grand Junction Railway, alongside a turnpike. Contemporaries say that the roads linking it with the outside world suffered from 'excessively deep' ruts. But it was the point at which the railway lines to Birmingham, Manchester, Liverpool and Chester were to meet — later to be joined by routes to Stoke, Shrewsbury and Preston. In 1840, the Grand Junction Railway bought some land for the construction of a railway repair and construction works. It was certainly not the ready supply of labour that drew them there, since the population of the entire parish was then just some two hundred people. By 1844, the company had built 217 cottages for its workers, designed by the railway's engineer, Joseph Locke and Liverpool architect John Cunningham. The architecture of the new town faithfully reflected the hierarchy of the Grand Junction's employees. They built four classes of house, from villas for their senior officials to cottages for their labourers. Rents started off at an economic level, but the company soon found they had to subsidise them. The following year they added a church and a public baths, and moved their workshops there, from Edge Hill. By 1846, the population had swollen to 2,000 people, and the emerging new town had taken its name from the nearby stately home — Crewe Hall. By the early years of the twentieth century, the town's population had reached 50,000, over 7,000 of whom were employed at the works. Like the railway itself, the workshops were not the safest places of employment. Crewe even employed two men in the carpentry shop to make artificial limbs for employees who lost them through workplace injuries.

Other railway-based industries would follow — a Bessemer steel plant, a brickworks that supplied the needs of the railway company, printers and a clothing firm making uniforms for railway staff. Non-railway industries never took off in the same way — it was alleged that the railway charged punitive rates for the carriage of goods to and from Crewe, so as to discourage rival employers from competing for 'their' workforce. This left the town economically vulnerable. The railway company also got very involved in local politics, supplying several very Conservative mayors and threatening any employee who had the temerity to vote Liberal with pay cuts or dismissal. The railway company's grip on the town was only loosened as war approached in 1938, when Rolls-Royce built a shadow factory there to manufacture aircraft engines.

Crewe was perhaps the most dramatic example of a railway town growing from nothing, but there were others whose rise was scarcely less meteoric. Swindon had a population of just 1,747 in 1831, but the railway works for the Great Western were opened in 1843. Initially, the works were for repairs only, but they began manufacturing locomotives from 1846. Swindon was roughly the mid-point on the railway, the location of the junction for the Gloucester branch and the point at which the railway's character changed. To the east, it was a largely level track; to the west was the relatively steeper descent to Bath. Each section required different types of locomotives.

The railway company got the contractors J. & C. Rigby to build three hundred cottages, as part of the disastrous deal described earlier that gave the Rigbys the monopoly on Great Western catering. The contractors built the cottages at their own expense and rented them to the railway company, who in turn rented them to their workers. As with Crewe, a church and school soon followed, in 1845. The church's tower was built on the north side, contrary to normal practice, to improve its appearance from the railway. Despite the building programme, there was soon a housing shortage and a local vicar in 1847 characterised the area as being 'a torrent of vice and drunkenness'. Both the old town and the new — which for a long time were kept separate — suffered from poor water supply and sanitation, and disease was rife. A doctor was provided only in 1847, after the employees agreed to pay for it through voluntary contributions. Initially 423 men were employed at the works, but it grew to over 14,000 by the early years of the twentieth century. By that time, the town had a population of over 40,000.

Even where railway companies were not creating new towns on a large scale, many of them still went in for building workers' housing. The Liverpool & Manchester, for example, provided a range of basic housing for its employees, at rents of between 2s and 3s 6d a week. Among the other benefits they provided were sick pay (later modified into a contributory benefit society), an employee savings bank and a circulating library and reading room.

Commuter suburbs and slum clearance

In addition to railway towns, the early railways also shaped the pattern of commuting into our major cities. Workers who could afford it moved out to the healthier environment of the suburbs, now within daily travelling distance of the centres of employment. The richer you were, the further you moved out:

> ***'... on the Crewe branch of the Manchester and Birmingham Railway, Alderley Edge became the***

village to which the most successful of Manchester's entrepreneurs gravitated, with successively more modest suburbs forming around the stations closer in to town. The railway company built a hotel in Alderley Edge and promoted the village as a tourist attraction for the people in Manchester. They even gave free railway passes **(for twenty-one years, in the form of a brass plate, to be worn on one's watch chain)** *to Manchester men who built homes of a specified minimum value near the railway station at Alderley.'*

(Hylton: *A History of Manchester*)

This had the effect of separating the classes, both physically and in terms of mutual understanding. In the pre-railway city, the entrepreneurs and their workforce were far more likely to live cheek by jowl around their shared places of work, their place of residence dictated by their lack of mobility. The railways and other public transport enabled those who could afford it to live hitherto unimaginable distances away from the city. This removed them as role models and potential civic leaders. Manchester, for example, had great difficulty in appointing a boroughreeve (a form of civic leader, dating back to mediaeval times) in the 1830s, partly because of the exodus of suitable candidates.

These were days when the prospect of housebuilding in your neighbourhood was seen as a benefit, rather than as the end of civilisation as the existing population knew it. Thus, Charles Saunders, the Secretary to the Great Western Railway, was able to win over the residents of Windsor to his proposed branch line into the town by promising them that:

'The land around the town may be cut up; it will not be by the railway, but with villas, which will spring up in all directions... The inns and hotels will also be much more frequented from the vast influx of visitors.'

The railways may have created large numbers of jobs for the urban poor and given them hitherto unimagined and affordable mobility, but at the same time they added to the congestion of the cities and took away part of the stock of cheaper housing, exacerbating overcrowding. Their impact on urban form as an agent of slum clearance was felt most strongly in the later part of the century, as they expanded their termini, marshalling yards and warehouses. By 1900, the railways directly controlled over 5% of central London and Birmingham, 7% of Glasgow and Manchester and 9% of Liverpool, and railway-related activities took up a similar percentage of the urban area.

The railways naturally gravitated towards the poorer parts of cities when planning their termini and other facilities. Land values were lower, the tenants of the houses had no statutory rights of objection to their proposals, and the large landlords and freeholders of slum housing land were easier to deal with than a host of individual owner-occupiers. It could also be more attractive for the landowner to sell out to the railway, rather than having to meet the expense of redeveloping his slum property or upgrading it to meet the latest public health requirements. However, the effect was to pack the poor into even more overcrowded conditions in the city's remaining slum areas, since none of the houses thus lost was replaced.

But the railways helped to draw public attention to the conditions in which people were living, in a number of ways. Not least, as Engels recognised, because those travelling across the railway viaducts in places like Manchester and Salford could look down and see 'plenty of dirt and poverty'. Charles Dickens' brother-in-law, Henry Austin, was the resident engineer to the Blackwall Company and gave evidence on housing conditions to an inquiry into life in large towns in 1844. The reformer Lord Shaftesbury persuaded the House of Lords in 1853 to adapt a parliamentary standing order, so that any promoter of a private Bill involving the demolition of more than thirty working-class houses in a single parish had to supply a return showing the numbers of people affected. In London alone, it was estimated from these returns that as many as 120,000 people were displaced by the railways during the second half of the century, whilst somewhere between 41,000 and 55,000 Mancunians were thought to have been displaced by the railways by 1900. Whilst this was useful in raising public awareness of the hardship involved, the railways were not the only developments of the day to result in large-scale disturbance of working-class communities. In 1827/28 a single scheme — the construction of St Katharine's Dock in London — involved the displacement of more than 11,000 people.

One criticism that might legitimately be laid at the railways' door was their role in destroying the individuality of towns, by making the same industrially produced building materials available across the nation. The sense of place that came from the use of local building materials began to be eroded from the time the railways opened the towns and cities to national markets.

'Cathedrals of the new humanity': the stations

> ***'These cathedrals of the new humanity are the meeting points of nations, the centre where all converges, the nucleus of the huge stars whose iron rays stretch out to the ends of the earth.'***
>
> *(Theophile Gautier, quoted in Richards and MacKenzie)*

> ***'The 19th century's distinctive contribution to architectural form.'***
>
> *(Richards and MacKenzie)*

Purpose-built stations were often not part of the original conception of railways. In many North East towns, such as Shildon, Sedgefield and South Shields, the old coaching inns continued to serve their traditional function for the new railways. The Darlington terminus of the Stockton & Darlington was, until 1842, a converted goods warehouse; Middlesbrough's first station was a run-down coach shed and Newcastle made do initially with an abandoned riverside mansion. Some early efforts were improvised in the extreme. The station at Hartlepool in 1840 consisted of 'the poop of an old Dutch galliot... its cabins housed the booking hall and stationmaster'. At Moreton-on-Lugg on the Shrewsbury & Hereford Railway, passengers had to make do with the hollow trunk of a dead tree as their only shelter.

The Liverpool & Manchester had purpose-built stations only at either end of the line (though even the Liverpool Road station in Manchester had no platform or weather protection until 1834). The intermediate stations on the railway were not identifiable by any structure, but were simply recognised stopping places, for example where the line crossed a road. Not until the 1840s were such amenities as platforms and shelters provided, nor was any timetable provided for the departure times from these stations. Among the excuses given for delays to services, one not heard today was 'waiting for important people'. The absence of a platform also made it all too easy to get out of the carriage on the wrong side, into the path of an oncoming train.

When purpose-built stations appeared in all their glory, they made quite an impact; Euston attracted busloads of visitors. But not everyone favoured the construction of grand edifices for this purpose. John Ruskin felt that such ornament ran counter to their entire purpose:

> ***'Another of the strange and evil tendencies of the present day is to the decoration of the railroad station.***

Now, if there be any place in the world in which people are deprived of that portion of temper and discretion which are necessary to the contemplation of beauty, it is there. It is the very temple of discomfort, and the only charity that the builder can extend to us is to show us, plainly as may be, how soonest to escape from it. The whole system of railroad travelling is addressed to people, who, being in a hurry, are therefore, for the time being, miserable... The railroad is in all its relations a matter of earnest business, to be got through as soon as possible. It transmutes a man from a traveller to a living parcel. For the time he has parted from the nobler characteristics of his humanity for the sake of a planetary power of locomotion. Do not ask him to admire anything. You might as well ask the wind... Better bury gold in the embankments, than put it in ornaments on the stations.'

(John Ruskin: *The Seven Lamps of Architecture — 1849*)

Among the curiosities of the Great Western were the one-sided stations Brunel planned for places such as Reading, Gloucester, Taunton and Exeter. (The principle was also used elsewhere, for example at Huddersfield.) The logic of these for Brunel was that all of the towns concerned lay entirely to one side of the railway, and he therefore provided two separate stations, both on the same side of the tracks; one for *up* trains and the other for *down*. Whilst this may have been convenient for the passengers, it meant that *up* trains had to cross the *down* lines twice, when entering and leaving the station. The policemen manning the points at either end of the station also had to be aware of which of the approaching trains were stopping, and therefore needed to be switched into the station, and which were through services. The consequence of getting it wrong, as happened at Reading on one occasion, was that an express service was sent thundering into the station at 55mph. It says much for the stability of broad gauge trains that the passengers on this occasion suffered nothing more than a bad shaking and having their luggage scattered from the tops of their carriages. The policeman manning the offending point was found, still standing upright and clutching his lever, but in a dead faint. The inconvenience of these one-sided stations was such that the first plans to redesign Reading station were being drawn up within twelve years of the railway opening.

London stations

'A village situated on the Edgware Road, about a mile from London.'

(Paddington, as described in 1814)

In the period 1836 to 1841, six railways came into London, giving us the stations at Euston, Paddington, Fenchurch Street, Nine Elms, London Bridge and Shoreditch. But none of them ever penetrated into the heart of the city (Euston station, for example, originally stood in open fields). But in 1846 a number of proposals came forward for a central London terminus. A Royal Commission was set up to establish *'whether the extension of railways into the centre of the metropolis is calculated to afford such additional convenience as will compensate for the sacrifice of property, the interruption of important thoroughfares and interference with plans of improvement already suggested.'*

They identified a number of adverse effects of those railways that had so far approached the city centre — such as inhibiting street improvements and rendering large numbers of poor people homeless. But a more immediate deterrent to a central London terminus, from the railway companies' point of view, was the cost of land and property. The extension of the London & Birmingham Railway from Camden Town to Euston (a distance of just one mile) cost them £380,000, and the Eastern Counties Railway was actually ruined financially by their extension from Mile End to Bishopsgate. However, the rewards could be equally great. The final section of the railway into Fenchurch Street, for example, cost £250,000 for 415 yards of track, but it increased that railway's traffic by 50%. But this reflected special circumstances, in that it wiped out the competition from riverboats that the railway had previously faced.

Despite the cost, there were plans to create one or more super termini in the centre of London — Euston would have been one such, though not strictly in the heart of the early Victorian city. The Great Western was originally intended to share the London & Birmingham's Euston terminus, but the negotiations were not successful and the Great Western was forced to construct a line from Acton to a new terminus which was at that time also virtually in open country, in Paddington. The GWR's original booking office was on Princes Street, near the Bank of England, and a 6d bus ride away from the actual station.

The Commission looked at a total of 19 railway projects for entering central London and concluded that approaches from the south side of the Thames were to be preferred, due to *the inferior nature of the properties that might be disturbed* and to the fact that there were more people on the Surrey side than on the Middlesex side who might wish to commute into central London. In this, the Commission showed an appreciation of the potential of London's local commuter traffic that seemed to evade many of the railway entrepreneurs of the time. However, the Commission put paid to any idea of a single terminus in 1846, when it defined a no-go area in central London. No railway should come within a quadrilateral, defined by New Road, Marylebone and Euston Road in the north, Paddington in the west, Euston in the east, and the River Thames in the south. That area is roughly defined today by the route of the Central Line on the London Underground, which was built between 1863 and 1884 to link London's scattered railway termini.

Other cities' stations

In Birmingham, the first station at Curzon Street was also about a mile (or a 1s cab fare) from the town centre. In this case, the local geography made it less difficult to get a line into the heart of the town and in April 1846, parliamentary consent was given for the railway to acquire an area of swampy land, containing some of the town's worst slum housing (and its worst criminal elements). The area was then known as the Froggary, a name which does not perhaps have quite the right ring for a major city's terminus, but the area was to be entered by means of a new street, and it was from this that Birmingham's station took its name.

In Liverpool, it was decided in August 1831 that a more central station was needed, requiring a tunnel over a mile long. As soon as the plans were announced, land speculators bought property along the route, increasing the cost of the project. The cost of the new station, at Lime Street, was shared with Liverpool Council, which was keen to ensure that it would be a building that befitted the prestige of the town. Locomotives and wagons were banned from the approach tunnel. Carriages travelled downhill into it by gravity, under the control of a brake wagon, and uphill by means of an ingenious geared counterweight, which dropped down a sixty-foot well.

Manchester also suffered from having its rail termini scattered around the edge of the city, but without the compensation (in the future) of a connecting underground railway. Liverpool Road station was considered to be so far from the centre that, as with Paddington, an office was opened in the heart of the town, at 57 Market Street, to sell tickets. The extra traffic the railway generated in the streets between the town centre and the station became a cause of complaint and, from the beginning of 1831, an omnibus service was provided between the two

— but for first-class passengers only. The search for a more central terminus led to a collaboration between the Liverpool & Manchester and Manchester & Leeds Railways to build a joint station at Hunts Bank. A number of the Liverpool & Manchester shareholders were none too happy at this, since they were also shareholders in Liverpool Docks. The Manchester & Leeds had an extension planned to Hull, and there were fears that the extended railway would enable Hull to take away some of Liverpool's port trade. Only after four years of bitter dispute was parliamentary approval for the scheme given in July 1842.

The great city termini, in London and elsewhere, became the showpieces of the railway companies. By 1890, over £100 million had been invested in the provision of termini (and gaining access to them). This represented more than an eighth of all the nation's railway capital investment.

Chapter 8:
The advance of railway technology

'There is no reason to expect any material improvement in the breed of horses in the future, while, in my judgement, the man is not living who knows what the breed of locomotives is to place at command.'

(An American engineer, visiting the Stockton & Darlington Railway in the 1820s)

'... the application of the loco-motive steam-engine, for propelling carriages on railways, has proved to be certain at all seasons of the year; and from the celerity of its motion and the very moderate expense attending its use, has been found to be more economical and advantageous for the transfer of goods than any other plan now adopted.'

(From the prospectus of the Bristol and Bath Rail Road — published in The Times, 8 January 1825)

'Does anyone in possession of his senses expect that this snorting, spluttering, hideous machine of iron, belching forth smoke and steam, can ever accomplish such a draught as is easily undertaken by the horses on the "Croydon Iron Road"?'

(An early critic of steam power, quoted in Carter, referring to the Surrey Iron Railway. Another contemporary described the 'lean and half-starved horses' working this early railway, which was never a commercial success and which closed in 1846.)

'The loco-motive monster': early opposition to steam

Thomas Creevey MP — an opponent of railways and friend of Lord Sefton, who helped throw out the first Liverpool & Manchester Railway

Bill — described his first — and, as he expected, last — railway trip to visit his step-daughter:

> ***'Today we have had a lark of a very high order. I had the satisfaction, for I can't call it a pleasure, of taking a trip of five miles in it, and we did it in just a quarter of an hour....***
>
> ***'But the quickest motion is to me frightful; it is really like flying, and it is impossible to divest yourself of the notion of instant death to all upon the least incident happening. It gave me a headache which has not left me yet. Sefton is convinced that some damnable thing must come of it; but he and I seem more struck with such apprehensions than others...'***

Creevey is better known for an often-quoted piece of invective dating from 1825, where he talks of 'the loco-motive monster carrying eighty tons of goods, and navigated by a tail of smoke and sulphur, coming through every man's grounds between Manchester and Liverpool'. The opponents of steam railways found no shortage of grounds for their opposition. Locomotive power on the Liverpool & Manchester Railway would, it was claimed, result in cows stopping grazing, hens ceasing to lay, country inns closing, birds being killed in the air, farmland being destroyed, farms and other properties being burnt to the ground, the air polluted, foxes and pheasants eradicated, fox-hunting prevented (the eradication of the fox would no doubt have been a major factor in the decline of fox-hunting), horses being extinguished as a species, and oats and hay becoming unmarketable.

A separate stream of opposition came from those who feared the health effects for humans of travelling at unprecedented speeds. Among the afflictions attributed to early rail travel were causing pregnant women to miscarry (Mrs Gamp in *Martin Chuzzlewit* was a prominent, if not authoritative, proponent of this school of thought), making women who were not pregnant barren, babies being born deformed, boiling, maiming, suffocation in tunnels due to carbonic acid exposure, colds, catarrhs and consumptions, weakening of the heart and brain, and premature ageing. It could lead to 'suicidal delirium' among those who were that way inclined. In addition, there was the risk to your health of being closeted in a carriage with a lunatic or a smallpox victim. If this were not enough, after the opening of the Liverpool & Manchester, a rumour spread among the travelling public that excess speed was bad for the eyes. A Doctor Chalmers had to be called upon to reassure people through the pages of the *Liverpool Mercury* that even speeds of 34mph would 'cause no inconvenience or alarm nor would the eye be disturbed while viewing the scenery'.

Those were just the physical symptoms. The *New York Gazette,* which was following the progress of the Liverpool & Manchester with interest, dwelt (perhaps not entirely seriously) on the effects on people's morals:

> ***'Grave plodding citizens will be flying around like comets. It will encourage flightiness of intellect. Various people will turn into the most immeasurable liars; all their conceptions will be exaggerated by their munificent notions of distance — "Only a hundred miles off! Tut, nonsense, I'll step across madam and bring your fan".'***
>
> (*Quoted in Garfield, page 57*)

Dr Dionysius Lardner, the so-called early expert of the railways and implacable opponent of Brunel and his Great Western, had his own health scare. He claimed that brake failure on a train passing through the Box Tunnel would result in it building up to a speed of 120mph, at which point the passengers would expire, being unable to breathe at such speeds. As he dismissively said of Brunel and his fellow engineers:

> ***'Engineers are merely judicial men, who do not have the extensive powers of generalisation, which is a matter of Arithmetic.'***

Brunel did not need medical help or mathematics to disprove Lardner's theory. As we have seen, he simply allowed a carriage on the Canterbury & Whitstable Railway to freewheel down the 1:49 Tyler Hill and through the tunnel, amply demonstrating the braking effects of friction and wind resistance.

Early sceptics about steam power could, however, find more rational bases for their opposition. The management of the Stratford & Moreton Railway discovered on testing one of Stephenson's pre-*Locomotion* engines in 1821 that it required a much heavier and more expensive track than a horse-drawn alternative, that it could not pull an adequate load up a 1:72 incline and would not run appreciably faster than a horse-drawn vehicle on the flat. They were also more dangerous — who ever heard of a horse exploding? Until John Rastrick came up with the water gauge in 1829, the crew had no way of knowing when the water supply needed refilling, making them prone to boiler explosions. *Locomotion* and another locomotive, *Hope*, both suffered this fate in 1828 (the dead crews could be conveniently blamed for tampering with the safety valves). It was perhaps small wonder that a number of railways, given the choice, opted for horses.

Even the allies of steam seemed to be prepared to talk down its potential. Nicholas Wood, the manager of Killingworth Colliery and one-time friend of George Stephenson, said in his *Treatise on Rail-Roads* (published — perhaps unhelpfully — in May 1825, as the first Liverpool & Manchester Bill was struggling to make its way through Parliament):

> ***'It is far from my wish to promulgate to the world that the ridiculous expectations, or rather professions, of the enthusiastic speculists be realised, and that we shall see them travelling at the rate of 12, 16, 18 or 20 miles an hour; nothing could do more harm towards their adoption, or general improvement, than the promulgation of such nonsense.'***

Others sought to have the ambitions of these speed-crazed fiends more strictly regulated. This from the *Quarterly Review* of March 1825:

> ***'We trust that Parliament will, in all railways it may sanction, limit the speed to 8 or 9 miles an hour.'***

It was therefore no wonder that George Stephenson was strictly warned by his Counsel not to over-state the case for steam locomotion in his presentation to Parliament — in particular, not to mention insane speeds like 20mph — or 'he would be regarded as a maniac fit for Bedlam and damn the whole thing'. In the event, Stephenson talked in terms of speeds of 4 to 8mph, but could not resist the speculation that much more was possible.

But speed was only one part of the argument. George Stephenson commissioned some cost comparisons on the Stockton & Darlington in 1826, which showed that locomotive traction cost less than a farthing (0.25d) per ton/mile. Fixed engines cost about a penny more. Perhaps more important, steam locomotives were estimated to be about 30% cheaper than horses.

But there were more alternatives to steam locomotives than just stationary engines and horsepower. A prototype electric vehicle was tested, sails were tried on the Stockton & Darlington, and a much more revolutionary new technique was anticipated in the *Manchester*

Guardian. After describing a new stagecoach service that would cut the travel time between London and Brighton to 'little more than five hours', they went on:

> ***'A more formidable rivalry, however, is expected in the Vacuum Tube Association, who are to convey passengers in one hour. This scheme is of course much laughed at; but thus argue the projectors — produce a species of vacuum or tube, with the general force of the common air excluded, and a body — say a coach, sledge or wooden horse — may be propelled, not merely 52, but about three hundred miles in one hour! Now it is ascertained (sayeth on dit) that human beings may exist in such a vacuity, as they would not have to cut against the air, when going at the rate of more than 52 miles an hour.'***
>
> (*Manchester Guardian — 3 September 1825*)

Even in 1825, it seems that visionaries were dreaming of commuting between London and Brighton on a daily basis. Experiments with atmospheric railways, worked on the vacuum principle, have been described earlier in the book.

Early Railway Acts could be vague or even inconsistent about the use of steam power. It was only the second Stockton & Darlington Act that permitted the carrying of passengers by steam locomotives. The revised prospectus for the Liverpool & Manchester actually volunteered that they would seek no clause empowering them to use locomotives, and offered environmental protection for their neighbours in the event of being given such powers. In the event, the first Liverpool and Manchester Act expressly forbade the use of locomotives on part of the route, but was unclear about their use elsewhere; and one clause in the Whitby & Pickering Railway Act (1833) permitted steam haulage, whilst another specifically forbade it. This last railway remained horse-drawn until 1846, when it was connected to the York & North Midland line.

In the case of the Newcastle & Carlisle Railway, clause 6 of the 1829 Act specified that 'No locomotive or moveable steam engine shall be used on the said railways or tramroads for drawing waggons or other carriages, or for any other purpose whatsoever'. It further required that no stationary steam engines be built within sight of a whole list of specific country residences. Only by this means was it possible to overcome the opposition of influential landowners to the scheme in Parliament. However, by the time the first phase of the scheme was nearing completion, in 1834, the advantages of steam traction were starting to become so obvious that the company ordered and began operating three steam locomotives, in anticipation of being able to change Parliament's mind on the matter. But within months of the line's official opening in March 1835, one of the dissenting landowners, one Charles Bacon Grey, obtained an order in the Court of Chancery that shut the railway down. However, this caused such a storm of local indignation that he was forced to back down. By June, a second Newcastle & Carlisle Railway Act sanctioned the use of steam locomotives, the only concession being that they had to burn coke, rather than coal, to prevent smoke.

Even after a railway was operating, its right to use locomotives could be challenged. In 1831, several landowners took the Stockton & Darlington to court, complaining of 'unwholesome and offensive smells, smokes and vapours as well as divers loud explosions, shocks and noises', not to mention 'terrific and alarming appearances when travelling at night'. The complainants wanted an end to 'those great snorting, roaring and mighty monsters, vomiting fire in all directions, which the horse by no means recognises as relations of his'. The case got as far as the King's Bench in London before being thrown out.

The progress of steam locomotives

Steam power had been around for a long time by the start of the railway age. The combination of steam and rail was also long established, if not commonplace. As we have seen, Richard Trevithick demonstrated a working example in South Wales in 1804, but the technology made little progress over the next twenty years. Between 1814 and 1826, Stephenson was just about the only man in Britain building locomotives. By 1823, only 28 steam locomotives had been built, and none of them had proved to be indisputably better than horse-drawn transport. So the evolution of steam locomotion was just as much a voyage of discovery as every other aspect of running the first railways. When a party from the Liverpool & Manchester Railway visited Killingworth Colliery in 1824, they found the locomotives there incapable of hauling more than 40 tons of coal at 4mph on a level track.

Locomotion No 1, the only steam locomotive at the opening of the Stockton & Darlington Railway, showed little development from those early colliery locomotives. Slow and lumbering, it had vertical cylinders driving the wheels through an elaborate and inefficient system of connecting rods that had echoes of the stationary beam engines of Boulton and Watt. It weighed almost $8^1/2$ tons in full operating order.

Locomotion and its three companions, bought during 1825/26, were not an unalloyed success. By June 1827, the company owned six locomotives, but they were proving very unreliable. They spent so much time under repair that the use of horses was actually increasing at this time. George Stephenson was so overloaded by his surveying work for this railway and the Liverpool & Manchester that he could devote no time to improving what were basically 1815 locomotive designs. Rumours circulated (incorrectly) that the Directors of the Stockton & Darlington were thinking about abandoning steam locomotion altogether, which may have coloured the judgement of the delegations from the Liverpool & Manchester Railway, who went to the Stockton & Darlington to compare the merits of locomotives and stationary engines.

Rocket, the victor of the Rainhill Trials, is probably the most famous locomotive in railway history. It was also an important advance in design in a number of respects, though none of them was entirely original. First, it had a multi-tube boiler, which meant that it had a much greater heating area for the water and could raise steam much more quickly. This was an idea on which many engineers of the day had been working, in one form or another. Versions of it had been patented by James Neville in March 1826 and Marc Séguin in France in 1828, and by others as long ago as 1776, but *Rocket* took the technology to a new level.

The second big idea was to discharge part of the waste steam up the locomotive's chimney through a blastpipe. This helped to make the fire burn more fiercely and thus take full advantage of the increased heating area of the multi-tube boiler. Again, this was not a new idea. Trevithick's 1804 locomotive had a form of blastpipe; as Trevithick quaintly said of it at the time:

> ***'The fire burns much better when the steam goes up the Chimney than what it do when the engine is idle.'***

Stephenson himself had used the idea since 1815, though not without problems. One of these was that the blast sucked burning coals up the chimney and spewed them onto the surrounding countryside, goods wagons and the passengers. Beaters were employed for the trackside fires, and tarpaulins to cover the goods wagons. Passengers, especially those travelling in the open, had to fend for themselves. Also, as one contemporary put it: *'the steam thrown in this manner into the chimney acts as a trumpet, and certainly makes a very disagreeable noise'*. So Stephenson's developments were evolution, not revolution. But combine these developments with *Rocket's* weight advantage —

it weighed just 4 tons 5 cwt to meet the Rainhill regulations — and it meant that *Rocket* was much more effective than its predecessors.

Another development that helped increase speed was the move from vertical to inclined cylinders, since the former caused a locomotive to pitch badly as soon as any sort of speed was reached. The early colliery engines could thus manage little more than walking pace.

Rocket was followed by a period of rapid innovation. The *Northumbrian*, built the following year, and others that followed, incorporated a host of further developments. There were also improvements in the use of materials. The hard particles in the coke the early locomotives burned led to rapid wear of the copper boiler tubes. Their replacement by brass increased the operating life of the locomotive. In later years (shortly after the period of our interest) the availability of affordable steel, in place of iron for key components, also helped the development process.

Until 1830, Stephenson had a virtual monopoly on locomotive production. But new manufacturers rapidly entered the field, starting with Fenton, Murray's *Vulcan*, supplied to the Liverpool & Manchester in May 1831. Within a year of opening, the railway was specifying locomotives of up to 8 tons, twice the weight of *Rocket*. These were too heavy for the original lightly built track. It was re-laid and reinforced and, by 1838, *Lion* was weighing in at about 27 tons. The company by then bought locomotives from a dozen different manufacturers. Above all else, the locomotives had to be reliable; they were already averaging 20,000 miles a year by the early 1830s and, from 1833, the Liverpool & Manchester demanded a twelve-month guarantee from their manufacturers.

One of the ways in which performance was improved, about which the railway industry was understandably coy, was by increasing the boiler pressure. *Rocket* worked on a maximum of 50 pounds per square inch; by 1845 pressures of more than twice this were in use. The public was particularly nervous about high-pressure boilers, and it was not at all unknown for a manufacturer to quote one operating figure for the public record and another, higher, one to those driving the locomotive. This problem was compounded by the locomotive drivers themselves, who could get more performance out of their machines by screwing the safety valves down. The number of boiler explosions that occurred on the Great Western and elsewhere suggests that this practice was far from uncommon.

As well as making locomotives go faster, the manufacturers struggled to find a way of making them stop. The earliest ones had no brakes at all, except perhaps on the tenders, and these were fitted with primitive wooden brake-blocks. If they needed to stop quickly, the driver would throw the locomotive into reverse, a somewhat brutal and tricky manoeuvre (it was said that only one of the Stockton & Darlington drivers could perform it in the dark, without the aid of a light). But it was still not particularly effective. For many years, manufacturers resisted having any brakes at all on the driving wheels, for fear that they would overheat the rims and cause them to part company with the wheel.

The *Patentee* of 1833 was fitted with a prototype steam brake; up until then, any braking had been limited to human power — no more than a lever pulled by the driver, which pressed wooden brake shoes against the wheels. It took some time before the steam brake — or its main alternative, the air brake — was made to work properly. From the mid-1840s, experiments were also made with continuous brakes, linking all the vehicles in the train, but again the technology that would allow the system to be disconnected and re-set each time a new train was formed took a long time to get right.

'Skinny chickens — all wings and legs': Great Western locomotives

> ***'In the whole history of British railways there has never existed such an extraordinary collection of freak locomotives as those that were built for the Great Western and delivered in a period of about 18 months from November 1837.'***
>
> (*MacDermot — page 372*)

By 1836, the workings of standard gauge steam locomotives were starting to become much better understood. The Comte de Pambour had carried out exhaustive experiments on the Liverpool & Manchester Railway, and the consequences of varying key aspects of their design could now be predicted much more accurately. But Brunel was not working within the confines of the standard gauge. One of the central purposes of his broad gauge was to enable him to use larger, faster and more powerful locomotives. At the time the locomotives for the Great Western had to be ordered, the company had not yet employed a locomotive superintendent and it fell to Brunel to set out a specification.

It was not Brunel's finest hour; he had had little experience of steam engines, apart perhaps with the slow and ponderous steam pumps that he no doubt used on his Thames tunnel project. It may have been from these devices that he got his unrealistic ideas about a low maximum piston speed (he specified as a maximum about two-thirds of the piston speeds already being successfully achieved by standard gauge locomotives). This in turn generated the need for huge driving wheels to achieve the speeds he required. (Mysteriously, Brunel specified that his locomotives should have a 'standard velocity' of 30mph, whatever that meant. He later explained, hardly less obtusely, that he wanted them to be 'capable of adaptation to run at up to 40 miles per hour'). These giant driving wheels used up a disproportionate amount of the meagre weight limit of 10.5 tons allowed by Brunel and in turn forced the manufacturers to skimp on the size and weight of the boilers.

His specification thus produced ill-matched freaks with under-sized boilers and pistons and grotesquely large driving wheels of up to ten feet in diameter — so large that they were badly affected by side winds. One example had six foot driving wheels, but with a gear ratio of 3:1, so that the driving wheels were the equivalent of 18 feet in diameter! In another ill-advised attempt to get round the weight limit, R. & W. Hawthorn had the engine and the boiler mounted on separate carriages. Seventeen of these freaks were built to Brunel's specification. They scarcely had the power to drag themselves, let alone a train, along the line. Gibson describes them as being 'like skinny chickens — all legs and wings'; and O. S. Nock suggests that Brunel's interest in atmospheric railways may have been encouraged by this unhappy early experience with steam traction.

Daniel Gooch was appointed locomotive superintendent in August 1837, not yet past his twenty-first birthday. It was his unenviable task to sort out this mess and, initially, to take the blame for what he had inherited. As G. H. Gibbs, one of the Company's directors, put it: 'Our engines are in very bad order and Gooch seems to be very unfit for the superintendence of that Department'. Fortunately for the Great Western, Gooch proved to be more than capable of sorting it out, giving rise to the saying 'Brunel built the Great Western but Gooch made it work'.

His initial salvation came in the form of two locomotives built by the Stephensons for an American railway with a 5 foot 6 inch gauge. The order was cancelled, Gooch snapped them up and Stephenson widened them to 7-foot gauge. These *Star* class locomotives were initially the only reliable ones the railway had, and bought Gooch the time he needed to sort the rest of the mess out. Ten of the seventeen freaks were scrapped by the end of 1840, others were rebuilt, and from 1839 Gooch himself did the specifications for the new locomotives. His first designs — the '*Fire Fly*' class — were enlarged versions of *Star* class, and were the world's first genuine express locomotives, capable of 60mph. These were ordered in large numbers — a total of 62 were delivered, 17 in 1840 alone. One of the great contributions Gooch made to locomotive manufacture was the idea of key parts being interchangeable between locomotives. Manufacturers would be supplied with detailed specifications and templates to ensure that this could be done.

'The wings of the wind': the quest for speed

> ***'What can be more palpably absurd and ridiculous than the prospect held out of locomotives travelling twice as fast as stagecoaches? We should as soon expect the people of Woolwich to suffer themselves to be fired off upon one of Congreve's ricochet rockets as trust themselves to the mercy of such a machine going at such a rate.'***
>
> (*Quarterly Review — March 1825*)

At the start of our period, locomotives could manage little more than walking pace and even talk of speeds as modest as 15mph terrified many people. But the Liverpool & Manchester locomotive *Northumbrian* soon set what must be one of the earliest railway speed records, on the opening day of the Liverpool & Manchester Railway in 1830, by reaching 36mph as it rushed the mortally wounded William Huskisson to the nearest medical aid. By the late 1830s, the trunk railways were the epitome of speed, most of the express services routinely averaging around 25mph, including stops. This was between two and three times the speed of stagecoaches.

Within 15 years of the Liverpool & Manchester opening, timetabled average speeds on much of the Great Western line between London and Bristol were 47 to 48mph, with a number of standard gauge services on other lines only a few miles per hour slower. In the gauge trials of 1845, discussed below, the Great Western locomotive *Ixion* managed to average 61mph for the journey between Paddington and Didcot, and standard gauge trains achieved maximum speeds of 60 to 62mph between Darlington and York. Claims (albeit of doubtful reliability) were even made of 68.2mph achieved on the Madeley Bank, approaching Crewe, and speeds of 74mph were recorded on the Great Western the following year.

It was the broad gauge locomotives of the Great Western that led the way in those early years. As early as 1847, their *Great Britain* exceeded 80mph — a speed that was not achieved on the standard gauge until the 1890s. This was not some freak result, achieved momentarily on a downhill stretch. The following year, one of their trains (admittedly on another test run) completed the 53 miles between Paddington and Didcot in just 47½ minutes, an average speed of 67mph, despite having to slow down for the passage through Reading station. This would not look too far out of place on a present-day timetable, and was achieved on a locomotive without either weather protection or effective brakes. It is perhaps worth noting that the driver on both these occasions was a man known to his colleagues as 'Mad Sandy'. By the time of the Great Exhibition in 1851, the most powerful of the Great Western locomotives on display there was developing as much as 1,140 horsepower.

But these high speeds could not be built into regular schedules, not least because of the imperfections of signalling to warn of dangers ahead, and the difficulties facing the driver in stopping the train in the event of danger. There were also problems in that the track could not always be relied upon, that the locomotives were not yet particularly reliable, and that many of the locomotives could not manage more than 20 or 30 miles without stopping for water. Anti-speed lobbyists filled the newspapers with complaints, and suggested elaborate solutions, involving maximum speed signs along the length of the route, or the locomotive automatically sounding its whistle every quarter of a mile, to give an indication of speed.

At the other extreme, the record for slowness — at least in the popular imagination — was held by the ill-fated Eastern Counties Railway. A malicious rumour was spread that one of its express trains had been raced — and beaten — by a costermonger's cart pulled by a donkey. Or, as Thackeray put it in *Punch:* 'Even a journey on the Eastern Counties must have an end at last'. The magazine suggested that 'every criminal awaiting execution should have his sentence commuted to a journey on the Eastern Counties Railway'.

Wave your arms about: the first signals

The arrangements for the return journey from Manchester on the opening day of the Liverpool & Manchester Railway illustrate the extent to which signalling had been thought about beforehand by the early railways. It was decided on the day to couple several locomotives together, to pull a single long train of carriages, rather than take the risk of running several separate trains along the unregulated tracks as darkness fell. The long train could not get up the inclines and the male passengers were forced to get out and walk up the slope. Part of the way back, they decided to detach one locomotive, which went ahead as a lookout pilot, with one man holding aloft a length of flaming tarred rope as a warning signal. At Rainhill, this lookout ran over a wheelbarrow, placed (possibly deliberately) across the tracks.

In the earliest days of the railways, the only signals were human ones, waving hands or flags in the daytime, or lights at night. On the Stockton & Darlington, white was for 'go on', red for 'go slowly' and purple 'stop'. In the case of the Great Western, it was some months after the opening before the need to provide the officials with lamps at night was appreciated, and these were belatedly ordered. the Liverpool & Manchester used burning braziers or lengths of flaming tarred rope, which were hauled up poles on a rope and pulley as signals at night. Even a year after the opening of the Great Western, Charles Saunders told a parliamentary committee that 'the policemen make signals with their arms; by this the Engine Men are principally governed'.

This early account describes in detail the code to which they worked on the Liverpool & Manchester:

> ***'When a train approaches within a certain distance of a station, the policeman presents himself, and signifies a clear road by assuming an erect posture with his arm outstretched: should he take the position of "stand at ease", the engineer is aware that some obstruction exists. When a passenger is waiting at the station, a red flag is hoisted by day, and a swinging light exhibited at night. In travelling in the dark, the last carriage of every train carries "astern" — to use a nautical expression — a revolving lamp, one side of which is red and the other blue. As long as the train is in motion the red light presents itself to whatever follows, but at the instant of stopping, the blue light is turned outward; the engineer of the next train instantly sees this change, and is enabled, by checking the velocity of his engine, to avoid a collision that would be tremendous. The fire of the engine is sufficient to give warning to the policeman or to any object upon the road of the approach of a train.'***
>
> (*'A Tourist', 1833 — page 24*)

This system is based on several layers of supreme optimism — it trusted that the drivers would be able to see these faint lights, even in adverse conditions; that, having seen the signal, they would be able to stop in time; even that 'objects' on the track would be warned of an oncoming train by the glow of its fire. (What would the objects then do? Leap out of the way by themselves?) The reality was that, even in good weather, smoke and steam could obscure the signaller's efforts. There was also no means of communication between the policemen and they were rarely even visible to each other. In 1831, recognising public concern about the dangers of speed, the Liverpool & Manchester introduced a speed limit of 20mph. Roads were gated (the men employed to tend them working a 15-hour day for around £1 a week). From about 1833, a labour-saving device — flagpoles — began to be introduced, to save the effort of manual waving.

One interesting variation on light signals in the early days was the use of the locomotive's fire. On the Stockton & Darlington, in the event of a breakdown, the fireman would run back down the track, carrying a shovelful of burning coals from the fire, which he would throw into the air at the appropriate moment to attract attention. This was not without its problems, since the track-bed often contained a significant proportion of inflammable waste material from the local mines, and they could end up setting the track alight. This would at least have the advantage of attracting the undivided attention of the driver of any oncoming train. The Great Western had its own version, where the fireman of a stationary train raked out the fire and deposited it on the track. This was done away with after the introduction of detonators.

Such methods only worked at all so long as trains were slow and infrequent, and railway junctions few and far between. According to Allen, the first recorded signalling of any kind at a railway junction was at the crossing of the Brandling Junction and Stanhope & Tyne railways. He describes its none-too simple rules thus:

> ***'At the approach to the crossing, there were three posts in succession on each line. On reaching the first post, the driver had to whistle; at the second, he reduced speed; at the third, if a white flag were hoisted at the crossing a Brandling Junction train could pass at half speed, and if a red flag, a Stanhope & Tyne train. If both flags were hoisted together and waved, or if no flag was shown, the driver had to stop at the third post, clear of the crossing. At night, lamps replaced flags.'***
>
> (*Allen, 1964 — page 222*)

Sometimes it was the locomotives that carried the signals. After the opening of the Grand Junction in 1837, Newton on the Liverpool & Manchester became a busy junction, making it difficult for the policemen on the points to identify the destination of approaching trains. Trains going onto the Warrington & Newton Railway, also served off the junction, therefore took to carrying a diamond symbol on the front, to help the policemen identify them.

If the policemen could get confused, then so too could the men on the locomotives. Drivers approaching the newly opened Reading station in 1840 were advised:

> ***'A signal ball will be seen at the entrance to Reading Station when the Line is right for the Train to go in. If the Ball is not visible the Train must not pass it.'***
>
> (*Daniel Gooch — Regulations for the Engines working the trains on and after the 30th March 1840*)

The advice not to pass something in the event that you cannot see it does not seem the safest method of controlling traffic. Moreover, these bewildering written instructions were being issued to a workforce many of whom would be illiterate. Gooch held it that locomotive drivers did not need to be able to read and Brunel actively preferred them to be illiterate, on the grounds that their minds were less likely to become distracted. This view was shared by Edward Bury, the Superintendent of Locomotives on the London & Birmingham Railway. Asked in Parliament in 1839 how his drivers gained sufficient practical knowledge to do their job, he told them: 'We do not want them to have much; I would rather the men did not touch the engine themselves.'

The first fixed signals were thought to have been installed on the Liverpool & Manchester in 1834. These consisted of a board on pivots, which would be turned at right-angles to the track to face an oncoming train to tell it to stop. If it were parallel to the track it was safe to proceed. The idea of signals gradually caught on and, by about 1840, Brunel was introducing them on the Great Western. A common problem with many of the early signalling systems was that they lacked a positive signal to proceed. The early disc signals were effectively invisible to the driver when set at 'proceed'. Similarly, with early semaphore signals, the 'proceed' signal entailed the arm of the signal disappearing onto a slot in its post. This would be indistinguishable to the driver from a signal that had broken. Another shortcoming of this system would later be illustrated at Abbotts Ripton in January 1876, when driven snow was blown into the slots of these semaphore signals, preventing them from working and resulting in a fatal accident.

Brunel addressed this by attaching a crossbar at right-angles to the disc on the signal pole. Thus, either the disc or the crossbar should be visible to tell the driver either to 'stop' or 'go'. Brunel's early signals were praised by the Board of Trade for the fact that they gave this positive 'all clear', and variants of them were adopted by railways in this country and overseas. One problem with them was that they still lacked a signal for 'proceed with caution'. Brunel attempted to solve this with a flag signal that opened like a fan. However, these soon got blown to tatters in the wind, and Brunel replaced them with an arrow-shaped fantail signal. This had three settings:

- an arrow pointing to the track and showing a red face meant 'danger';
- an arrow pointing away from the track and showing green was 'proceed with caution';
- and an arrow pointing parallel to the track (invisible again) was 'all clear'.

The signals were mounted on the top of tall posts, 40 or 60 feet high, to give them maximum visibility. Even so, their lack of remote operation in the early days was a problem. It meant that the signal was erected where it was convenient for the operator to use. This could mean that the train was not given time to stop, or that it ended up stopping in the wrong place.

Semaphore signals were first introduced on the London & Croydon Railway in 1841. They were a variation of a form of signalling devised for military use in 1792. When the signal was horizontal, at right-angles to the post, it meant 'stop'. Lowered through 45 degrees was 'proceed with caution', whilst lowered through 90 degrees into a slot in the post was 'all clear'. The system was substituted by red, green and white lights at night.

Early signals worked on standard time intervals. In the case of the Liverpool & Manchester, the signal remained at 'danger' for five minutes after a train had passed. Since the policemen operating the signals were unlikely to possess a watch, they were each issued with an egg timer to ensure a correct interval. In similar vein, signals on the Great Western would, until 1852, automatically remain at 'danger' for three minutes and 'caution' for seven minutes after the passage of a train. This meant that, if a train broke down or was delayed, the next one would carry on into the back of it, unless someone ran back from the first train to give warning. The danger of this kind of rear-end collision was learned by the Liverpool & Manchester in the early, pre-signal, days of its operation.

One day in November 1832, the 7.15am train from Manchester had stopped at Rainhill to pick up passengers. The 8am train, which, according to the contemporary report in *The Times*: 'must have travelled with tremendous velocity to reach Rainhill at so early an hour, was observed coming along the road with great speed'. Calls for it to stop were in vain. It hit the rear of the first train with tremendous force, killing one of the passengers before crashing into the station and tearing the front off the building.

The railway company explained that the first train had been running half an hour late, and had been further delayed loading passengers' luggage at Rainhill. The driver of the second train had presumed that the first would have virtually arrived in Liverpool by this time and was consequently going too fast in the fog. The company described it as the first serious accident to be caused by fog (as distinct from one caused by any shortcoming in their operating practices). Nonetheless they gave instructions to their gatemen that in future, under similar circumstances, they were to give up duties such as ticket collecting or loading luggage, and were instead to run back three hundred yards to warn any oncoming trains. Detonators were invented in 1841 and came into use soon afterwards as a means of warning of hazards ahead in fog. One problem with them was that many railway companies specified distances for spacing them that were clearly inadequate to enable the trains of the day to stop, and rear-end collisions were still far more common than they needed to be.

The Yarmouth & Norwich Railway, which opened in 1844, became the first to begin to replace the use of time intervals for signals with a version of the modern block system, in which the railway was divided into sections and no two trains were allowed to be in the same section at once. However, its use did not become universal for many years afterwards. It was resisted by the railway companies on the perverse grounds that, by transferring responsibility away from the locomotive drivers, it would increase, rather than decrease, the risk of accidents. Often, however, such arguments masked concerns about the cost of its installation.

The earliest signalboxes, if they can be so described, were the miserable huts provided as shelter for the men who worked individual signals or points. The very first staff on the Great Western did not have even these for several months after the opening. Even then, it took some time for them to be fixed on a pivot, so that they could at least be turned to face out of the wind. The first real signalbox, as the term is currently understood, was probably at the junction of the London & Croydon and London & Greenwich Railways, just south of London Bridge. From 1839, the signals at that junction were operated remotely from a structure resembling a lighthouse. Until proper signalboxes were introduced onto the GWR in 1874, signals and points both required individual lineside policemen to operate them. This was a tremendously piecemeal system and depended upon each of them knowing the timetable by heart, and which train needed to be switched in which direction. This was further complicated after dual gauge operation was introduced on the Great Western, when the operators had to remember not just the destination of the next train but also its gauge, so as to switch the right set of rails.

The telegraph

A proposal to link Liverpool and Manchester by telegraph was announced in the *Manchester Guardian* of 24 September 1825, by the Imperial Telegraphic Company. The capital cost was estimated at £2,500, with running costs of £3,200 per annum and an estimated cost of 6d (2½p) a signal. This was some 12 years before Cooke and Wheatstone, generally credited with its invention, came up with their improved version. During 1837, this latter system was installed in the Liverpool railway tunnel and also linked Euston station with the engine house in Camden that provided the stationary steam power along that stretch of line. It would be another decade before the rest of the London & Birmingham line was linked by telegraph.

Prior to the opening of the Great Western, it was agreed to organise a trial of the telegraph between Slough and West Drayton, as a demonstration project. The company would install the wires, at a cost of between £250 and £300 per mile, and the patentees would in return grant them a free licence to install it throughout the GWR. It rapidly became more of a tourist attraction than a useful working tool for the railway. MacDermot reports that, on 24 August 1840, the Duke of Wellington, Lord Bathurst, Lord Fitzroy Somerset 'and some ladies' called at Paddington for a demonstration. For much of the time it appears to have been out of order and, even when it was working, there appeared to be no clear idea of what exactly it was for. The lack of literacy among railway staff may have been part of the reason for this. When on one occasion it was used to report danger on the line, the fact was deemed sufficiently unusual to warrant reporting it to the Directors.

Despite this, installation of the system went ahead across the rail network. By 1846, there were 1,048 miles of railway telegraph in place, over half of it installed by three companies — the Midland, the Eastern Counties and the South Eastern Railway. It made it possible for the railways to operate an early form of block working on particularly dangerous sections of track, such as where there were long tunnels. The South Eastern enterprisingly found a commercial outlet for it, licensing *The Times* to send its reports — encrypted — along it. Many members of the public were apparently bewildered by the miracle of the telegraph, and turned up at railway stations thinking it could be used to transmit banknotes or parcels.

Chapter 9:
A national network takes shape

'They will be joined together some day.'

George Stephenson's prediction of a national network of railways, c1825.

We have looked at the construction of a number of the most important lines, but many other major parts of the railway network were approved and built in the period to 1845. The London & Southampton Railway was approved in 1834, but the poor organisation of its first engineer, Francis Giles, helped delay its opening until 1840. Giles was eventually dismissed and his replacement, Joseph Locke, had to tell the shareholders that the 78-mile line was going to cost about three times Giles' initial estimate of £800-900,000.

The oddest thing about this railway, for O. S. Nock, was the choice of Southampton as a terminus, which he describes as being at that time 'a sleepy old market town, far eclipsed as a seaport by Poole and Bournemouth'. It had, however, enjoyed something of a renaissance in the 1820s, as a result of steamships running services to the Channel Islands and the Continent. The railway also meant that boat passengers disembarking here could replace a long and sometimes dangerous voyage around Kent to the Port of London with a three-hour rail journey.

A branch from this line was planned to Portsmouth/Gosport. This was authorised by Parliament in 1839 and opened in 1842, but the people of Portsmouth objected to being served by a mere branch line of something called the London & Southampton Railway. The company was therefore forced to change its name to the London & South Western Railway. A further branch was planned to Bath and Bristol, putting it in direct competition with the Great Western, but this was not pursued.

The Newcastle & Carlisle Railway had been authorised much earlier, in 1829, but various difficulties with it delayed the opening until 1838. This 62-mile line was originally to have been entirely worked by horses. The Birmingham & Derby and the North Midland Railways were both authorised in 1836 and provided a route between the towns named and Leeds. These by-passed such major centres along the route as Sheffield and Wakefield, partly on the grounds that some major engineering works would be needed to get into them. The Midland Counties Railway was approved in the same year, and ran from Rugby, where it was linked to the London & Birmingham Railway, to Derby. This, together with two other routes approved in that year, meant that there would soon be a continuous rail link between London and Teesside. The outlines of a national network were beginning to take shape.

The idea of a direct linkage between England and Scotland seemed to arouse differing views. A Commission of the Board of Trade noted in 1839 that it was possible to travel by rail to Fleetwood, from which a new steamer service went to Ardrossan, from which in turn a rail service ran to Glasgow. This reduced the journey time between London and Glasgow to around 24 hours and, as the *Railway Times* of the day put it, 'What more can any reasonable man want?'. The Commission concluded that, if any route was to be favoured, it should be via one of the direct routes already surveyed between London and York. They doubted its viability at the time, but the financial markets and the climate for investment had both changed radically by 1844.

As we have seen, there was no overall strategic plan for the development of a national rail network. Parliament judged schemes on their individual merits. But while this laissez-faire approach could lead to wasteful duplication of services, its general effect was to ensure that most of the locations with the biggest market potential were linked by rail services first. By 1845, many parts of the national trunk rail system were in place, or in prospect. In many cases, these links were the cumulative results of a lot of small, localised investments. There were several reasons for this: first, it was difficult in the 1830s to raise the scale of finance needed for something like a strategic rail route; smaller-scale schemes, mobilising local capital and civic pride, were a more realistic prospect. Second, many investors were understandably cautious about such novel investments as railways, until more was known about the robustness of the capital assets like rails and rolling stock, and the hidden costs of operating them. Third, it was difficult, until the technology such as the telegraph and the railways themselves were in place, to organise and run large and complex businesses over long distances. One of the things the railways themselves made possible was the establishment of national businesses with multiple branches, such as banks and retail stores — and strategic rail services.

The early railways had the same problems as the canals in dealing with through traffic. Nonetheless, the railways more quickly saw the potential for a national network and worked towards it to a far greater extent than the canal operators ever had. The demand for a national network of mail trains was one of the first pressures for co-operation between railway companies. The development of standard ticketing, discussed elsewhere, made it easier to develop through booking. Then came the Railway Clearing House, also discussed in more detail elsewhere. Nine companies set it up in 1842 to handle the accounts on through traffic and, by 1845, about half the nation's railway mileage was in the scheme, with almost half a million passengers being carried by an average of three different companies. But it was not until 1847 that they turned their minds to encouraging through traffic, rather than just dealing with its consequences. Most of them were very small — the average length of route operated by the railways in the Clearing House in 1846 was 41 miles.

Amalgamation

The other great unifying force was amalgamation, something that happened increasingly often as companies got experience in running railways and the evidence of economies of scale became clearer. By the end of 1844, 104 separate railway companies existed in Britain; a further 110 would join them by 1850 and fifty or more had also been sanctioned by Parliament but never came to fruition. Only 11 of these operated more than fifty miles of line. Although places were physically joined by lines, the piecemeal way in which the network had emerged often meant that the services provided, and their timetabling, did not initially provide convenient through travel. Even if the passengers were not inconvenienced, fierce rivalry between competing companies could undermine those rivals' finances to the point where bankruptcy threatened them both. Nonetheless, amalgamation was far from enjoying universal public support. *Punch* attacked it in 1848 as leading to higher fares, fewer trains and poorer facilities.

As we have seen, one of the great amalgamators was George Hudson, who brought together a number of small Midland and Yorkshire railway companies in 1844 to form the Midland Railway, with over 200 miles of track. This in turn went on to incorporate many smaller companies. These included the Midland Counties and the Birmingham & Derby Junction Railways, who until then were engaged in a cut-throat competition for the trade between Derby and Rugby that was bleeding them both to death. The Grand Junction Railway merged with the Liverpool & Manchester in 1845, which in turn merged the following year with the London & Birmingham and the Manchester & Birmingham. The result of this union was Britain's largest joint-stock company, the London & North Western Railway. With 10,000 employees and a share capital of more than £17 million, it took about a quarter of the total amount that British people spent on railways. By 1848, the Great Western, the Midland and the London & North Western together accounted for over half the route mileage then in existence.

Other amalgamations would be approved by Parliament in 1846/47: among them, the companies providing services between Manchester and Grimsby came together to form the Manchester, Sheffield & Lincolnshire Railway, and the Manchester & Leeds amalgamated with other local services as the Lancashire & Yorkshire Railway.

For other companies, joint purchases and leases, falling short of complete amalgamation, provided a quicker and relatively cheap alternative. Sharp operators would spot a route a major trunk railway might wish to follow and would plant a small railway on that line, to enable it to extract a ransom from its bigger rival. As with so much in the period of railway mania, absurdly high prices were sometimes paid for these arrangements.

Broad gauge and the gauge war

When George Stephenson was building a railway, one aspect of the design was in no doubt — the gauge of the track. Stephenson had based the Stockton & Darlington on the average gauge of local farm wagons — four feet eight and a half inches — as a means of allowing the maximum number of vehicles to operate on what were supposed to be public railways for use by all-comers, in the same way that roads were. There are suggestions that this gauge — or something similar to it — has its origins in antiquity, on wagons used by the Romans or Babylonians. This is entirely possible, since it is an ergonomically convenient size for use with a single horse. But Stephenson had a clear vision of a national network of railways in his mind from the start. At the time when he was involved in the construction of the Stockton & Darlington, the Liverpool & Manchester and the Canterbury & Whitstable Railways — three of the first railways, and schemes which were almost as remote from each other as it was possible to get within England — he said:

> ***'Make them of the same width; though they may be a long way apart now, depend upon it, they will be joined together some day.'***

A further development of this was that the gap between the two pairs of rails on the Liverpool & Manchester (the Stockton & Darlington was largely single-track) was also to be 4 feet $8^1/2$ inches, rather than the 6 feet or so of a modern railway. The logic of this was that Stephenson intended to run extra wide loads along the two central rails, outside peak hours, giving them additional clearance. This did, however, have an unexpected consequence — the relative lack of space between the tracks was said to have been a contributory factor to the railways' first famous fatality, William Huskisson.

There were other rival gauges. The Eastern Counties Railway — promoted in 1836 — was built to a five-foot gauge, as was the London & Blackwall; the Dundee & Arbroath was 5 feet 6 inches, the same gauge as the Rennies had planned to use on the Liverpool & Manchester; the Garnkirk & Glasgow was 4 feet 6 inches and the Dundee & Arbroath 5 feet 6 inches. But Brunel and his 7 feet 0 inches Great Western represented the major opposition to the standard (or as the Great Western lobby preferred to call it, *cart*) gauge. Brunel could mount an impressive-looking technical argument for his chosen gauge (though he missed a trick by not allowing his railway to have greater clearance in height, corresponding to its width).

However, at least part of Brunel's case was based upon special pleading; he had been able to create, and all credit to his skill in doing so, a remarkably flat and straight route between London and Bristol. With some of the more winding and undulating routes he was later asked to develop, further to the southwest, the advantages for his broad gauge (in terms, for example, of straight line speed) were far less apparent.

More important, the lack of a standard gauge for the railways was a major obstacle to a truly national network. One omission from the Great Western Bill had been any reference to its gauge. Brunel persuaded the Chairman of the House of Lords Committee to leave it out, quoting as a precedent the recent London & Southampton Railway Act (where it was probably omitted in error — most railway Acts specified the standard Stephenson gauge). This allowed Brunel to make the case for his seven-foot broad gauge to his Directors. A further impediment to it was removed when negotiations to share the track into Euston with the standard gauge London & Birmingham collapsed and the company became free to establish an independent London terminus.

Even after its adoption by the company, the broad gauge was not a *fait accompli*. Brunel came under fire early on from the Great Western shareholders when the first phases of the Great Western were found to give a rough ride and the railway's locomotives proved unreliable. In August 1838, John Hawkshaw, the Engineer of the Manchester & Leeds Railway, was called in to inspect the works carried out so far. His report called for the line to be converted immediately to the standard gauge, promising a net saving of over £30,000, even after the costs of conversion were taken into account. Hawkshaw's case was based largely upon the benefits of standardisation, but he also argued (oddly) that the broad gauge locomotives were too heavy and too powerful. For once, Brunel's vision failed him, as he argued for the separateness of the Great Western:

> ***'Such is the position of the Great Western Railway. It could have no connection with any other of the main lines, and the principal branches likely to be made were well considered and almost formed part of the original plan; nor can these be dependent upon any existing lines for the traffic which they will bring to the main trunk.'***
>
> *(Quoted in MacDermot (1964) — page 42 of revised edition)*

This argument seems particularly odd, given that the Great Western had ambitions to take the broad gauge into the Midlands. However, this was thwarted by its implacable opponent, George Hudson, who gradually acquired the lines between Birmingham and Bristol. The reality was that the Great Western could not exist in isolation. As the network grew, it continually found itself linking up to — or competing for routes with — standard gauge railways. One solution, first employed on the line between Cheltenham and Gloucester in 1844, was the construction of a dual gauge railway, over which both types of train could pass, but this presented operational difficulties. The tensions eventually became sufficient to warrant the setting up of a Royal Commission in 1845, to investigate the respective merits of the two gauges and the issues raised by the possibility of standardising on one or the other.

There were over 30 points in the network where a break in gauge made necessary the transhipment of goods and passengers. Brunel tried to make light of this, claiming that, in some cases:

> ***'... a very simple arrangement may effect the transfer of the entire load of goods from the wagon of one Company to that of the other while the passengers can merely step from one carriage into the other in the same station and on the same platform.'***

Few believed him, including (as his diaries subsequently showed) his colleague Daniel Gooch. Certainly these so-called 'simple arrangements' were never put into practice by the Great Western itself and the overcrowded transfer sheds at places like Gloucester became a byword for delay and the mis-sorting of goods. The Royal Commission went to see these in action and the Goods Manager of the Birmingham & Gloucester Railway made sure the point was not lost on them. Just to add to the impression of confusion, he sent two trains that had already been sorted back through the shed, causing a most gratifying degree of chaos and overloading. The Commission not surprisingly concluded that breaks of gauge were:

> ***'a very serious evil* and that *no method has been proposed to them which is calculated to remedy in any important degree the inconvenience attending a break of gauge.'***

Similar chicanery was used in the comparative tests of broad and standard gauge locomotives. Flying starts were used to improve journey times and hot water was added to the tenders to improve performance.

The Commission agreed the undesirability of having different gauges. Transhipment was expensive and inefficient. The Railway Clearing House estimated that a break of gauge added a cost equivalent to an extra twenty miles on the journey. It was not even a real option for minerals traffic or for the movement of livestock (the argument in the latter case being that once you had let the terrified animals out of one set of pitching, solid-buffered wagons, there was no easy prospect of herding them straight into another set). They considered and rejected the various compromise solutions that were put forward: telescopic axles on the wagons, low-loader broad gauge flat-trucks, on which narrow gauge trucks could travel, mixed gauge trains, and an early version of containers.

Among the impacts the Commission had on services was a marked reduction in journey times, as broad and standard gauges competed to prove their superior speed. Companies would put on one or two crack trains a day, in an effort to provide them with headlines for the Commission. As with the stagecoaches' earlier bid for speed, this also increased the accident rate. The seven months leading up to the Gauge Commissioners' report saw more derailments than in the previous five years put together. The net result of this was to lead the Commission to question the value of further increases in speed. They suggested that the power and capacity of broad gauge trains was 'greatly in excess of the requirements of traffic', whilst the recent improvements in standard gauge locomotives had, they thought, brought them almost to the limits of the power for that gauge.

Come their report and, in the finest tradition of Royal Commissions, they equivocated. Whilst they recognised the superiority of the broad gauge for pulling heavy loads and achieving high speeds, they understood the impracticality of converting the nation's growing infrastructure of standard gauge lines to broad gauge (conversion the other way held no such problems) and concluded that standard gauge was best suited to the 'general needs of the country'. They recommended the extinction of the broad gauge 'if equitable means could be forthcoming'. Of course, they could not do so, since that would either have involved the lubricant of public money (anathema to the governments of the day) or the Great Western paying for the conversion itself (intolerable interference with the freedom of competition).

The Gauge Act of 1846, which flowed from the Commission's report, was another fudge. It standardised future railways on 4 feet $8^1/2$ inches, but excluded any new railway whose gauge was specified separately by an individual Act of Parliament. By this loophole, the Great Western, which had just 274 miles of broad gauge track at the time of the Commission, was able to continue building it until 1863, by which time its network amounted to 1,040 miles of broad gauge and 387 miles of mixed gauge track. This made the process of conversion (finally completed only in 1892) a much more expensive one than it might otherwise have been.

Chapter 10:
The economic effects of the railways

'What was distant is now near'

> ***'Notions we have received from our ancestors, and verified by our own experience, are thrown over in a day, and new standards erected, by which to form our ideas for the future. Speed — despatch — distance — are still relative terms, but their meaning has been totally changed within a few months: what was quick is now slow; what was distant is now near; and this change in our ideas will not be limited to the environs of Liverpool and Manchester — it will pervade society at large.'***
>
> (*Henry Booth — Company Secretary of the Liverpool & Manchester Railway, 1830*)

Effects on communities

There was by no means universal agreement in the early days that the railways would bring economic benefits to the communities they touched. Certainly, they were not seen as an absolute guarantee that a town would grow. Simmons (1986) quotes the examples of Bath (connected to the main line in 1840/41) and Cambridge (1845), both of which experienced a fall in population over the following years; but they were perhaps exceptions to a general trend in the opposite direction. The first period of rapid railway expansion closely followed some of the most sweeping political reforms in over a century. Numbers of small towns lost their status as parliamentary boroughs in the Reform Act of 1832 and had their local government powers changed by the Municipal Reform Act of 1835. Many people were unsure about their community's future in a changing world and it was by no means clear that a railway linking them to larger and economically more powerful areas would be to their advantage. The shopkeepers of Ashton-under-Lyne, Stockport and other small towns around Manchester all complained about how their customers travelled by rail into the city to shop.

Even a community as relatively large and prosperous as Reading had its doubters:

> ***'The opening of the (Great Western) railway to (Reading) will positively take place on Monday next, when, from the novelty of this mode of travelling, a considerable influx of visitors from the metropolis &c., may be anticipated; and, as regards the commercial relations of this borough, it may be considered one of the most important events in the history of the town. Public opinion is, as might be expected, much divided on the question, whether the prosperity of the Borough will eventually be increased or diminished by the facility of communication with London, which the railways will produce; much uncertainty on this subject must of necessity prevail, but it is generally remarked that the greatest advocates for the railway are much less sanguine of success than formerly.'***
>
> (*Berkshire Chronicle — 28 March 1840*)

To some extent, it depended on which newspaper you read. The *Berkshire Chronicle*, quoted above, was the mouthpiece of the Conservative landowners of Berkshire, who generally opposed the railway. Its rival, the *Reading Mercury*, spoke for the more liberal factions who supported it.

Some communities were strongly in favour of the railway, and towns like Aylesbury and Bedford even went so far as to promote and help raise the finance for branches linking them to the nearest main line. Some changed their mind. Abingdon twice petitioned against the Great Western coming to their town. Eventually, when they saw the benefits other towns derived from a railway, they had to form their own local Abingdon Railway Company to connect them to the Great Western. In some cases, the railways were keener to come to a town than the town was to have them. The prestige of possible royal patronage meant that Windsor got two lines in the same year (1849) but not before the Commissioners of Woods and Forests had extracted — one hesitates to say extorted — large sums of money from both of them, for works supposedly necessitated by their coming.

Even after the opening of a railway, the benefits to the towns served by it were sometimes far from clear-cut:

> ***'Maidenhead is now in miserable plight. The glories of The Bear, where a good twenty minutes were allowed to the traveller to stow away three or four shillings' worth of boiled fowls and ham to support his inward man during the night, are fast fading away forever. This celebrated hostelry is about to be permanently closed as a public inn.'***
>
> *(Quoted in Acworth. In fact, The Bear has survived as an inn to this day)*

One significant (but as yet unquantified) impact of the railways was on the fortunes of small market towns. The number of markets in England halved between 1792 and 1888. Part of this may have been a process of rationalisation that would have gone on with or without the railways, but they are thought to have helped concentrate business in the larger centres — in particular, those served by rail.

Effects on individual industries

The early railway era gave a tremendous boost to a variety of British industries. At the height of railway activity in the 1830s and 1840s, it was estimated that about a fifth of the engineering industry's output went to domestic railways, which also provided a wonderful training experience for a whole generation of engineers during a time of rapid technological innovation.

The railways also became a major consumer of raw materials. Between 1844 and 1851 the demand for new rails alone consumed 18% of the nation's output of pig iron. Whilst the cyclical nature of this demand was thought by some commentators to have been less than helpful to the industry, Gourvish points out that when the demand for other iron products from the railway, the demand from overseas railway companies and the influence the railways had on the development of iron-industry technology are taken into account, the picture is much more positive. Overall, well over a third of UK iron production between 1844 and 1851 went into railway-related products, for use at home and overseas.

A third of national brick production, some 740 million bricks, was consumed by the railways in 1847. Entire new brickworks grew up, for example in parts of Essex and in Slough, to feed the needs of the railway. Whilst the demand for coal for railways was not particularly large in overall terms (about 3% of total production in 1855) the search for the right quality of coal for use in steam locomotives had some locally beneficial effects, for example in developing the coalfields of south Durham. A larger proportion of national coal production (about 5% in the period from 1844 to 1851) went to the iron industry to satisfy railway-related orders for their products.

Businesses not directly related to the railways also benefited from a swifter and more reliable mode of transport, which meant that manufacturers no longer needed to tie up so much capital in excessive stocks of raw materials against the possibility of late deliveries. Cheaper deliveries at all stages in the manufacturing process also helped the competitive position of British industry, especially against less industrialised overseas competition. Bulk goods, in particular, could be moved at unimaginably low prices, and the opening up of much larger markets made possible new economies of scale. The railways thus played an important part in ushering in the age of mass manufacture (and, correspondingly, the decline of the individual local craftsman).

The railways also had an indirect impact on the cost of living, by undermining local monopolies built upon the high cost of transport. In few industries was this truer than in agriculture. Some of the most vocal opposition to the early railways came from farmers in the areas immediately around the major towns and cities. The high cost of transport before railways meant that the markets for farm produce were relatively localised, and those close to urban areas could sell at monopolistic prices. In a paper read to the Statistical Society in 1843, Middlesex farmers complained that:

> ***'... in consequence of the facility that (the railway) afforded for the rapid transfer of stock from one county to another, they had been deprived of the advantages which they formerly possessed from their proximity to London. Five hundred head of sheep and a hundred head of cattle had upon more than one occasion been suddenly introduced into the market from the west of England, and prices had been proportionately forced down.'***

They were potential losers, but farmers in more remote areas could now begin to sell their perishable products to hitherto inaccessible urban markets, and the value of farmland could increase by 25% or more with the arrival of a railway in the area. Not only that, but the farmland could also become more productive. Before the railways, the transport costs of bringing in large volumes of fertiliser were prohibitive. Suddenly, lime, guano and even fertiliser based on sewage from the urban areas became affordable to transport. A Parliamentary Select Committee in 1846 reported 'a great agricultural improvement' in rural areas near to the newly opened railways.

Livestock could now be moved to urban markets without having to walk them there. Animals destined to feed London could, before the railways, be made to walk from as far away as Lincolnshire. In the course of the journey, a sheep might shed 8 pounds in weight and an ox some $3^{1}/_{2}$ stones. One Norfolk farmer complained that his cattle walked off three guineas-worth of weight in the two-week journey to market in London. This, along with the drovers' wages and lodgings and the cost of feeding and penning the animals overnight on their journey, all added to the cost of urban foodstuffs. Livestock soon became a major cargo for the railways. In 1843, the London & Birmingham Railway alone brought 263 wagonloads of livestock to London for the Christmas cattle market. Slaughtered animals, as distinct from livestock, were sent to London from as far away as Darlington by this time. At most rural stations, and many urban ones, animal pens would be found alongside the coal yard and goods shed.

For some, like Thomas Gray, the benefits derived from using fewer horses were an important agricultural argument for the steam engine. He estimated that there were 10,000 stationary steam engines in use in Britain in 1820, and that they were doing the work of over 200,000 horses. Those horses would otherwise have required a million acres to grow their feed, and the steam engine thus freed up enough land to feed 1,500,000 people.

Last but not least, the railways made it easier for individual farmers to attend agricultural shows and exhibitions, and learn about the many developments that were taking place in farming techniques. All in all, improvements in transport probably had at least as much impact on farming as the radical changes in agricultural practices that were taking place during the period.

Employment in building and running the railways

The railways also created new industries of their own. Contracting firms grew up to undertake the large-scale civil engineering required. As we have seen, some, such as those of Thomas Brassey and Samuel Peto, were major national employers. In the late 1830s, it was estimated that one in seven workers in the building industry was employed on the railways (or about 1% of the total male workforce). This rose to about 4% in the boom of 1847.

During the period of railway mania before 1850, the employment generated by the construction of the railways substantially exceeded that of the staff employed to run the completed lines. At its peak, in 1847, about 257,000 people were employed in railway construction. Their wage bill was around £16 million, or 3% of GNP. The multiplier effect of this income, in a time of national recession, and paid as it was to a largely unskilled and often locally recruited labour force who might otherwise have looked to the provisions of the Poor Law, was particularly significant to some local economies.

Railways were also huge direct employers of labour once they were operational. By the 1850s, railway staff totalled some 56,000, compared with a civil service of fewer than 20,000 and a similar number of Post Office employees. The railways also offered much more secure employment than many manufacturing industries, which were subject to trade cycles and lay-offs. By the 1890s, the total number of employees would exceed a third of a million.

Numerically less significant, but important in other ways, was the threefold increase in the number of practising civil engineers between 1841 and 1851, by which time the Census listed some 3,000 members of the profession. Other growth areas of employment included the parliamentary agent, who handled the submission of private bills to Parliament. There were twenty-nine of these in 1841, but 141 a decade later. Some of today's leading firms of commercial lawyers and accountants also have their origins (or at least periods of substantial growth) in the development of the early railways. By 1860, the railways would employ as many accountants and cashiers as engineers. The surveying profession was also re-shaped by the railways, developing new areas of expertise in valuation and the negotiation of compensation, beyond its traditional skills.

Effects on the competition: passenger travel

> **'The railway holds out *the fair prospect of a public accommodation* but its *magnitude and importance… cannot be immediately ascertained.*'**
>
> (*Some of just thirty-two words in the Liverpool & Manchester Railway prospectus given over to the scope for it to promote passenger travel*)

The original *raison d'être* for the first railways was the carriage of bulk cargoes. The surprise for their operators was that they unleashed a huge pent-up demand for passenger travel and for the movement of high-value cargoes, transported until then by road. The impact of the railways on their competition was often swift and devastating. By the end of 1830, just three months after the opening of the railway, 14 of the 26 coaches running between Manchester and Liverpool had been taken off and the mail had switched to rail. By 1832, just one coach was left running, and that was carrying parcels. In similar manner, 23 coach services were operating between London and Brighton in 1839. The railway opened in September 1841 and, by the summer of 1845, only one was still in business. Many rival businesses were obliterated in this way, but the full picture is rather more complex.

The conventional explanation was that road transport simply could not compete, on price or speed. Even after the stagecoaches cut their fares between Manchester and Liverpool to 10s inside and 5s outside, they still could not beat the railway's offer of a 5s first-class fare for a journey which, at two hours, was substantially quicker. This popular view on price competition has been somewhat qualified by Gourvish. Once the railways had removed the stagecoaches from longer routes, he claims that they were able to maintain first- and second-class fares of around 3 1/2d and 2 1/2d a mile respectively, not dissimilar to inside and outside rates for coach travel. However, he also makes the claim that even second-class rail travel offered standards of comfort that were more comparable with inside coach travel, and was a lot quicker. (The point about speed is incontrovertible, but Chapter 5 casts some doubt on how comfortable some of the second-class accommodation was.) On this basis, at least, the railway can still be said to offer a substantial saving against the comparable coach journey. The really big difference in cost came with the introduction of the Parliamentary trains. Third-class passenger travel would grow from 20% of passenger receipts for the major companies in 1845/46 to 61% in 1875. Volumes increased, even if profit margins shrank.

But the railways did not just steal existing trade from the roads; they created a vast new market. The total capacity of the coaches running between Liverpool and Manchester in 1830 was around 250 passengers a day, with doubtless a few extra travelling more slowly by wagon. Within weeks of its opening, the railway was carrying 1,000 passengers a day. It was calculated that the number of passengers being conveyed by rail nationally in 1848 would have required over 140,000 horses, had they all been travelling by road.

The impact was of course greatest where the new railway was in direct competition with a coach route. Even if a coach operator tried to compete on cost in these circumstances, he found that the travelling public was, for the most part, even more interested in saving time than money, and speed was something on which they could not compete.

As if their natural competitive disadvantages were not severe enough, the coaching industry was also more heavily taxed than the railways; the railways being newer, the Government had not yet worked out how best to maximise the tax revenue from them.

All sorts of compensating advantages were claimed by the coach operators. Perhaps the oddest example followed a spate of railway accidents in 1840. This led coach operators between Derby and Nottingham to promote themselves (rather unjustifiably, in view of their own track record) as the safe mode of travel. Their advertisement talked of:

> ***'...going by coaches combining safety and expedition with comfort and economy'***

(approximately none of which claims were borne out by the facts) and went on to argue that:

> ***'it must be evident to all that the Old Mode of Travelling is still the most preferable, and the only one to escape the Dreadful Railway Accidents, too awful to describe.'***
>
> (*Derby Mercury — 2 December 1840*)

A similar attempt was made to prey on the fears of the claustrophobic (and followers of Dionysius Lardner — see Chapter 3) in this advertisement for the *Star* coach, offering a tunnel-free route for London-bound travellers:

> ***'Persons fearful of Box Tunnel may go to Chippenham by this coach and proceed by the line of the railway by the eleven o' clock train.'***

The fear of tunnels — which were a new phenomenon for the travelling public to encounter — was a very real one. The Liverpool & Manchester painted the walls of the Edge Hill Tunnel white and illuminated it with gaslights in an effort to overcome this. Stationary engines outside the tunnel were used instead of locomotives to move trains through it, as much to keep out the smoke and reassure the public as for the slopes involved. When an engraving appeared, showing (courtesy of some artistic licence) a locomotive in the tunnel, it caused such an outcry that the picture had to be withdrawn and the locomotive replaced by a wagon.

As stagecoach operators tried to reduce their journey times in a vain effort to compete with the railways, it led to them having more accidents. A similar approach to play up the safety angle — but this time in rhyme — was adopted by horse bus proprietor George Shillibeer, when the London & Greenwich Railway threatened his business:

> ***'These pleasure with comfort and safety combine,***
>
> ***They will neither blow up nor explode like a mine;***
>
> ***Those who ride on the railroad might half die with fear,***
>
> ***You can come to no harm with the safe Shillibeer'***
>
> (Quoted in R. H. G. Thomas: *London's First Railway — 1972*)

Some coach operators saw the writing on the wall sooner than others. The very day, in July 1844, that the railway between Bristol and Gloucester opened, the *North Mail* coach made its final journey, with its horses wearing black plumes and the coachmen in full funeral regalia.

But the coaching companies did not necessarily go out of business. There were new markets that were not yet served by the railway, and short-haul routes to be developed, linking businesses to the railway network. For example, once the Great Western got as far as Maidenhead, in 1838, a new shuttle coach called *The Railway* began to operate between Reading and the new railhead. As we have seen, this could be a particularly lucrative trade in the case of those stations, like Oxford, where the station was built some distance from the town. With the greater overall volume of travel that the railway age promoted, some coach operators even found that their profitability improved with the coming of the railways. In perhaps the most integrated example of the two modes working together, one stagecoach took passengers to the railway station, where the coach itself went onto a truck behind the train and was carried down the line, where it disembarked and its passengers completed their journey as they had started, by horse power.

Like the coach operators, those turnpikes feeding the railway network thrived, while those in direct competition with it went under. A number of turnpikes tried to recoup their losses by introducing additional tollgates to milk their remaining custom, sometimes to the point where people found a way to circumvent the road entirely. In general, they were too small and too inefficient to survive, though it took a long time for a publicly funded system of road maintenance to take their place.

Effects on the competition: freight and the canals

Freight still represented just 26% of total railway revenue in 1845, though it would grow to 51% by 1850. The relatively slow early growth of freight traffic is perhaps surprising, but a numbers of factors may help to explain it. One is that, for many parts of the country, the inland waterways could still provide a reasonably satisfactory alternative means of moving freight. Their upkeep was lower, their infrastructure (barges as against wagons) cheaper and longer lasting, and a given unit of power — such as a horse — could draw a heavier load on a canal than a railway. For goods that were not time-sensitive, there was a complementary niche in the market that they could fill.

There was also a good deal of substantial investment associated with the canals — in particular, the canalside warehouses — which the operators were unwilling to abandon while they still had some economic life in them. The fact that so many business premises were situated along the canalside also reduced the amount of transhipment canal-borne traffic required, which counter-balanced some of the competitive edge the railways might have had. Only as new generations of businesses began to locate around railheads did the canals' advantage in this respect begin to erode. The canal companies — after their initial Canute-like efforts to stop the spread of the railways — also responded to the challenge and took positive steps to improve their attractions as an alternative to rail. A number of factors prevented them from doing so to the extent that they might have done, including the fact that they lacked a George Hudson figure to secure their amalgamation and the standardisation of operating practices.

The effects on the canals were therefore not as immediately catastrophic as might have been expected. By forcing the canal companies to improve their service and lower their costs, the railways were probably instrumental in getting some of the canals' customers to stick with them, rather than shift onto rail, and they also benefited from the general uplift in the volume of trade. Certainly this can be seen in the case of the Bridgewater. Before 1825, its highest annual volume of trade had been 730,000 tons. This figure was regularly exceeded after 1833; by 1838, it was up to 900,000 tons and it remained over a million tons a year after 1843. By 1850, the Bridgewater Canal was still carrying two-thirds of the goods trade between Liverpool and Manchester. Profit margins on canals were reduced, but some of them could still provide a good income to their shareholders. The Trent & Mersey paid its shareholders a dividend of 32½% in 1838/39 and 30% in 1846. In those same years, shareholders in the Coventry Canal received 46% and 25% on their investment.

From many railways' point of view, the unexpected bonus of a booming passenger market presented so much of a challenge to them that they did not find it imperative to try and corner the freight market as well. Only after the boom years of railway mania did they start to make serious inroads into it.

It was during the railway mania of the 1840s that the joining of railway and canal interests first took off. In 1846 alone, some 200 Bills involving the unification of railways and canals came before Parliament. If the legislators hoped that it would produce some kind of rational division of traffic, they would be greatly disappointed. The railway companies generally had little financial incentive to direct trade to the canals. They often neglected their maintenance or, when they did undertake it, closed the canals during the busiest period of the year, after which they would take an inordinate time to complete the works. Acquisition was all too often the first step in a long process of neglect and decay.

While rail passenger revenues (which included income from the mails) increased by 140% between 1843 and 1852, freight income grew by 470% in the same period. By the early 1850s, freight revenues on the nation's railways exceeded those from passengers by a ratio of 55:45.

One further effect of the railways was to open up wider markets for goods. The average distance travelled by rail freight was about twice that on canals. The railways also opened up whole new areas of production, one notable example being inland coalmining in those areas hitherto inaccessible by waterways and thus unviable.

Effects on the wider economy

The railways contributed to the mobility of labour. Robert Peel, speaking in support of the Birmingham & Derby Junction Railway in 1835, said:

> ***'Whatever improvement in communication will enable the poor man... to carry his labour, perhaps the only valuable property he possesses, to the best market, and where it is most wanted, must be a decided advantage, not only to him but to the community at large.'***

But it would be mistaken to think that labour mobility started with the railways. The settlement laws, designed to keep workers within the parish of their birth, had been widely ignored since the 18th century. Nor was this new labour mobility an undiluted blessing for everyone.

Employment on the railways stripped low-wage farming areas like south Devon of much of their labour force, offering as it did up to three times an agricultural worker's wage.

Railway equipment and railway expertise became a major export. British-made rolling stock ran on British rails laid by British engineers throughout Europe, the Americas and the colonies. Often their construction was financed from Britain; by 1914, some 40% of British foreign investment, estimated at £4,000 million, was in railway companies and a further 30% was in overseas government and municipal loans, which included publicly financed railways.

Construction costs and the economy

High construction costs were a feature of British railways well before the period of railway mania. Schemes like the London & Birmingham Railway came in at over £50,000 a mile and the United Kingdom average in 1844 was £33,000 a mile. A combination of factors contributed to this — the sometimes ruinous cost of obtaining a private Act of Parliament and the costs associated with the compulsory purchase of land accounted for about a third; the relatively higher standard of construction caused much of the rest. There was also the conservatism of some of the engineers, who incurred additional costs to avoid gradients that would have been a problem to early locomotives, but not to those that quickly superseded them. Gourvish quotes a Board of Trade submission to the 1844 Select Committee on Railways, which argued that British construction costs were, on average, eight times higher than in the USA and three to four times those of Germany. This inevitably had its effect on freight charges and meant that the competitive advantage of Britain's pioneering role in the railway age was eroded. Whilst the level of investment sucked into the railways in the middle of the century probably had a negative impact on other areas of national investment, such as house building, the very existence of the railways was, in overall terms, undoubtedly a major compensating benefit to the wider economy.

Railways and the private investor

The building of the canal network had done much to stimulate the idea of private investment in capital projects, and the railway era increased investment opportunities to a far greater extent. The London & Birmingham Railway, for example, cost four times as much as its canal equivalent, the Grand Junction. Investment in canals had tended to be the preserve of the rich, the shares normally being sold in large denominations. The voracious demand for investment in the railways made it necessary to trawl a rather wider market, and led to the promoters reducing the cost of entry to shareholding. The railway boom of 1836 led to the establishment of Stock Exchanges in Manchester and Liverpool, and the mania of the mid-1840s spread them to many other towns and cities, such as Leeds, Glasgow and Edinburgh.

This was not yet fully the era of the small private investor, but *The Times* suggested in November 1845 that these Stock Exchanges had the effect of 'fomenting all over the country the fatal passion for speculating in railways'. Perhaps more importantly, the railways changed the climate for investment generally. In pre-railway days, only 5% of national wealth was invested. By the middle of the century, the figure was more like 10%, and this helped to accelerate economic growth.

In addition to the direct boost they gave to the economy, the early railways are also thought to have benefited it by working to some extent against the cycles in the economy generally. Although the railways made their greatest initial demand for investors to commit to expenditure while the economy was in an upswing, construction tended to have a built-in time lag, which meant that the actual calling up of that expenditure was spread well beyond the peaks in the economic cycle, into periods when competing investment pressures were reduced.

Newspapers and mail

Everything could now circulate faster — including news, ideas and scandal. Some 252 more or less local newspapers were circulating in the United Kingdom in 1815. The introduction of steam printing presses in 1814 had increased printing capacity three-fold and lowered production costs, but Government stamp duty was raised the following year to 4d, pushing the total cost of a newspaper to 7d. Only after 1836 did stamp duty start to be reduced, bringing newspapers back within the financial reach of less wealthy readers.

The railways meant that newspapers could now enjoy a far wider circulation and the idea of a genuinely national newspaper became a possibility. The railway companies encouraged the delivery of newspapers by rail. The Liverpool & Manchester even allowed them to travel free for a time, provided the publishers delivered them at one end and the newsagents collected them at the other.

Britain already had a relatively efficient mail service before the railway era. Since about 1784, specialist mail-coaches left London daily, heading along the main turnpikes to Scotland, Wales, Ireland, the Continent and the regions. These coaches were among the fastest things on the road, averaging around 10mph and, from 1836, pulling a fleet of new, high-specification coaches. But they had reached the limits of their potential, and their end had been foreshadowed as early as 1827, when the first rail-borne mail deliveries were made. the Liverpool & Manchester Railway secured the mail business between the two towns within months of its opening and the carriage of mail by the railways nationally was eventually regulated by the Railways (Conveyance of Mails) Act of 1838. This required the railways to lay on special mail services at whatever hour of the day or night the Postmaster General deemed fit.

With the introduction of the flat-rate Penny Post in 1840, the volume of mail doubled overnight and would increase five-fold by the early 1850s. The first travelling sorting office — a converted horsebox — appeared in 1838 on the Grand Junction Railway between Birmingham and Liverpool. The idea of a net that folded out from the wagon to catch the sack of mail from a trackside post appeared at about the same time, but it took a decade — and many dropped mailbags — to perfect it. By 1842, mail services ran over 1,400 route miles, in some cases carrying the mail coaches on low wagons, and by 1850 all long-distance movement of mail was by rail, where a line existed.

The relationship was not without its tensions, however; during a recession in 1837 the Royal Mail even introduced a Bill to Parliament, proposing that it should run its own trains over the network, free of charge. A furious railway lobby soon killed off this piece of opportunism. But there was one other negative factor in their relationship. The growth in popularity of a swift and reliable rail-borne Penny Post enabled business to conduct many more of its transactions by mail, rather than face to face, resulting in a significant loss of passenger revenues to the railways.

Railway mania

In 1825, investment in railways nationally stood at a modest £170,000. By 1844 it had risen to more than £67 million, more than had been invested in the cotton industry. In their day, there had been bouts of canal mania, when the nation queued up to invest in canal schemes. The railways were no different, except in scale. The first, relatively modest, outbreak was in 1824, when some 20 schemes, costed at almost £14 million, were being promoted. Had they all been built, they would (among other things) have linked London and Edinburgh (by two different routes) and provided a railway linking London, Birmingham, Manchester, Derby, Nottingham and Hull. Most of them never happened. Even at this early stage, George Stephenson anticipated the consequences of full-blown railway mania. As he predicted in 1824: 'the rage for railroads is so great that many will be laid in parts where they will not pay'.

A further boom in 1836/37 was fuelled by a combination of good harvests, relative political stability and low returns on Government stocks, one of the main alternatives to railway investment. By now, some of the pioneer railways were showing promising returns — dividends on the Stockton & Darlington had risen from 6% in 1831 to 14% in 1837 — and other prospective railway schemes benefited from their apparent Midas touch. This boom was rapidly killed off by the American trade recession of 1837 and a poor harvest in 1838, but the major outbreak of railway mania was not far behind.

Good harvests in 1842 and 1843 coincided with a reduction in tariff duties and a liberal policy towards lending by the Bank of England. The nation's investors suddenly became convinced that railways were a licence to print money and Parliament found itself swamped by proposals, many of them hopelessly unviable or technically unrealistic. *Punch's* joke about the 'Eel-Pie Island Railway, with a branch to the Chelsea Bun-House' was scarcely more fanciful (and possibly less comical) than some of the schemes put to Parliament. Simmons cites insanely optimistic schemes along such unlikely routes as Yarmouth to Swansea, and Bristol to Dover. In a single parliamentary session in 1845, 2,816 miles of railway were approved, roughly equivalent to all the mileage approved between 1821 (the year of the Stockton & Darlington consent) and 1843. The funding of the 240 railway Bills presented to Parliament in the 1844 session would have involved a total investment of about £100 million. This was, as Lewin put it, 'a figure impossible to raise without serious financial derangement', given that it was almost twice the current national income, and impossible to deliver, in terms of the amount of labour and skills required. At its height in 1847, railway investment in fact claimed 6.7% of national income, equivalent to:

> ***'about two thirds of the value of all domestic exports, and... over twice as great as the maximum level of the Bank of England's bullion reserve in the decade.'***
>
> (B. R. Mitchell: *The Coming of the Railway and United Kingdom Economic Growth — Journal of Economic History XXIV, 1964 page 322*)

Hugely inflated estimates of the potential traffic would be produced to support the proposed schemes. Sometimes this would be done by stationing some poor junior engineer along the line of the proposed railway for days, recording every passing farm cart to add to his tally of potential traffic. Leading Victorian railway promoter Sir Edward Watkin gave an account of the even more dubious research that went into some of these proposals:

> ***'Between 1837 and 1845 inclusive, there were gentlemen who rode in their carriages and kept fine establishments, who were called "traffic takers". He stumbled over one of these gentlemen in 1844, who was sent to take the traffic on a railway called the Manchester and Southampton. It did not go to Manchester and it did not go to Southampton; but it was certainly an intermediate link between these places. This gentleman went to a place in Wilts where there was a fair, and there took the number of sheep on the fair day and assuming that there would be the same number all the days of the year, he doubled or trebled the amount for what he called "development" and the result was that he calculated that by sheep alone the Manchester and Southampton line would pay 15 per cent.'***
>
> (*Bagwell — page 82*)

A further 4,541 miles were approved in 1846 and 1,295 in 1847. Although many of these were never built, 3,411 more miles were opened by the end of 1849 and a further 877 miles by 1851. In the course of six years, the railway network roughly trebled in size and the majority of the modern railway network was in place (along with many routes that would not survive in the longer term).

During the period of railway mania, railway shares became the subject of a huge speculative bubble. Initially, investors merely had to promise to subscribe to the share issue. Railway companies wishing to get a Bill through Parliament, had to secure the signatures of subscribers, who together promised to underwrite at least three-quarters of its estimated capital cost. Becoming a subscriber entitled you to a 'scrip' — a document that enabled you to buy shares in the railway at their face value, once they were issued. In a market where railway share prices were booming, a scrip became a licence to print money, and would often be sold on immediately at a profit. Even so, with so many railway schemes vying for investment, companies competed desperately to secure the necessary level of subscription. All too often, the 'subscribers' were men of no financial substance, whose only interest was to sell the scrip on before any call was made on them to fund the railway. Some were even paid five shillings to sign up for a given number of shares. In some cases, the names on the list of subscribers were unauthorised or even fictitious. Parliament — swamped with railway Bills — had no time to check them. Allen quotes one example:

> ***'Lord Clanricarde told the House of Lords of a broker's clerk, son of a charwoman and earning no more than twelve shillings a week, who by some means or other had his name down for shares on the London and York Railway to a total of £52,000!'***
>
> (C. J. Allen: *The North Eastern Railway*)

As we have seen, because the call from the shareholders for the funds that actually paid for the railway came later, as it was being built, the railways approved by Parliament in 1835 to 1837 were not making their maximum call on investment funds until the late 1830s and early 1840s (by which time virtually no new railway Bills were coming before Parliament).

But in the period 1844 to 1848 alone, the total *additional* route mileage of the network would have been around 12,000 miles. A collapse was inevitable, and was foreseen by the shrewder investors in the railways:

> ***'I am alarmed at the number of new lines before Parliament and continuing to be brought forward. A panic will come. That is unquestionable, but I think it will be staved off so long as we have 15 millions in the Bank of England; as soon as a bad harvest comes, then the gold will be withdrawn, accommodation at the bankers' will decrease, instalments [of payments on shares] continue to be called for, shareholders will not be able to sell, and then for the crash.'***
>
> (*The 1845 diary of Francis Mewburn, one of the original investors in the Stockton & Darlington, quoted in Simmons — 1961, page 10*)

When the crash came and railway share prices plummeted, many investors caught a cold. From October 1845, panic-stricken speculators were desperate to offload financial commitments they could not meet, but were unable to sell on at a profit. One major victim was the

Caledonian Railway, incorporated in 1845 and operated with a policy of 'reckless optimism quite out of keeping with the financial resources of the district to be served'. George Hudson would have been proud. Their directors invested £380,000 of the money raised for its own construction in the shares of other railway companies. When the prices of those shares fell, they had no money to complete their own railway. But for those railway companies with more conventional financial arrangements, a greater problem was calling up the capital payments to which their investors had committed.

Non-payment of calls became a growing problem for many companies. In October 1846, the Manchester & Leeds resolved that shares in one of their subsidiaries whose owners had defaulted on their payments were to be forfeited. By the spring of 1847, this one company alone had arrears of calls running to over £250,000. Another projected line that called in deposits that should have yielded £700,000 received just £60. Railway debtors fled the country; others committed suicide. One gentleman was served with no fewer than four hundred writs. The lawyers were one of the few groups to benefit from the blitz of lawsuits generated by railway mania.

Many railway companies at this time suffered from liquidity problems, and a variety of devices were employed to overcome them. Not uncommon was paying the contractor in the railway company's own bonds, rather than money. For example, Thomas Brassey built the North Staffordshire Railway at his own expense, in return for £45,000 in the company's bonds. One potential downside to this was that the contractor might engineer the line to the absolute minimum standards, with severe gradients, in order to keep the construction costs down. The Portsmouth Direct line, built and funded by Brassey, was for many years described as 'the curse of the engine man'. Some companies just went under. By 1853, some 2,000 miles of railway line, sanctioned by Parliament, had been abandoned by their promoters.

By the end of this period of railway mania, large parts of the national network were in place, or in prospect, but there were still significant gaps. Most of Wales and large parts of Scotland were still without rail services. There were no railways to the east of Nottingham or the west of Birmingham, and all the traffic between London and the north ran on just a single pair of tracks as far north as Rugby. The railways in Scotland were not yet connected to those in England. Much had been achieved, but there was still much to be done.

Chapter 11: 'A dangerous tendency towards equality' — the politics of the railways

'No public good whatever could possibly come from such an undertaking, and I should be wanting in my duty to the establishment over which I preside if I did not oppose it to the utmost of my ability.'

(The Provost of Eton College, voicing his opposition to the proposed Great Western Railway)

'I fear the railroad has a dangerous tendency towards equality.'

(Benjamin Disraeli: *Sybil — 1845*)

The railways and national security

Britain's defence as an island nation was traditionally based on the Royal Navy. However, the recent threat from Napoleon had prompted some major investments in land-based defences. These included the seventy-four Martello Towers built along the south and east coasts to ward off invaders. One further example, which combined defence with the transport of troops and equipment, was the Royal Military Canal, which ran the 28 miles between Hythe and Rye on the Kent/Sussex coast. The Government had spent some £200,000 of public money on this project by 1806, when the Napoleonic threat was at its height. Other canals had been promoted around the country as being in the interests of national security, in that they reduced the need for coastal shipping to be exposed to the danger of French privateers.

On the Continent, railways were seen from the early 1830s as a vital instrument of warfare, and were planned in part with military strategy in mind. Britain had less need for strategic railway lines for military purposes although, from the Crimean War onwards, troops and their equipment were dispatched to their points of embarkation by rail, and, as we saw, the big railway contractors built overseas lines in the Crimea and elsewhere to support British war efforts.

This is not to say that military considerations did not enter into domestic railway planning. When Parliament was considering lines in Dorset and Devon, the Great Western saw them as their — and broad gauge's — natural territory, since Parliament had specifically excluded railways in these counties from the provisions of the Gauge Act. However, Parliament preferred standard gauge for them, not least on the grounds that it could link seamlessly with the lines between Dover and Portsmouth. This would be important in supporting military operations along the coast in the event of an attempted invasion.

Brunel attempted to counter these arguments by claiming that the greater carrying capacity of broad gauge meant that they could move 15,000 troops in a shorter time than standard gauge would take to move 10,000. Military requirements also dictated the route of some railways. In vulnerable coastal areas, they specified that the main line should follow a more defensible line some miles from the coast, with ports being served by branch lines. This influenced Brunel's designs for the Devon & Dorset railway which, contrary to good railway practice, left even major stops like Bridport stranded on a branch line, four miles from the main route.

But the railways were more important as an instrument for maintaining internal order. For the governments of the day, the railways were more about protection from its own citizens. The British people were considered a turbulent bunch by their political masters in 1820. Their track record over the past couple of centuries gave the Government some legitimate grounds for concern: two revolutions (the Civil War and 1688); two attempted rebellions (1715 and 1745); and numberless cases of civil disorder, large and small, from the Luddites to the very recent demonstrations in Manchester that had led to the Peterloo Massacre. More to the point, governments saw what had happened to the established order overseas, in France in particular, and were understandably nervous.

One of the root causes of the Peterloo Massacre, though the Government might not admit it, was the authorities' use of ill-trained, ill-disciplined local militias to keep order. This was sometimes unavoidable, given the time it took to move troops around the country to respond to what the Government saw as threats to public order. The railways changed all this and the Government was not slow to see their potential. Early use was made of them in moving troops during the disturbances of 1839 and 1842. In 1842, Peel had legislation passed, requiring the trunk railways to transport troops or police to the

Government's orders. This was reinforced in further legislation in 1844. As part of the contract, women 'belonging to the regiment' were allowed to travel free, up to a rate of ten women for every hundred men. The Government could also require telegraph lines to be laid alongside any railway line, giving it instant communication with the farthest corners of the country.

Together, the railways and the telegraph gave the Government the ability to respond much more quickly to unrest. During the Chartist disorders of 1842, the Government was able within hours to move 700 troops via Birmingham to Manchester. There were demonstrations by working-class people at Euston station as the troops were being entrained for the journey. In the turbulent year of 1848, three companies of troops were kept in readiness at Weedon Barracks in Northamptonshire, to be dispatched to Liverpool or Manchester, as events required. The railways' appreciation of this role may have been helped by the presence of several former military men (most notably, Captain Mark Huish of the Grand Junction) at the head of railway companies. In a more covert example of centralisation, the railways also made practical the establishment of a national system of school inspectors, imposing a greater degree of uniformity upon the nation's educational establishments.

Subversion could come from the most unexpected sources. On one occasion, rail-borne troops had to go and help put down an outbreak of militant Sabbatarianism in the West Highlands. But a more common cause of urban rioting was food shortages. The military, for example, had been called in to quell food riots in Manchester in 1757 and 1812. The railways could thus both address the root cause of the rioting by providing a more efficient means of getting the food into the cities and, if rioting broke out, by carrying the military in with greater speed to quell the disorder.

The railways and parliamentary representation

One change the railways may have helped to bring about was in parliamentary representation. Prior to reform, representation in Parliament was hopelessly unequal. Only about 435,000 (possibly as little as 366,000) out of a population of 14 million had the vote. Some 276 parliamentary seats were controlled by landed patrons, and impoverished and depopulated Cornwall had 44 seats, compared with the 14 allocated to the emerging economic powerhouse of Lancashire. The system of rotten boroughs and unrepresented industrial cities could not long survive the greater mobility of the railway age and the insights that came with it. As one Manchester man wrote, around the time of the opening of the Liverpool & Manchester Railway:

> ***'Parliamentary reform must follow soon after the opening of this road. A million of persons will pass over it in the course of this year, and see that hitherto unseen village of Newton; and they must be convinced of the absurdity of its sending two Members to Parliament, whilst Manchester sends none.'***

A murderer apprehended

The railway telegraph also had important ramifications for more conventional law enforcement. The best-known example occurred at Slough station, which had been linked to Paddington by telegraph by 1843. On New Year's Day 1845, a man called John Tawell put cyanide in his former mistress's stout, then made his way to nearby Slough station for his rail-borne getaway. However, suspicions had been raised when her screams were heard, he was followed and railway staff at Slough were able to telegraph ahead to Paddington about a man dressed as a Quaker, travelling in a first-class compartment. Police met the train at Paddington, leading eventually to Tawell's appointment with the gallows. Despite this priceless piece of publicity, the Great Western Railway's telegraph system was allowed to fall into disuse and was removed entirely, prior to being re-installed throughout the railway in the 1850s.

'A dangerous tendency to equality' — landowner opposition

We considered earlier some of the early opposition to the railway, including the Duke of Wellington's disparaging thoughts on how it encouraged working class mobility. Disraeli's novel *Sybil* (1845) contains a good parody of the hypocritical nature of some aristocratic opposition to the railways:

> ***' "I fear (the railroad) has a dangerous tendency to equality" said his Lordship, shaking his head: "I suppose Lord Marney gives them all the opposition in his power?"***
>
> ***' "There is nobody so violent against the railroads as George'" said Lady Marney, "I cannot tell you what***

Star class locomotives bought by the Great Western Railway in 1837, which did much to save the company's reputation.

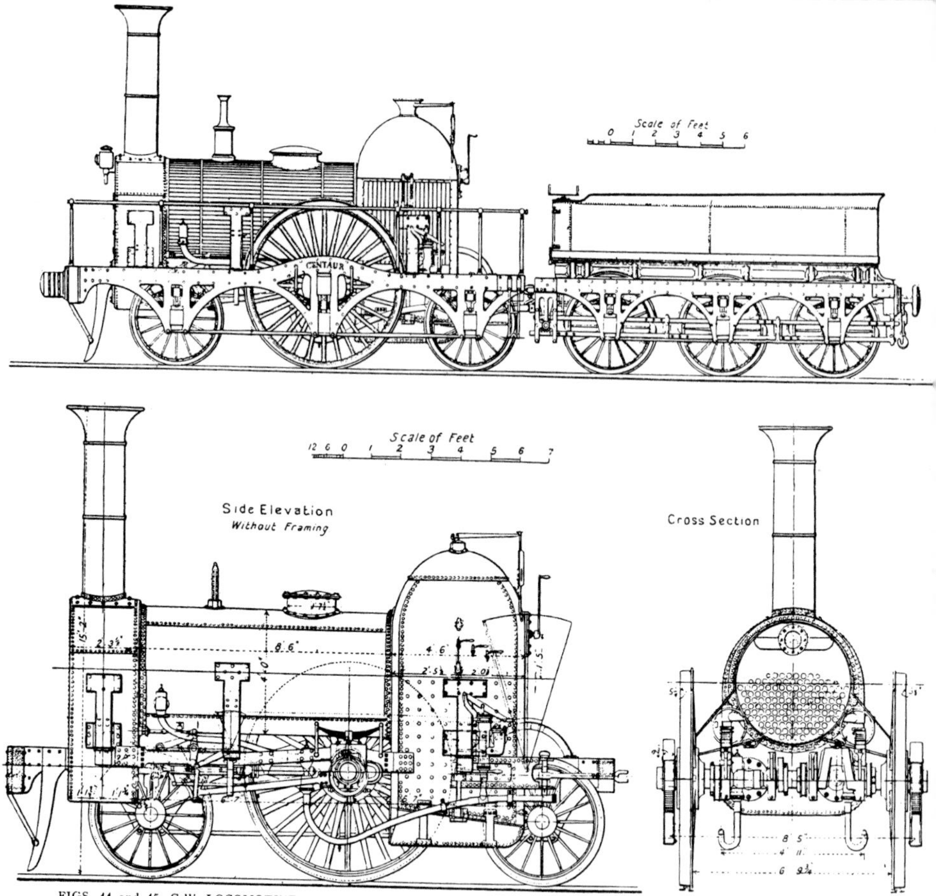

FIGS. 44 and 45—G.W. LOCOMOTIVE "CENTAUR," ELEVATIONS AND SECTION, BUILT BY NASMYTH, GASKELL & CO., 1841

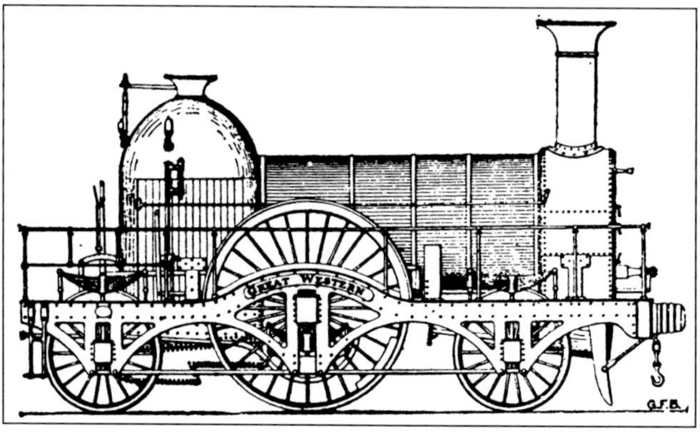

Above: Elevations and section of the Great Western locomotive *Centaur*, dating from 1841. (from Ahrons)

Left: The *Great Western* of 1846, the first locomotive to be built entirely at Swindon. It was built in just thirteen weeks, to demonstrate the superiority of the broad gauge to the Gauge Commissioners. It had eight-foot driving wheels, but at least its cylinders and boiler were in proportion. In June 1846, it completed the 194 miles from London to Exeter in 208 minutes, and covered a total of 307,687 miles before its retirement in 187 (from MacDermot).

op: In this 1831 Ackermann print, a locomotive takes on water at arkside, the point on the Liverpool & Manchester line where William uskisson suffered his fatal injury.

bove: A Stephenson locomotive from the end of our period — a long-oiler outside-cylinder engine built for the Yarmouth & Norwich ailway in 1844 (from a drawing originally published in *The Engineer*).

Above: The Great Western's conventions for hand signalling, as set out by MacDermot.

Right: Different railway companies used different signalling conventions. These, from the London & Birmingham Railway, show: (left) All clear; (far left) slacken speed — engine; (below left) caution — rails; and (below far left) caution — rails for trains on the Dover branch. *Illustrated London News,* December 1844

bove: A disc signal on the Somerset & Dorset Railway, which
ırvived until this photograph was taken in about 1900. (190/1/55)

ight: The ball signal,
f the type used on the
reat Western Railway
rom MacDermot).

entre right: The Great
/estern flag signal, set
t caution (from
lacDermot).

ar right: The original
rm of the Great
/estern disc and
rossbar signal
rom MacDermot).

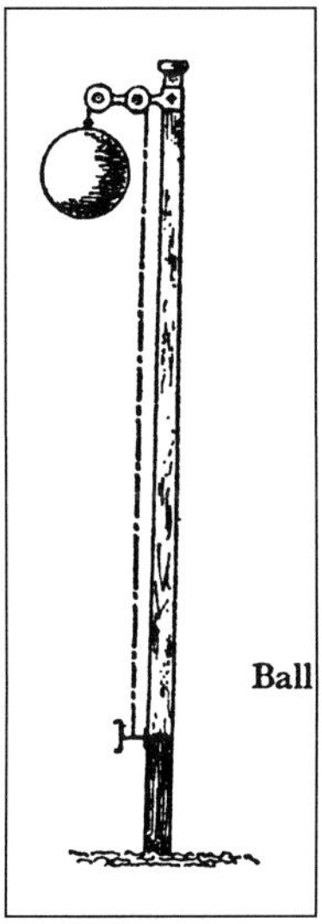

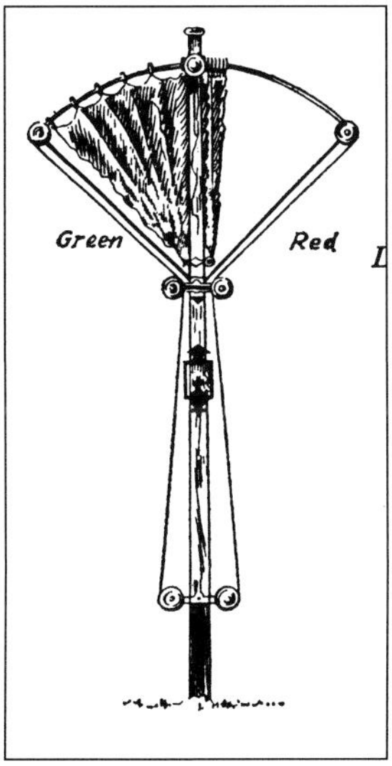

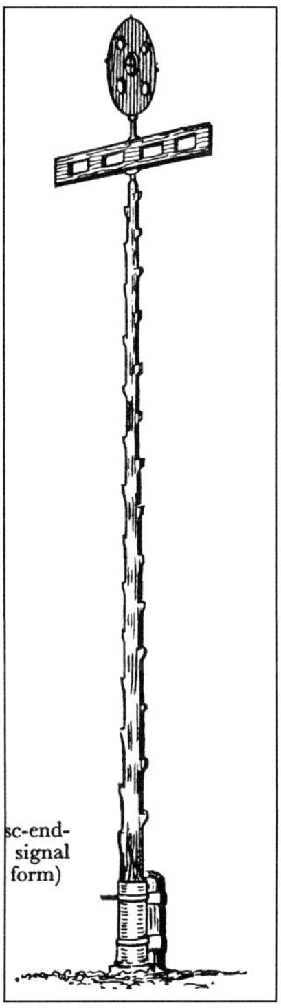

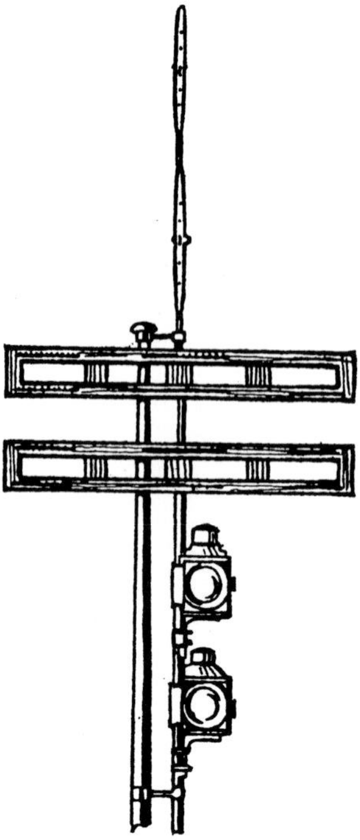

Up junction signal at DANGER

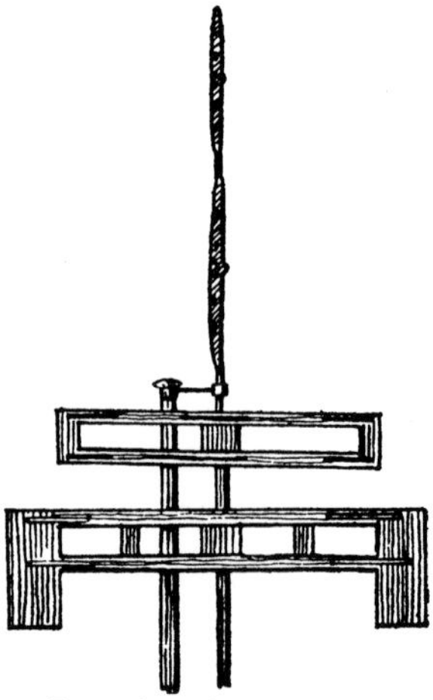

Down junction signal at DANGER

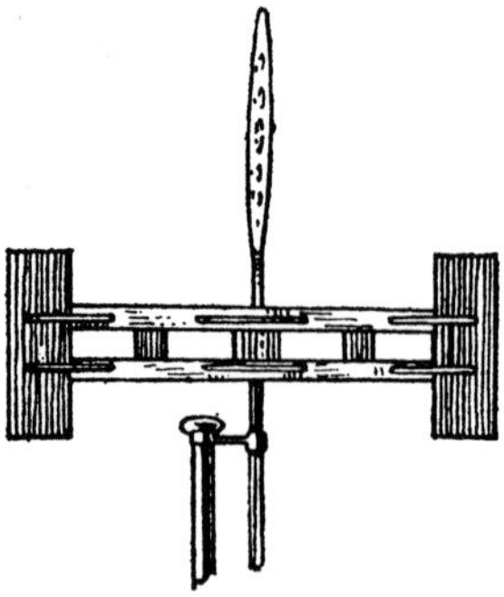

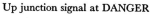

Level crossing signal for both lines at DANGER

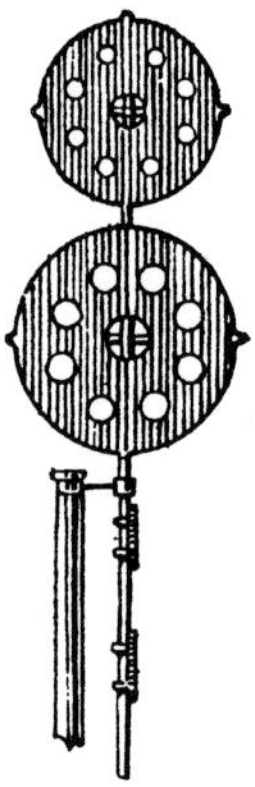

Up or down junction signal at ALL RIGHT

Right: 'Worcester' lever

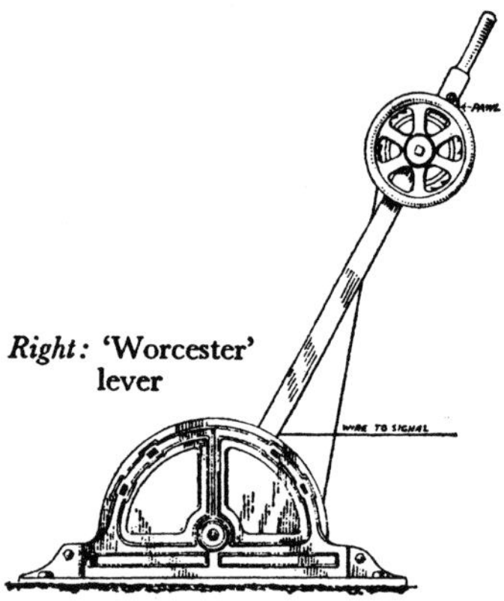

Illustrations of the different Great Western signals at danger and all clear (from MacDermot).

Right, top to bottom: Hand signals used on the Great Western Railway: 1: All right; 2: Caution; 3: Stop. *Illustrated London News*, December 1844

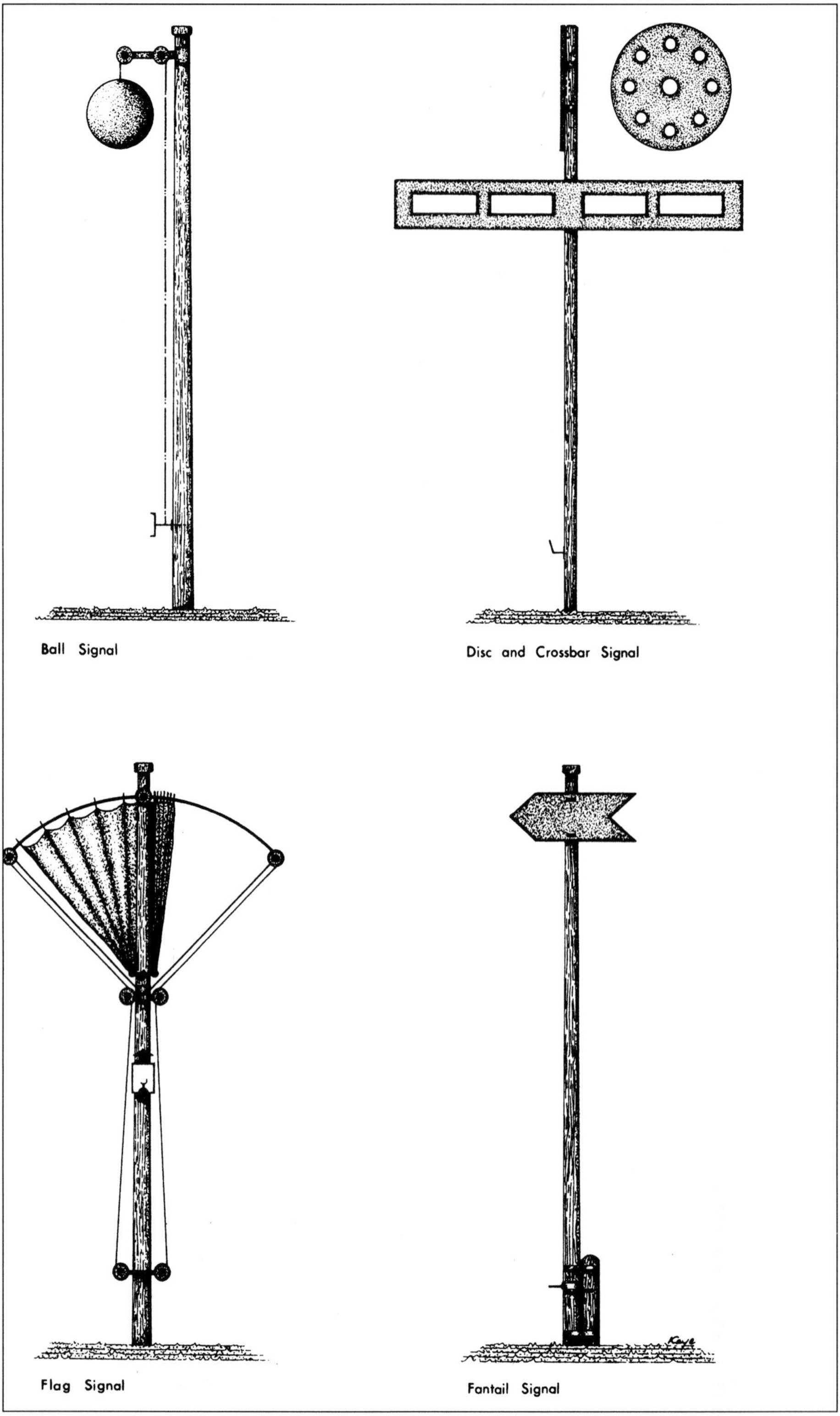

Examples of the ball, disc and crossbar, flag and fantail types of early signal (from Beckett)

PLACING A FOG SIGNAL.

bove: A railway employee places one of the new fog detonators on the track, to warn of danger ahead.
lustrated London News

elow: The electric telegraph room at Nine Elms station. Its appearance in the *Illustrated London News* in April 845 was less to do with its value to the railway and more related to a chess game played with the participants 8 miles apart.

Above: A trackside view of the electric telegraph line, running alongside the South Western Railway. *Illustrated London News*

Below: Goods being transhipped from broad to standard gauge wagons. *Illustrated London News* (p116)

Right: The equivocation of the Gauge Commissioners meant it was 1892 befor the railways were finally standardised onto the Stephenson gauge. Here, the broad gauge lines are being taken up at Plymouth. (355/780/51)

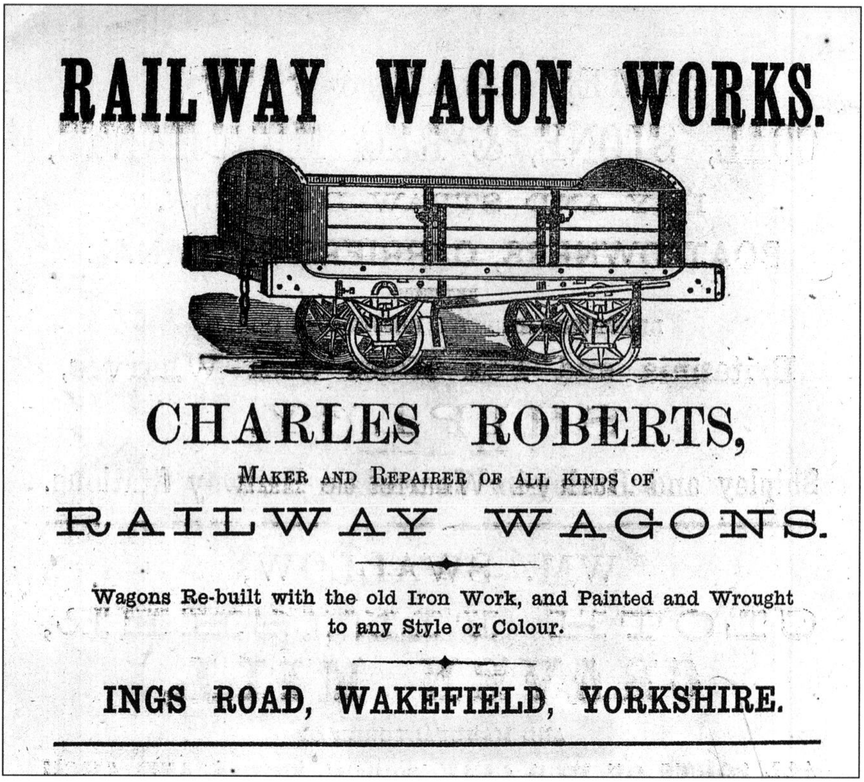

RAILWAY WAGON WORKS.
CHARLES ROBERTS,
MAKER AND REPAIRER OF ALL KINDS OF
RAILWAY WAGONS.
Wagons Re-built with the old Iron Work, and Painted and Wrought to any Style or Colour.
INGS ROAD, WAKEFIELD, YORKSHIRE.

Above: The maintenance of railway rolling stock provided a new industry in itself.

Right: The most successful of the coach operators were those who learned to integrate with the railways and provide feeder services to them, as in this example.

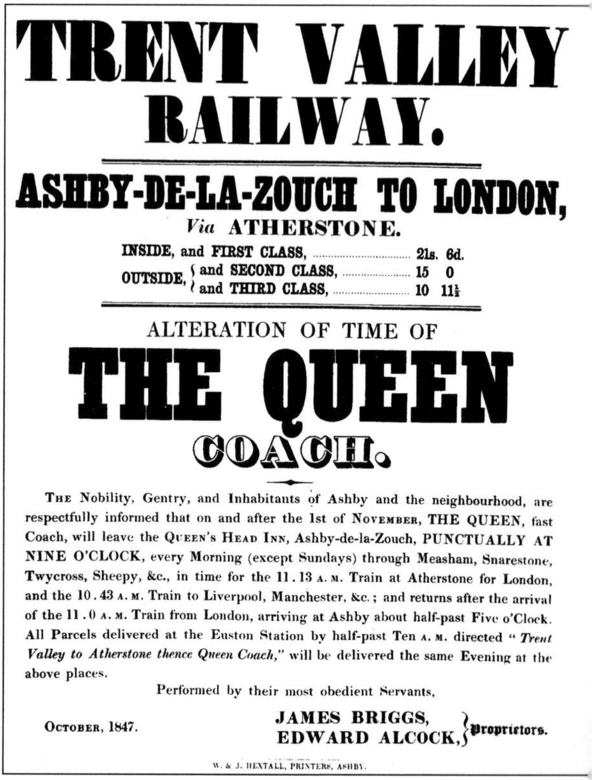

TRENT VALLEY RAILWAY.

ASHBY-DE-LA-ZOUCH TO LONDON,

Via ATHERSTONE.

INSIDE, and FIRST CLASS,		21s. 6d.
OUTSIDE,	and SECOND CLASS,	15 0
	and THIRD CLASS,	10 11½

ALTERATION OF TIME OF

THE QUEEN COACH.

THE Nobility, Gentry, and Inhabitants of Ashby and the neighbourhood, are respectfully informed that on and after the 1st of NOVEMBER, THE QUEEN, fast Coach, will leave the QUEEN'S HEAD INN, Ashby-de-la-Zouch, PUNCTUALLY AT NINE O'CLOCK, every Morning (except Sundays) through Measham, Snarestone, Twycross, Sheepy, &c., in time for the 11 . 13 A. M. Train at Atherstone for London, and the 10 . 43 A. M. Train to Liverpool, Manchester, &c. ; and returns after the arrival of the 11 . 0 A. M. Train from London, arriving at Ashby about half-past Five o'Clock. All Parcels delivered at the Euston Station by half-past Ten A. M. directed "*Trent Valley to Atherstone thence Queen Coach,*" will be delivered the same Evening at the above places.

Performed by their most obedient Servants,

OCTOBER, 1847.

JAMES BRIGGS,
EDWARD ALCOCK, } Proprietors.

W. & J. HEXTALL, PRINTERS, ASHBY.

Within a few years of the opening of the Stockton & Darlington, railway building had spread to other continents. This is the *Atlantic* of 1832, on the Baltimore & Ohio Railway. It is known as a grasshopper type of locomotive, due to its long vertical driveshafts resembling grasshopper legs.

The *Illustrated London News* captures the frantic rush to get railway plans deposited for the next parliamentary session, in December 1845.

THE GREAT WESTERN ELECTRIC TELEGRAPH.

THE MURDER AT SALT-HILL.—THE ELECTRO-MAGNETIC TELEGRAPH, AT SLOUGH.

An extraordinary instance of the working of the newly-applied power of electro-magnetism will be found in the details of the "Murder at Salt-Hill," in another portion of our journal. The eventful circumstance is of such interest as to induce us to submit to our readers a series of illustrations of the detailed means by which the intelligence of a suspected person being in a railway train, has been conveyed from Slough to the metropolis, after the train itself had started from the former place. The instrument of this important result is the Electro-Magnetic Telegraph on the Great Western Railway between Paddington and Slough, a distance of eighteen miles; by which any communication can be made from one point to the other in an almost inappreciably short space of time. To Professor Wheatstone and Mr. Cooke are we indebted for this valuable application of electro-magnetism;

BODMIN AND WADEBRIDGE RAILWAY.

CAUTION.

HORSES ON THE RAILWAY.

Any Person using a Horse or Carriage drawn by a Horse or Horses on the Railway, without the previous consent of the Superintendent, will be prosecuted for the recovery of the full Penalty of

FIVE POUNDS.

PRESTON WALLIS, Clerk.

LIDDELL and SON, Printers, BODMIN.

Top: The success of the telegraph in aiding the apprehension of a murderer prompted this detailed explanation of its operation in the *Illustrated London News* in January 1845.

Above: Even the freest of enterprise needed some degree of regulation, as this notice from the Bodmin & Wadebridge Railway shows.

Left: When the railway boom of 1845 collapsed, thousands of impoverished speculators were left holding scrip — the commitment to buy shares that rapidly turned from a licence to print money into a financial millstone around their necks. *Illustrated London News*

The view down from the railway viaduct gave many passengers their first insight into the lives of the urban poor, as this engraving of inner London by Gustave Doré and Blanchard Jerrold shows. (AE185.5296)

he does not do! He organised the whole of our division against our Marham line".

' "I rather counted on him," said Lord de Mowbray, "to assist me in resisting this joint branch line here; but I was surprised to learn that he had consented."

' "Not until the compensation was settled," innocently remarked Lady Marney: "George never opposes them after that. He gave up all opposition to the Marham line when they agreed to his terms." '

Truth being stranger than fiction, Bagwell also quotes a letter from a group of aristocratic landlords on the Isle of Wight, opposing a railway on the island and written in the year in which *Sybil* was published. Its clinching argument was that the opponents of the scheme owned property amounting to 76,000 acres, whereas its supporters could lay claim to only about 8,000 acres. This anti-democratic argument was apparently good enough to prevent the railway age coming to the island for 17 years. As we have seen, one of the fears expressed within conservative rural Britain was that the railways would bring urban radicals and dissenters out from the towns to poison the minds of the locals.

Parliamentary delay was widely used by the opponents of railways and added significantly to their cost. The legal expenses of the parliamentary process were estimated to have cost the Great Western some £87,197, or £775 for every mile of track. But the heaviest costs of all fell on the Great Northern Railway of 1845/46, whose passage through Parliament cost the company £433,000.

Landowners also held the companies to ransom with the threat of delay and opposition. The Eastern Counties Railway paid Lord Petre of Ingatestone Hall £120,000 for land worth no more than £5,000. Shameful to relate, the Dean and Chapter of Durham proved to be, as Allen put it, 'among the most grasping of all the landowners with whom the various railways in the County of Durham had to deal'. For example, they forced the Newcastle & Darlington Junction Company to put in an extra branch to Durham City in order to get their Act approved by Parliament, then charged them an extortionate price for the land needed to do so. On a more modest scale, one landowner near Oxford erected a 'house', consisting of an insubstantial framework of timber battens covered with brown paper, but complete with a fireplace, near to the proposed line of a branch of the Great Western. His hope was to obtain compensation for his 'loss of amenity' as a result of the railway building.

As we have seen, all of this led to markedly higher construction costs than the overseas competition. Freight transport rates were correspondingly higher and this was to be to the nation's disadvantage later in the century.

The authorities at Eton College, fearful of the attractions the fleshpots of London could hold for their pupils, sought to have the four miles of the railway nearest to the College screened by a ten-foot boy-proof fence. When the Windsor branch of the GWR was opened in 1848, they obliged the railway to have staff — under the control of the Provost of the College — to patrol the line, in case their pupils trespassed.

The Provost was right to be concerned. On 5 June 1838, the 5pm from Maidenhead was hijacked by a mob of Eton boys at Slough, who literally fought their way onto the train past railway staff, police and anyone else who got in their way. After a solid twenty-five minutes' brawling, they established themselves on board (or in some cases, on top of) the train. The officials decided that the safest thing was to allow it to depart for London, where the boys could find their own way to moral ruin.

At the other end of the country, Lord Eldon was concerned about any mineral rights which might exist beneath the line of the Stockton & Darlington Railway, were it to be built on his land:

> ***'If the soil on which the railway is built belongs to the railway, and there is a seam of coal passing beneath the railway, then this too will belong to the railway and the owner must stop his workings or the railway may make him pay what they please for passing under their line.'***
>
> (Vaughan, 1997 — *page 61*)

This was a bit rich, coming from one of the great northern landowners who for years had demanded large annual payments from any wagonway or canal that crossed his land. This system of wayleaves was described by Vaughan as 'little better than highway robbery' and was one of the factors that contributed greatly to the high price of coal for the consumer. The landowner's share of the price of coal was often more than the colliery owner got. Suffice it to say that his Lordship's opposition was bought off with large sums of money, which no doubt contributed to the parlous state of the Railway's finances in its early days. In similar manner, the Duke of Northumberland tried to introduce a clause into the Newcastle & North Shields Railway Bill that would prevent the railway carrying coal without the consent of adjoining landowners, so as to prevent any traffic being diverted from existing wagonways. This outrageous demand was later commuted into a toll of 3/4d per ton of coal per mile, payable to the landowners.

There was also municipal opposition. The local authorities (there were at that time several competing municipal bodies) in Manchester refused to allow steam locomotives to be used there, except on the railway line over Water Street and on the company's own property, unless it had their prior consent. There was a fine of £20 for each breach of this rule, half going to the informer and half to relieve the Poor Rate. In 1830, when the railway wanted to cross Liverpool Road in Manchester at grade, the Police Commissioners were told to oppose the introduction of 'any loco-motive engine moved by steam-air' into the town by every means at their disposal. At the other end of the line, Liverpool Town Council had a strong canal interest among its membership. They gave at best a qualified support for the railway, and specifically forbade steam locomotives from travelling on the town's streets.

Chapter 12:
All Change

'The men who made the railways were not merely creating a revolutionary means of transport. They were helping to create a new society and a new world. They were... men ahead of their time, visionary, energetic, self-reliant individuals, scornful of difficulties, ruthless with rivals and opponents, moving what they considered prejudice and reaction as they moved mountains of earth and rock to smooth the road into the future.'

(H. Perkin: *The Age of the Railway*)

Within a generation, everything had changed. From a world where the country's legislators did not know the meaning of the word 'locomotive', we had become a nation — and increasingly a world — in which railways dominated people's lives in all sorts of ways. Twenty-five years after the opening of the Stockton & Darlington, railways were being built on five continents. No other revolution in transport before or since — the canals, the turnpikes, the motorcar or the aeroplane — changed so much so quickly.

The railways widened people's horizons to a degree that is almost impossible for us to understand today. They changed people's whole perception of time, space and speed, opening their eyes to the possibility of travel, for work or for leisure, over distances that they could not previously have imagined. Travel became the new recreation of the working classes. By the end of our period, some 300,000 passengers were being carried each week. *The Economist* in 1851 described the railways as the Magna Carta of the poor's motive freedom, and *The Times* the previous year said:

'There are thousands of our readers, we are sure, who in the last three years have travelled more and seen more than in all their previous life taken together.'

THE FOUNDATION OF THE RAILWAY SYSTEM

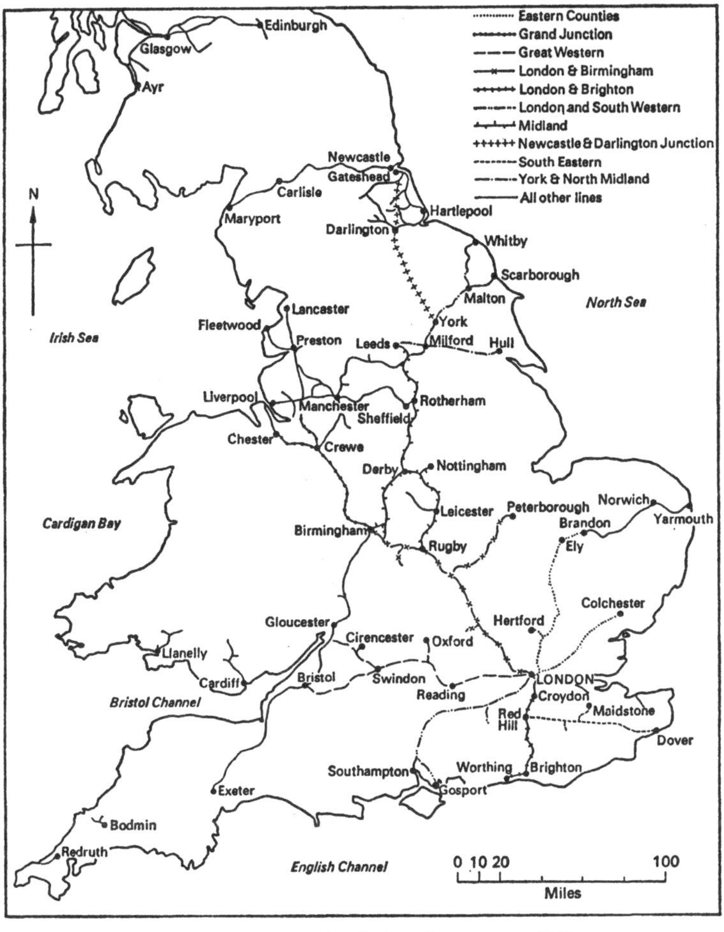

Source: Dyos and Aldcroft, *British Transport*, 1969.
Map 6 The Railway System in 1845

The railway network in 1845.

F. S. Williams described the shrinking of the world in the following terms in 1852:

> ***'The extremities of the island are now, to all intents and purposes, as near the metropolis as Sussex or Buckinghamshire were two centuries ago. ...For questions of distance, we are as mere a spot as Malta, St Helena or one of the Channel Isles.'***

The railways underpinned the mass migration to the cities. At the start of our period, there were seven provincial towns with a population of more than 100,000. By 1901, the number had risen to 40. Whilst they did not begin the process of urbanisation, the railways made the rapid growth of towns and cities a much more feasible proposition. Without the railways, how would the massive populations that flocked to the cities have been fed and clothed efficiently? Certainly, the availability of fresh and perishable foodstuffs, however imperfect it may have been in practice (for other reasons), would have been infinitely worse without the railways. How would the urbanised industries on which the city dwellers depended for their livelihoods have been sustained with coal and essential raw materials? How would their finished products have been transported reliably to the national markets on which so many of them depended, and to the ports that were the gateways to world trade?

At the same time, the railways opened the door to the flight from the cities by those residents with the money to do so. No longer did the entrepreneur have to live over the shop. As whole areas of cities disappeared beneath railways or rail-related activities, new suburbs, residential dormitories and entire new towns grew up around the railway lines, with profound effects for the social structure and governance of established towns and cities. Whole new railway landscapes appeared and the great railway stations became one of the most important parts of the architectural heritage passed on to us by the Victorians.

The railways also opened people up to a world of ideas. The journey from Manchester to Liverpool was an object lesson in the iniquities of early Victorian society. The viaducts that cut through inner-city Manchester and Salford opened the eyes of the commuter — however unwillingly — to the realities of slum living that were, for the most part, concealed behind the respectable façades lining the main thoroughfares into town. The section of the line that passed the rotten borough of Newton revealed the truth about a hamlet that returned two Members of Parliament, at a time when Manchester had none.

The railways carried a contagion of ideas. They made national newspapers a possibility and conveyed the literature and speakers of movements like the Anti-Corn Law League around the country with hitherto unimaginable speed; the railway was a major factor in the effectiveness of their campaigning. There was, in fact, a deal of sympathy between railway interests and the Anti-Corn Law League. Railway supporters saw parallels between the landowning interests' efforts to artificially inflate bread prices and their grasping attempts to extract unreasonable compensation for the loss of their land to railway companies.

The railways' other major contribution to political thought was the realisation — however slowly and painfully arrived at in some quarters — that the free market and competition could not always be relied upon to regulate private enterprise. The railways were a prime and early example of where tight regulation and a monopoly of control over operations were essential to a safe and efficient undertaking. In its own way, the spectacular fall of George Hudson was another good illustration of the shortcomings of an excessively free market, for those who were prepared to learn the lesson. Despite the laissez-faire tendencies of successive Victorian governments, a considerable body of statutory control was gradually built up, covering the financing, planning and operation of the railways — a model for the more interventionist twentieth century.

The whole pace of life was transformed, as the early railways were variously credited with the great increase in the ownership of pocket watches in the first half of the century, and blamed for the increase in deaths through heart failure in the mid-Victorian period. News, ideas, scandal — everything circulated faster and, with the coming of the network of telegraph lines that grew up along the railways, instant communication across the nation became a possibility. But this did not work entirely in the cause of freedom, for it also gave the governments of the day a far more efficient means of responding to and suppressing civil disobedience.

The railways transformed the working of the economy. Businesses could now reach far wider markets, creating new possibilities for industrialisation and mass production. By overcoming distance and opening up markets, they made possible new ways of conducting business. It also became feasible to locate businesses in a variety of centres, opening up the possibility of the chain store and of regional or national banking businesses, among others. As we have seen, they worked their transformation in agriculture, no less than in manufacturing or other industries. The railways fostered technological development; not just that related directly to their own activities, but in wider fields, such as surveying and civil and mechanical engineering. They changed the shape of investment in the economy — introducing a whole new class, for good or ill, to the idea of share ownership, and the largest of the railways became public joint stock companies, with limited liability and a separation between their ownership and their day-to-day management — the prototype of the structure of a modern business.

By the end of the period, the railways were no longer 'one of the greatest curiosities in the Kingdom'. They had become the centre of a whole new way of living, whose influence was to be seen wherever you looked:

'There were railway patterns in the drapers' shops, and railway journals in the windows of its newsmen. There were railway hotels, coffee houses, lodging houses, boarding houses; railway plans, maps, views, wrappers, bottles, sandwich bottles and timetables; railway hackney coach and cabstands; railway omnibuses, railway streets and buildings, railway hangers-on and parasites, and flatterers out of all calculation. There was even railway time observed in clocks, as if the sun itself had given in.'

(Charles Dickens: *Dombey and Son* — 1848)

A new generation of children were being raised with railways as a familiar part of their lives, just as the children of today are far more at home with computers than their forebears. The child of 1845 would learn to read with *Cousin Chatterbox's Railway Alphabet*, play with *Wallis's Locomotive Game of Railway Adventures,* make jigsaw puzzles depicting the London & Birmingham Railway or (the really fortunate ones) play with toy trains, some even powered by steam. What had been the wonder of the age was now an accepted part of the fabric of life, so much so that it was all too easy to take the wonder for granted.

'Railways have rendered more services, and have received less gratitude, than any other institution in the land.'

(John Bright)

The Grand Experiment was complete.

Bibliography

Acworth, W. M.: *The Railways of England* (John Murray 1900)

Ahrons, E. L.: *The British Steam Railway Locomotive 1825-1925* (Locomotive Publishing Company 1927)

Allen, Cecil J.: *The North Eastern Railway* (Ian Allan 1964)

Bagwell, Philip S.: *The Transport Revolution* (Routledge 1974)

Balkwill, Richard and Marshall, John (editors): *The Guinness Book of Railway Facts and Feats* (Guinness 1993)

Barker, T. C. and Savage, C. I.: *An Economic History of Transport in Britain* (Hutchinson 1974)

Barrett, Revd D. W.: *Life and Work Among the Navvies* (SPCK 1884)

Beaumont, Robert: *The Railway King* (Review 2002)

Beckett, Derrick: *Brunel's Britain* (David and Charles 1981)

Belchem, John and Price, Richard (editors): *A Dictionary of 19th Century History* (Basil Blackwell 1994)

Berkshire Chronicle

Blythe, Richard: *Danger Ahead — the dramatic story of railway signalling* (Newman Neame 1951)

Board of Trade: *Report of the Officers of the Railway Department to the President of the Board of Trade for 1842 and 1843* (HMSO 1843 and 1844)

Body, Geoffrey: *The Railway Era* (Moorland 1982)

Booth, Henry: *An Account of the Liverpool & Manchester Railway* (Liverpool 1830)

Broadridge, Seymour: *Studies in railway expansion and the capital market in England 1825-1873* (Frank Cass 1970)

Buck, Alan: *The Little Giant: A Life of I. K. Brunel* (David and Charles 1986)

Burton, Anthony: *The Railway Builders* (John Murray 1992)

Burton, Anthony: *The Rainhill Story* (BBC 1980)

Burton, Anthony: *On the Rails — Two Centuries of Railways* (Aurum Press 2004)

The Cambrian

Carlson, Robert E.: *the Liverpool & Manchester Railway Project 1821-1831* (David and Charles 1969)

Carter, Ernest F.: *An Historical Geography of the Railways of the British Isles* (Cassell 1959)

Davies, Hunter: *George Stephenson* (Weidenfeld and Nicolson 1975)

Dendy-Marshall C. F.: *A History of Railway Locomotives down to the end of the year 1831* (Locomotive Publishing Company 1953)

Dyos, H. J. and Aldcroft, D. H.: *British Transport* (Leicester University Press 1969)

Ellis, C. Hamilton: *Railway Carriages in the British Isles from 1830 to 1914* (George Allen & Unwin 1965)

Emett, Charlie: *The Stockton & Darlington Railway — 175 years* (Sutton 2000)

Evans, Eric J.: *Britain before the Reform Act — Policy and Society 1815-1832* (Longman 1989)

Ferneyhough, Frank: *Liverpool and Manchester Railway 1830-1980* (Robert Hale 1980)

Fields, N., Gilbert, A. C. and Knight, N. R.: *Liverpool to Manchester* (Manchester Transport Museum Society 1980)

Francis, John: *A History of the British Railway* (1851)

Freeman, M. J. and Aldcroft, D. H.: *Transport in Victorian Britain* (Manchester University Press 1988)

Freeman, Michael: *Railways and the Victorian Imagination* (Yale University Press 1999)

Garfield, Simon: *The Last Journey of William Huskisson* (Faber 2002)

Gibson, John C.: *Great Western Locomotive Design* (David and Charles 1984)

Gourvish, T. R.: *Railways and the British Economy 1830-1914* (London 1980)

Grahame, Thomas: *A Treatise on Internal Intercourse and Communication in Civilised States, and Particularly in Great Britain* (1834)

Gray, Thomas: *Observations on a General Iron Rail-Way* (Baldwin, Craddock and Joy 1825 5th edition)

Great Western Railway Magazine XVVII — September 1935

Hadrill, John: *Rails to the Sea* (Atlantic 1999)

Haresnape, Brian: *Railway Design since 1830 — Volume 1* (Ian Allan 1968)

Hart, Brian: *The Canterbury & Whitstable Railway* (Wild Swan 1991)

Heath Robinson, W.: *Railway Ribaldry* (Great Western Railway 1935)

Holt, G. O.: *A Short History of the Liverpool & Manchester Railway* (Railway and Canal Historical Society 1965)

Holt, G. O.: *A Regional History of the Railways of Great Britain — Volume 10, The North West* (David and Charles 1978)

Hylton, Stuart: *A History of Manchester* (Phillimore 2003)

Illustrated London News

Joby, R. S.: *The Railway Builders* (David and Charles 1983)

Lambert, Anthony, J: *19th Century Railway History through the Illustrated London News* (David and Charles 1984)

Lewin, Henry Grote: *The Railway Mania and its Aftermath* (The Railway Gazette 1936)

Liverpool Times

MacDermot E. T. (revised by Clinker, C. R.): *A History of the Great Western Railway — Volume 1 1833-1863* (Ian Allan 1964)

Makepeace, Chris (editor): *Oldest in the World — The Story of Liverpool Road Station, Manchester* (Liverpool Road Station Society 1980)

Manchester Guardian

Manchester Mercury

May, Trevor: *The Victorian Railway Worker* (Shire 2000)

Measom, George: *The Illustrated Guide to the Great Western Railway 1852* (Marshall 1852)

Mitchell, B. R.: 'The Coming of the Railway and United Kingdom Economic Growth' — (*Journal of Economic History XXIV* 1964)

Morgan, Bryan (editor): *The Railway Lover's Companion* (Eyre and Spottiswoode 1963)

Newcastle Chronicle

Nock, O. S.: *150 Years of Mainline Railways* (David and Charles 1980)

Perkin, H.: *The Age of the Railway* (London 1970)

Phillips, Daphne: *How the Great Western Came to Berkshire* (Berkshire County Libraries, undated)

Pratt, Ian S. (editor): *By Rocket to Rainhill* (Privately published 1979)

Pudney, John: *Brunel and his World* (Thames and Hudson 1974)

Pugsley, Sir Alfred (editor): *The Works of Isambard Kingdom Brunel* (Institution of Civil Engineers 1976)

Ransom, P. J. G.: *The Victorian Railway and how it evolved* (Heinemann 1990)

Reading Mercury

Rees, Gareth: *Early Railway Prints* (Phaidon 1980)

Richards, Geoffrey and MacKenzie, John M.: *The Railway Station — A Social History* (Oxford University Press 1986)

Robbins, Michael: *The Railway Age in Britain and Its Impact on the World* (Routledge & Kegan Paul 1962)

Simmons, Jack and Biddle, Gordon (editors): *The Oxford Companion to British Railway History* (Oxford University Press 1997)

Simmons, Jack: *The Railways of Britain* (Routledge & Kegan Paul 1961)

Simmons, Jack (editor): *Rail 150* (Eyre Methuen 1975)

Simmons, Jack: *The Railway in Town and Country 1830-1914* (David and Charles 1986)

Simmons, Jack: *The Victorian Railway* (Thames and Hudson 1991)

Smith, Martin: *Great Western Passenger Locomotives* (Argus 1992)

Stockton Reference Library: *Notes of incidents connected with the Stockton & Darlington Railway* (Reference NE/-/385.24F)

'A Tourist': *The Railway Companion* (1833, reprinted 1980 by the Liverpool Road Station Society)

Thomson, David: *England in the 19th Century* (Penguin 1960)

The Times

Upton, Chris: *A History of Birmingham* (Phillimore 1993)

Vaughan, Adrian: *Grub, Water and Relief — Tales of the Great Western 1835-1892* (John Murray 1985)

Vaughan, Adrian: *Isambard Kingdom Brunel — Engineering Knight Errant* (John Murray 1991)

Vaughan, Adrian: *Railwaymen, Politics and Money* (John Murray 1997)

Walker, Scott James: *An accurate description of the Liverpool & Manchester Railway* (J. F. Cannell 1830)

Wilson, A. N.: *The Victorians* (Arrow 2003)

Wood, Anthony: *19th Century Britain 1815-1914* (Longman 1982)

Woodward, Llewellyn: *The Age of Reform — England 1815-1870* (Oxford University Press 1962)

Wooler, Neil: *Dinner in the Diner — The History of Railway Catering* (David and Charles 1987)

Young, R.: *Timothy Hackworth and the Locomotive* (Shildon 1975)

Index

S

T

V

W

Y